Daniel Dennett

Daniel Dennett

Reconciling Science and Our Self-Conception

Matthew Elton

polity

First published in 2003 by Polity Press in association with Blackwell Publishing Ltd

Editorial office:
Polity Press
65 Bridge Street
Cambridge CB2 1UR, UK

Marketing and production:
Blackwell Publishing Ltd
108 Cowley Road
Oxford OX4 1JF, UK

Distributed in the USA by
Blackwell Publishing Inc.
350 Main Street
Malden, MA 02148, USA

A catalogue record for this book is available from the British Library.

Library of Congress Cataloging-in-Publication Data
Elton, Matthew.
    Daniel Dennett : reconciling science and our self-conception /
      Matthew Elton.
      p.   cm. – (Key contemporary thinkers)
    Includes bibliographical references and index.
    ISBN 0–7456–2116–3 (alk. paper) – ISBN 0–7456–2117–1 (pbk. : alk. paper)
      1. Dennett, Daniel Clement.   I. Title.   II. Key contemporary thinkers
(Cambridge, England)
B945.D394 E48   2003
191 – dc21

                                                                    2002156336

Typeset in 10.5 on 12 pt Palatino by SNP Best-set Typesetter Ltd., Hong Kong
Printed and bound in Great Britain by MPG Books Ltd, Bodmin, Cornwall

For further information on Polity, visit our website: www.polity.co.uk

Key Contemporary Thinkers

Published

Jeremy Ahearne, *Michel de Certeau: Interpretation and its Other*
Peter Burke, *The French Historical Revolution: The* Annales *School 1929–1989*
Michael Caesar, *Umberto Eco: Philosophy, Semiotics and the Work of Fiction*
M. J. Cain, *Fodor: Language, Mind and Philosophy*
Rosemary Cowan, *Cornel West: The Politics of Redemption*
Colin Davis, *Levinas: An Introduction*
Matthew Elton, *Daniel Dennett: Reconciling Science and Our Self-Conception*
Simon Evnine, *Donald Davidson*
Edward Fullbrook and Kate Fullbrook, *Simone de Beauvoir: A Critical Introduction*
Andrew Gamble, *Hayek: The Iron Cage of Liberty*
Nigel Gibson, *Fanon: The Postcolonial Imagination*
Graeme Gilloch, *Walter Benjamin: Critical Constellations*
Karen Green, *Dummett: Philosophy of Language*
Espen Hammer, *Stanley Cavell: Skepticism, Subjectivity, and the Ordinary*
Phillip Hansen, *Hannah Arendt: Politics, History and Citizenship*
Sean Homer, *Fredric Jameson: Marxism, Hermeneutics, Postmodernism*
Christopher Hookway, *Quine: Language, Experience and Reality*
Christina Howells, *Derrida: Deconstruction from Phenomenology to Ethics*
Fred Inglis, *Clifford Geertz: Culture, Custom and Ethics*
Simon Jarvis, *Adorno: A Critical Introduction*
Sarah Kay, *Žižek: A Critical Introduction*
Douglas Kellner, *Jean Baudrillard: From Marxism to Post-Modernism and Beyond*
Valerie Kennedy, *Edward Said: A Critical Introduction*
Chandran Kukathas and Philip Pettit, *Rawls: A Theory of Justice and its Critics*
James McGilvray, *Chomsky: Language, Mind and Politics*
Lois McNay, *Foucault: A Critical Introduction*
Philip Manning, *Erving Goffman and Modern Sociology*
Michael Moriarty, *Roland Barthes*
Harold W. Noonan, *Frege: A Critical Introduction*

William Outhwaite, *Habermas: A Critical Introduction*
Kari Palonen, *Quentin Skinner: History, Politics, Rhetoric*
John Preston, *Feyerabend: Philosophy, Science and Society*
Chris Rojek, *Stuart Hall*
Susan Sellers, *Hélène Cixous: Authorship, Autobiography and Love*
Wes Sharrock and Rupert Read, *Kuhn: Philosopher of Scientific Revolution*
David Silverman, *Harvey Sacks: Social Science and Conversation Analysis*
Dennis Smith, *Zygmunt Bauman: Prophet of Postmodernity*
Nicholas H. Smith, *Charles Taylor: Meaning, Morals and Modernity*
Geoffrey Stokes, *Popper: Philosophy, Politics and Scientific Method*
Georgia Warnke, *Gadamer: Hermeneutics, Tradition and Reason*
James Williams, *Lyotard: Towards a Postmodern Philosophy*
Jonathan Wolff, *Robert Nozick: Property, Justice and the Minimal State*

Forthcoming

Maria Baghramian, *Hilary Putnam*
Sara Beardsworth, *Kristeva*
James Carey, *Innis and McLuhan*
George Crowder, *Isaiah Berlin*
Thomas D'Andrea, *Alasdair MacIntyre*
Maximilian de Gaynesford, *John McDowell*
Reidar Andreas Due, *Deleuze*
Jocelyn Dunphy, *Ricoeur*
Eric Dunning, *Norbert Elias*
Chris Fleming, *René Girard*
Paul Kelly, *Ronald Dworkin*
Carl Levy, *Antonio Gramsci*
Moya Lloyd, *Judith Butler*
Nigel Mapp, *Paul de Man*
Dermot Moran, *Edmund Husserl*
Jim Murray, *C. L. R. James*
James O'Shea, *Wilfrid Sellars*
Nicholas Walker, *Heidegger*

Contents

Acknowledgements

Thanks to all the many friends and colleagues, especially the now dispersed members of the Monboddo Group, who in a variety of ways have helped bring this project to fruition. Thanks to Jennifer Hornsby, for opening up the world of philosophy to me and, along the way, introducing me to Dennett's work. Thanks also to Professor Dennett for reading some of my work in progress and giving me valuable feedback and encouragement. Finally, a special thanks to Darren Brierton for suggesting that I write this book in the first place.

Assorted quotations from *Consciousness Explained* by Daniel Dennett. Copyright © 1991 by Daniel C. Dennett. By permission of Little, Brown and Company (Inc.); also reproduced by permission of Penguin Books Ltd (London: Allen Lane, 1992 © 1992 Daniel C. Dennett).

Abbreviations

Books and key papers by Dennett (both collected and uncollected) are referenced by letter codes. Other papers are referenced by date (see Bibliography). Where a paper has been collected I refer always to the collected version.

Books

CC   1969 (2nd edn, 1986) *Content and Consciousness*. London: Routledge and Kegan Paul.

BS   1978 *Brainstorms: Philosophical Essays on Mind and Psychology*. Cambridge, Mass.: MIT Press.

ER   1984 *Elbow Room: The Varieties of Free Will Worth Wanting*. Oxford: Clarendon Press.

IS   1987 *The Intentional Stance*. Cambridge, Mass.: MIT Press.

CE   1991 *Consciousness Explained*. Boston: Little, Brown & Company.

DDI   1995 *Darwin's Dangerous Idea: Evolution and the Meanings of Life*. New York: Simon and Schuster.

KM   1996 *Kinds of Minds: Towards an Understanding of Consciousness*. London: Weidenfeld and Nicolson.

BC   1998 *Brainchildren: Essays on Designing Minds*. London: Penguin.

Key papers

ISY   'Intentional Systems'. First published in 1971. Reprinted in *BS*, ch. 1.

MR   'Mechanism and Responsibility'. First published in 1973. Reprinted in *BS*, ch. 12.

CP   'Conditions of Personhood'. First published in 1976. Reprinted in *BS*, ch. 14.

TCTC 'Towards a Cognitive Theory of Consciousness'. First published in 1978. Reprinted in *BS*, ch. 9.

MSO   'Making Sense of Ourselves'. First published in 1981. Reprinted in *IS*, ch. 4.

TB   'True Believers'. First published in 1981. Reprinted in *IS*, ch. 2.

TK   'Three Kinds of Intentional Psychology'. First published in 1981. Reprinted in *IS*, ch. 3.

ISCE   'Intentional Systems in Cognitive Ethology: The "Panglossian Paradigm" Defended'. First published in 1983. Reprinted in *IS*, ch. 7.

QQ   'Quining Qualia'. First published in Marcel and Bisiach (1988). Reprinted in Block et al. (1997). (Page references are to this reprint.)

RP   'Real Patterns'. First published in 1991. Reprinted in *BC*, ch. 5.

BDB   'Back from the Drawing Board', in Bo Dahlbom (ed.) (1993) *Dennett and His Critics: Demystifying the Mind*. Oxford: Blackwell.

TO   'Time and the Observer: The Where and When of Consciousness in the Brain'. Co-authored with Marcel Kinsbourne. First published, with peer commentaries, in *Behavioral and Brain Sciences* 15, 183–247. Reprinted in Block et al. (1997).

Preface

We understand ourselves as agents who are conscious, who can exercise free will, and who can be moved not merely by causes but by reasons. It is barely imaginable, perhaps barely coherent, to think that we could give up such a self-conception. Yet this very self-conception appears to be in conflict with the claims of science. On the one hand science seems to undermine our self-conception, for example, by denying that we are genuinely free. On the other, the explanatory adequacy of science seems to be undermined by phenomena such as consciousness, meaning, and the sheer diversity and complexity of biological organisms.

Throughout his career, Daniel Dennett's mission has been to show how science and our self-conception can be reconciled, and, indeed, how both can be made stronger by reaching rapprochement. To this end he, firstly, talks up the power of scientific explanation, showing how rich such explanation can be. And, secondly, he talks down some aspects of our self-conception. So he tells us that some varieties of free will, some varieties of consciousness – those that fiercely resist accommodation with science – just aren't worth having. When placed under a philosophical microscope, they turn out either to be incoherent or to fail to give us what we really want.

The resistance to a reconciliation of science and our self-conception is not, Dennett argues, the preserve only of those who unhesitatingly endorse the supernatural, such as those who admit of a designing God or of immaterial souls. It is also at work within science and philosophy that thinks of itself as naturalist, that is, as eschewing supernature altogether. The resistance can take two forms. First, there are those who, while officially rejecting supernature, are in fact committed to a self-conception that would make it impossible for us to be natural entities. To achieve reconciliation, such thinkers must temper their understanding of our self-conception. Second, there are those who are so zealously committed to naturalism, and more particularly to reductionism, that they are prepared to accept quite startling revisions to our self-conception, revisions that make it impossible to be the entities we manifestly are. To achieve reconciliation, such thinkers must accept the distinctive nature of persons.

It is characteristic of Dennett's work that he employs not only formal philosophical argument, but also 'more artful methods' (*DDI*, 12) which are designed to break down his audience's resistance to his message and to expose unwitting prejudice. He offers, for example, short tutorials on this or that scientific theory. And he tells imaginative stories that aim to stretch our self-conception. This, combined with the fact that in his many writings he has used a raft of different labels to describe his philosophical views, can sometimes make it hard to discern a clear and consistent Dennettian philosophy.

Nonetheless, amidst the stories and anecdotes, and through the shifts of terminology and the tweaking of detail, I contend that Dennett's basic claims and arguments are remarkably consistent. Dennett's output is large, and he often tackles the same topic in a variety of ways. I have not here attempted to be wholly comprehensive in my coverage of his work, nor of his critics' engagement with it. But, to use a Dennettian turn of phrase, I have attempted to trace and cast into clear relief the 'real patterns' that persist throughout his writings.

1

Dennett and the Philosophy of Mind

1.1 Dennett's project

Out of the armchair and into the field

It is sometimes said that philosophers work mostly from the armchair. This is not because they are overly fond of their creature comforts but because the questions they investigate turn on the relations of ideas rather than matters of fact. Are there objective facts about right and wrong? What is meaning? What is truth? None of these questions, it would seem, turns on facts that we could gather by going into the world, undertaking surveys, carrying out experiments, and so forth. Daniel Dennett's work has its origins in the armchair tradition. Following in the footsteps of his key influences, Gilbert Ryle, Ludwig Wittgenstein, and W. V. O. Quine, he has done his fair share of working slowly and carefully through difficult concepts, showing how some apparent puzzles are mere chimera and how others require us to rethink our grasp of our own nature, the world's nature, and the relation between the two. Ryle and Wittgenstein both thought that philosophical questions were best settled in the armchair. Quine, although an armchair thinker himself, argued that philosophical questions and the questions of natural science were fundamentally of the same kind. For Quine, then, science can always bear on the answers to what were once thought of as purely philosophical questions.

Inspired by this idea, or at least some form of it, Daniel Dennett's philosophical work is characterized by the fact that he is prepared to move out of the armchair and into the field. Hence he, as a philosopher, has accompanied ethologists as they observe vervet monkeys and study their communication skills. He has followed and contributed to work in psychology, in brain science, and in evolutionary theory. But his closest association is with the field of artificial intelligence: the attempt to build mechanistic devices that behave in intelligent ways. As a result, Dennett has even been recruited as a consultant on a highly ambitious artificial intelligence project – the COG project based at MIT – a project to build an intelligent human-like robot, capable of responding in many human-like ways and doing so in real time.

Dennett is a champion of science and of what science tells us about the nature of our world. But for all that, he carries with him the clear legacy of Ryle and Wittgenstein. So he thinks that some of what we know about the world and ourselves is independent of any of the facts that science might turn up. In spite of sometimes paying lip-service to Quine's radical agenda, Dennett's work shows that he rejects the idea that the questions of philosophy and of natural science are of the same kind. Making clear just how Dennett sees the relationship between philosophy and science is one of the major burdens of this book. But, as Dennett so often does, I want to begin with a story, an imaginary successor to the COG project. The story will lead us into the set of questions and issues which form the subject matter of Dennett's philosophical work, and to a survey of how Dennett's approach sits with other leading ideas in the field.

Cogit-8

Imagine a robot with a complex computer for a brain, metal and plastic limbs, small TV-cameras for eyes, and so on. And imagine that the robot can interact with you in very much the same way as a person. It can speak to you, discuss the weather, play catch, and wonder about the meaning of existence. And it does this in a rich and interesting way. You do not discover, after half an hour's conversation, that it is simply parroting phrases. Rather, you find that, like you, it is responsive to the pattern of conversation, to arguments and observations you have put forward, to jokes you have shared. It even has a name: 'Cog-Improved-Type-8' or 'Cogit-8' for short.

Now think how you might answer the following kinds of question. Is Cogit-8 a rational agent? Does Cogit-8 think? Does Cogit-8 have free will? Does it have conscious experiences? Would it be wrong to switch it off? Could we read off Cogit-8's thoughts simply by examining the circuits in its electronic brain?

For some thinkers it seems obvious that, however sophisticated Cogit-8 may be, it lacks a certain kind of specialness that human persons have, and hence it is not a rational agent, and could have no thoughts, no free will, and no conscious experience. It could be switched off without a twinge of misgiving. Dennett disagrees. He thinks that Cogit-8 would be a rational agent with thoughts, a free will, and conscious experiences, that switching off Cogit-8 without good reason would be deeply suspect, and that the best way to learn what Cogit-8 is thinking is to ask.

The Cogit-8 question matters to Dennett not especially for its own sake, but as a means of examining our concepts of rational agency, thought, free will, consciousness, and so forth. For Dennett, as for the history of philosophy, there is a striking tension between these concepts and the concepts of science. Our self-conception portrays us as creatures moved by reasons, working towards purposes, making free choices, and enjoying conscious experience. But, at first glance, the scientific picture of the world seems to make no space for any of these things. Atoms and molecules are not moved by reasons. They have no purpose; they just are. And, it would seem, nothing made of atoms and molecules could exercise free will, for whatever such a thing does is determined by its prior state and the laws of nature. Finally, conscious experiences – itches, tickles, hearing, tasting, and seeing – appear to be utterly unlike anything we encounter in the scientific picture. And yet science seems to leave nothing out: every occupant of space, every possible causal factor or force, is, if real at all, capable of capture in science's grasp. Given this, how can we, made from material parts as we are, be counted as exceptions? There is, then, a serious tension between science and our self-conception.

There are many ways to respond to this tension. One kind of response is simply to give up on one or other side. So, for example, we can reject the idea that science is complete and claim that in addition to the material world there is an immaterial world, a world in which minds reside. This, famously, was the option exercised by René Descartes (1596–1650). But if we say this, then we must accept that science is not complete; we must accept that there are some things which have causal effects, and are affected by causes, that stand outside of what science can account for. Or, by contrast, some of Dennett's contemporaries, such as Paul Churchland, argue that our self-conception is radically mistaken. Rather than resolve the tension between our current self-conception and science, Churchland proposes that we ditch the former and replace it with a radically new self-conception based on a scientific investigation of the ways in which our brains work.

Dennett finds neither of these responses acceptable. On the first response, Dennett believes we have overwhelming evidence to think that science is complete in the sense that every occupant of space, and every causal factor, can be accounted for by science. For him, it is a non-negotiable premise that science is complete in this sense, that everything in nature can be accommodated within the scientific world view. Thinkers, like Dennett, who insist on this premise are often described as subscribing to the doctrine of naturalism. Descartes' view is unacceptable to the naturalist because it appeals to factors that are, by her lights, supernatural. On the second response, Dennett thinks it just makes no sense to sacrifice the core elements of our self-conception. To sacrifice them would not, for Dennett, be to discover the real truth about ourselves but, if it were possible, to transform us into something else altogether. Rejecting both these kinds of response, Dennett's aim is to find some sort of reconciliation. He seeks to show how we can embrace science and retain if not the whole at least a substantial part of our self-conception. He wants to show how our self-conception can be naturalized, that is, reconciled with the scientific world view.

Reconciliation could be achieved if we could somehow identify the categories of our self-conception with the categories of science. This approach, reduction, is how many otherwise problematic phenomena have been shown to fit into science. Through reduction, for example, we can show that stars and planets are not supernatural entities, made from different stuff and obeying different laws from the things we find here on earth. Rather, they are just very large and very distant lumps of matter, obeying the very same laws as the lumps of matter that surround us. Can the same sort of trick be applied to persons, their thoughts, choices, and experiences? For Dennett the answer is no. (But see Glossary on 'reduction'.) The case of persons is importantly different from the case of the stars and another, more subtle trick is required.

Dennett's rejection of reduction as a method of reconciliation, and his need for a different method, makes his approach highly distinctive. He presents a radical account of our self-conception. He asks us to think differently about thought, free will, and consciousness. For some critics, this is too much, and they see Dennett's account as not reconciling science and our self-conception, but simply setting aside essential elements of that self-conception. What is certainly true is that Dennett presses for a deflation, a cutting down to size, of a number of aspects of our self-conception. But if our self-conception is in some ways over-inflated our under-standing of science is often too austere. Dennett argues that distinct modes of description are needed for an adequate vision of what goes on in the world. The rough thought here – which shall be refined throughout the book – is that there is more to saying what is in the world than describing the particles that fill up space and time. There are patterns amongst those particles that, while fixed by the description of the language of science, are not discernible within the vocabulary of that language. These patterns are not in any way supernatural, but nor can they be described in the canonical language of science, the language of regular, law-governed causal structures.[1]

Intentionality

One way in which much recent philosophy of mind, including Dennett's, has characterized our self-conception is by appeal to the technical notion of intentionality. Because it is a technical notion it can be tricky for non-specialists to get a good grip on its meaning – a process not helped by the fact that different authors use the word in subtly different ways. Roughly, we can say that intentionality is the property of being 'about' something. This is a property most clearly exemplified by thoughts, hopes, fears, and so forth. So, for example, the thought that the sandwich is seasoned with parsley exhibits intentionality because it is *about* the sandwich, and *about* the parsley, and *about* the relationship between the two. The hope that I will see a unicorn when I visit the Land of Narnia is a hope that is *about* a unicorn and *about* the Land of Narnia. And it is *about* these things notwithstanding the fact that, at least so far as I am aware, neither exists. Such thoughts and hopes somehow reach from the person and point to things that either are in or could be in the world. Indeed, the term intentionality is derived from the Latin word for pointing.

Intentionality is a necessary property of our thoughts and perhaps also of our experiences. Controversially, Dennett thinks that intentionality is a widespread phenomenon. Not only do people's thoughts have intentionality, but so do the cognitive and motivational states of animals. We predict and explain what an animal does by referring to states that are about the world, such as the dog 'thinking' that the bone is buried under the tree. Dennett goes even further. As we shall see in the following chapter, he is prepared to ascribe intentionality to artefacts, such as chess machines. When we say that the machine 'thinks' its queen is in danger, for Dennett there is genuine intentionality here, even if the 'thoughts' the machine has are in other ways very different from the thoughts that persons have.

With the idea of intentionality in place – and there will be much more to say about that idea as we go – we can outline the basic shape of Dennett's reconciliation project. The first stage of the project is to show how intentionality can be naturalized. Dennett needs to show how we can believe that there is intentionality in the world and yet, at the same time, believe that the world is built up of nothing more than complex mechanisms. Describing how Dennett tackles this is the task of the first four chapters of the book.

The second stage of Dennett's project is to show that the other concepts of our common-sense conception, and in particular freedom of the will and consciousness, can also be naturalized. His strategy here is to give an account of consciousness and of freedom of the will in terms of intentionality. For Dennett, all of these concepts are, at root, intentional concepts. And this, as we shall see, is controversial. For example, it is often argued that intentionality should be understood in terms of consciousness and not the other way around. I shall note here that it is tendentious to describe consciousness and freedom as intentional concepts – the issues will receive their due discussion in chapters 5, 6, and 8 – but describe them so nonetheless in order to best represent Dennett's project.

Dennett's overall strategy is to show that modestly deflated accounts of the concepts of thought, freedom, and consciousness – what I am calling intentional concepts – still retain what matters as far as human dignity is concerned; they retain whatever 'special-ness' about persons is really 'worth wanting'. But because the deflated versions of our intentional concepts can be shown to be compatible with naturalism, they are much more attractive. For Dennett, the vision of us that they reflect is a better vision, indeed, a truer vision, of what we are.

But, as I have already noted, Dennett does not want to reduce these revised intentional concepts to the concepts of mechanistic science. His method of reconciliation is not reduction. Rather, he aims to show how, by looking and thinking in the right way, we can come to be satisfied that something intentional is built only from mechanical parts. Working from the other end, he aims to show how we can come to be satisfied that something built only from mechanical parts can, when looked at and thought about in the right way, come to be seen as something intentional.

To do this he has, on the one hand, to promote the power of scientific explanation. A casual glance can make it seem utterly impersonal, wholly unfit to ever have anything useful to say about the personal. But this, he aims to persuade us, is a mistaken impression. Mere mechanisms can operate in very subtle ways. His work aims to show that by reflecting on the technology of computing and robotics, as well as thinking clearly about the power of evolution by natural selection, we can come to a deeper appreciation of these subtleties.

On the other hand, although he is committed to preserving the 'specialness' of persons, and committed to maintaining that there is an important qualitative contrast between persons and mere machines, Dennett does want to temper our self-conception. Some analyses of intentional concepts, the concepts of freedom, thought, and consciousness, make us too special, so special that, were those analyses correct, at best they could apply only to supernatural entities. Dennett's contention is that a more modest self-conception, preserving but tempering specialness, yields concepts that can apply to wholly natural entities.

1.2   Locating Dennett's view

In this section I want to introduce Dennett's position on a number of key issues in the philosophy of mind and show how they differ from a number of other positions in the field. I shall make my way through a number of positions more or less in historical order. For each theory I shall ask three critical questions: (i) what makes it true that something is a conscious rational agent? (ii) what makes it true that an agent has a particular thought or experience? and (iii) how does the theory reconcile science and our self-conception?

Cartesian Dualism

Our philosophical culture is steeped in the influence of Descartes. Arguably, Descartes was the first philosopher to tackle seriously the tension between science and our self-conception. His solution, as briefly canvassed above, was a bold rejection of naturalism. This is surprising because Descartes himself was a fierce promoter of science. Indeed, he played a key role in articulating, and perhaps even driving forward, the shift from seeing the world as seamlessly infused with purpose – the world as understood by Aristotle and Aquinas – to seeing it as a clockwork engine that might, on occasion, be interfered with by non-clockwork factors. As far as plants and animals were concerned, as against the Aristotelian tradition dominant at the time, Descartes insisted that mechanism was all that was needed to fully account for their natures. Some of his contemporaries, notably Thomas Hobbes (1588–1678), extended the same kind of thinking to persons. But for Descartes the mind was something quite different from any material object or aggregation of material objects. Hence he postulated an immaterial realm to go along with the material realm. Thus we have dualism: the view that there are two quite different kinds of things in the world, the immaterial and the material, and that persons are a composite of the two. Minds exist in the immaterial realm and, by means unknowable to science, are causally connected to bodies. So, for Descartes, what makes something a conscious rational agent is the presence of an immaterial mind. What makes it true that an agent has a particular thought or a particular experience is that there is some mental object before the agent's mind.

It is instructive to ask how Descartes would respond to our imaginary robot Cogit-8. The historical Descartes would simply deny the coherence of the story. We might, he would say, be able to imagine this, but in fact no mere mechanism could give rise to the kinds of behaviour we say Cogit-8 would display. However the typical Cartesian Dualist, who follows the spirit if not the letter of Descartes' doctrine, takes a slightly different view. She allows that Cogit-8 could behave in exactly the way in which we describe, but argues that it does not follow from this that Cogit-8 has thoughts and experiences. And, indeed, she may decide that, on the balance of probabilities, we have no reason to believe that Cogit-8 is connected to an immaterial mind.

One of the merits of Cartesian Dualism is that it takes certain aspects of our self-conception very seriously. In particular, it places great emphasis on our sense of our own consciousness. When we think about consciousness – our awareness of our thoughts and feelings – it does seem to make sense to us that we could have these very thoughts and feelings even if, as the view allows, we lacked a body. And, further, it does seem to make sense that something could behave just as if it had all these thoughts and feelings, something like Cogit-8, and yet everything be 'dark inside'. And, of course, it makes sense of an intuition that is hard to shake, namely that consciousness is so different from anything in the material world that it could not possibly be a result of material processes.

However Cartesian Dualism is starkly at odds with naturalism. We have no good reason to believe that there are gaps in the causal chain via which, somehow, the mind could come to have an influence on our body. There are plenty of other problems with dualism, but, for our purposes here, this is enough to dismiss the view. Dennett's project is to give the best naturalist account of persons, the best account given the assumption that the basic tenets of the scientific world view are correct. Any theory that appeals to supernature can be ruled out from the off.

Rylean Behaviourism

For the Cartesian Dualist our behaviour is a sign or symptom of a certain kind of inner cause, i.e., a distinctively mental cause. So when the Cartesian Dualist addresses our questions – about persons, thoughts, and experiences – her answer is given in terms of something that lies behind behaviour, in terms of something that is, as it were, hidden on the inside. Behaviourism is a doctrine that takes the opposite tack. Behaviourists argue that to be a person is to be something with a certain kind of behavioural capacity, and that to have thoughts or experiences is to be disposed to behave in certain kinds of ways. The doctrine, like so many in philosophy, comes in a bewildering array of varieties. One of the few versions that are not obviously flawed, is that developed by Gilbert Ryle (1900–1976) in his 1949 book *The Concept of Mind*. It is this version that I describe here, and it is this version that forms the basis for Dennett's own account of the mental.

To get a firm grip on behaviourism it is worth drawing out a more general contrast. Let us call a Cartesian Theory one that answers various 'what makes it true' questions by appeal to factors that lie behind outward appearances, that is by appeal to things that are hidden on the inside. And let us call a Rylean Theory one that answers the same kinds of question by appeal to outward appearances. For some kinds of thing, it is clear that the Cartesian Theory is better placed than a Rylean Theory. A Rylean Theory of tigers, which I am sure no one would ever endorse, would say, if it looks like a tiger, and behaves like a tiger, then it is a tiger. The Rylean Theory is somehow failing to pick up on what really matters here. After all, a robot covered in fur may look and behave like a tiger, but it is not a tiger. The Cartesian Theory, by contrast, can tell fake tigers from real tigers by appealing to the structure of their insides, i.e., whether they have the right kind of biochemistry.

However, for other kinds of things it is clear that a Rylean Theory has more going for it. Imagine someone who thought that we could give an account of, say, clocks by means of a Cartesian Theory. Would she say, for example, that reliably telling the time was mere evidence that the something was a clock, but that what really decided the issue was some inner condition? Could she say that all and only 'real' clocks met some special inner condition? It seems fairly clear that the Cartesian Theory is a non-starter. All that matters about the inner workings of the clock are that they get the job done. What determines whether something is a clock or not is what it can do, not what is inside. Clearly, when it comes to clocks, a Rylean Theory is the right way to go.

According to Ryle's version of behaviourism, what makes it true that something is a conscious rational agent is that the something manifests rich, flexible, and intelligent behaviour, including behaviour such as the engagement in rational discourse. Anything that does this job is a conscious rational agent. The idea that there might be a fake that behaved in this way but was counted as a fake because it had the wrong kinds of insides is rejected. Of course, there must be something inside, just as there must be something inside a clock, but the internal details have no bearing on whether or not the thing in question is a conscious rational agent. Ryle writes:

> In judging that someone's performance is or is not intelligent, we have ... to look beyond the performance itself. ... But in looking beyond the performance itself, we are not trying to pry into some hidden counterpart performances enacted on the supposed secret stage of the agent's inner life. We are considering his abilities and propensities of which this performance was an actualisation. Our inquiry is not into causes (and *a fortiori* not into occult causes), but into capacities, skills, habits, liabilities and bents. (Ryle, 1949, 46)

In this passage, Ryle offers a derogatory characterization of Cartesian Dualism but also of any Cartesian Theory of the mind, such as those that replace Descartes' supernatural inner workings with mechanistic inner workings. Either kind of Cartesian Theory, presses Ryle, has a mistaken idea of what it is to have a mind, and what it is to have thoughts and experiences. In particular, having a thought or experience is not having something on some inner 'secret stage', whether that be a mental item before an immaterial mind or a physical state inside the brain.

Rather, to a first approximation, Ryle thinks that what it is to have a thought or experience is to be disposed to behave in certain ways. So we understand what it is to have, say, the belief that the ice is unsafe for skating, in terms of how having that belief will make an agent behave differently in different circumstances, for example, keeping to the edges, discouraging others from skating, saying 'The ice is not safe', and so forth. In spelling out what a belief is in this way, we make no reference to, nor imply any identity with, part of a person's inner workings. And Ryle offers a similar story about other kinds of thoughts, such as wants, and also about experiences.

Before mentioning some of the pros and cons of behaviourism, it is important to clear up a common confusion about the doctrine. It is sometimes said that behaviourism must be mistaken because, after all, people are quite capable of keeping their thoughts hidden from view. But if thoughts just are behaviour, this would be impossible. This criticism is confused. Behaviourism is a view about what conscious rational agents are, about what thoughts and experiences are. But it is not a foolproof recipe for working out whether something has a mind or what someone thinks or feels. The behaviourist, as much as the Cartesian Dualist, recognizes that we cannot always tell what an agent is thinking. So, for example, behaviourism does not deny that a person can keep secrets, or can behave in misleading ways. Rather, the theory simply claims that deception and acting are just more sophisticated ways of behaving. The way to unmask someone as a liar or as self-deceived is not to look inside her head, but to look and look more carefully at longer stretches of her behaviour.

Assessing behaviourism

If you read the philosophy of mind textbooks you find that behaviourism comes in for a great deal of criticism. Behaviourism is often treated as an obviously false doctrine. This is far too swift. Like most theories of mind, there are versions of the doctrine that are easy to knock down. For example, there are versions of behaviourism that seek to reduce the mental to behavioural dispositions expressed in terms of physically characterized input stimuli and physically characterized behaviour. Such an approach is very much in the spirit of naturalism: it shows immediately how to reconcile our self-conception with our scientific world view. But it is also desperately implausible. There is simply no good reason to think that such a reduction can be achieved, as a moment's reflection on the sheer diversity of physical inputs and outputs that may cause and be caused by, say, the belief that the ice is unsafe, reveals.

In Ryle's version of behaviourism, particular thoughts and experiences are analysed in terms of intentionally characterized perceptions and intentionally characterized behaviour. There is no attempt to reduce intentional concepts to non-intentional ones, just an attempt to show that when we use intentional concepts we are not referring to inner goings on, but to dispositions, capacities, and abilities.

There are versions of behaviourism that seek to show that any given mental state, such as the belief that the ice is unsafe, can be analysed without reference to any other mental state. But, as is quickly pointed out, how a given belief affects behaviour is dependent on other beliefs and desires. If you have an unusual desire, to harm the children for example, then the belief that the ice is unsafe may dispose you to encourage the children to skate. This worry, often put forward as a knock-down argument against behaviourism, mistakes the enterprise in which Ryle is engaged. Ryle has no interest in giving an account of individual beliefs or desires, in isolation from all others. To use the philosophical jargon, his theory is holistic as opposed to atomistic (see Glossary, and chapter 2, p. 47). His claim is only that, if you took all the mental states of a person together simultaneously, you could, as a theoretical if utterly pointless exercise, redescribe the condition of the agent entirely in terms of behavioural dispositions.

Cartesian Dualism allows that it is perfectly intelligible that something might display all the signs of having thoughts and feelings in its behaviour and yet lack thoughts and feelings on the inside. Because of this it can coherently question whether Cogit-8 has thoughts and feelings. But a consequence of this feature of Cartesian Dualism is that our contact with the minds of others is portrayed as being more tenuous than it seems to be. For example, Cartesian Dualism cannot easily shake off doubts about other minds. For given the nature of the position how can we ever justify our belief that something or someone else has a mind at all? We have no access to the fact that settles the question. We cannot observe another's mind directly: only she can do that through introspection.

Rylean Behaviourism makes the problem of other minds quite tractable. Minds are not hidden. That a person has a mind is a fact that is made manifest in what she does. Rich patterns of behaviour are not merely evidence for having a mind. Rather, such rich patterns of behaviour just are what it is to have a mind. An agent's capacities with respect to colour – the ability to discern different colours, along with the ability to talk about, compare, and comment on colours – is not so much evidence that she can have colour experiences. Rather, the exercise of these capacities just is what it is to have colour experiences.

The Cartesian Dualist will see this feature of Rylean Behaviourism as a failure to understand the nature of consciousness, namely, that consciousness is something that is inherently private and is only contingently connected to behaviour. The Rylean Behaviourist argues that we can still say all that we really want to say about consciousness using her theory, but that with her theory we avoid the problem of other minds, avoid the peculiar idea that we can never really be sure what someone else is thinking or feeling. Here we have something of a stand-off. The Cartesian will claim that the behaviourist does not take consciousness seriously enough. But in arguing for her view the behaviourist will claim that the Cartesian does not take seriously enough the self-evident fact that we often know very well what someone else is thinking and feeling.

For Dennett, the key weakness of Ryle's theory is that it makes no attempt to address the question of how our self-conception can be reconciled with our scientific world view. Ryle did not believe in supernature. But nor did he see it as part of his job to show how conscious rational agents could be correctly characterized by intentional concepts and yet be made out of parts that could be completely described using only the mechanistic concepts of science. This is the key issue on which Dennett's view differs from Ryle's.

First, unlike Ryle, Dennett thinks that there is a problem to be solved here: the problem of making sense of how it is possible for there to be things, made only from mechanistic parts, that have the behavioural dispositions, capacities, and abilities described by Ryle's theory. It is not enough to say, 'Oh well, since there is no such thing as supernature, it must be possible somehow or other.' We need to show how it is possible. We need to make the possibility intelligible.

Second, again unlike Ryle, Dennett thinks that when you take seriously the fact that conscious rational agents are made only from mechanistic parts, and take seriously the fact that the organization of these parts must have come about in natural ways too, primarily through the forces of Darwinian natural selection, this can have an impact on your account of our self-conception.

There is more to say about the pros and cons of Rylean Behaviourism both in this chapter, and indeed, given that Dennett's own view is a development of it, throughout the book. But the further pros and cons are best discussed in the context of some of the other key positions in the philosophy of mind. The next of these that I want to discuss is the identity theory.

The identity theory

The identity theory[2] claims that the mind is identical with the brain and that mental states – both thoughts and experiences – are identical to brain states. What makes it true that something is a conscious rational agent is that it has the right kind of physical insides, that, in other words, there is a suitable brain inside the body. What makes it true that an agent has a particular thought or experience is that the agent's brain is in this or that physical state or configuration. In the textbook philosophy of mind narrative the identity theory has three key merits.

The first is that, unlike Cartesian Dualism and Rylean Behaviourism, it gives a clear account as to how science and our self-conception are reconciled. The identity theory notes that although minds and mental states may initially appear to be non-physical, this is mere appearance: in reality they are just as physical as rocks and stones. One and the same physical item can be referred to in two different ways – a mental way and a physical way.

The second merit is that brain states, or brain events, are claimed to be more plausible bases for conscious experiences than the exercise of behavioural capacities. We can, so the textbook narrative goes, make good sense of the idea that the experience of pain is identical with the firing of C-fibres in the brain, and that the experience of a tickle is identical with stimulation of some neural sub-system. Quite why pains and experiences are more plausibly identified with a brain state than with the exercise of a capacity is not something that is ever made very clear. Nonetheless, this intuition has drawn many towards the identity theory.

Third, brain states, unlike dispositions and capacities, are said to be suitable causes of behaviour. The thought is that if we attempt to explain why someone said that the ice is unsafe for skating by reference to the belief that the ice is unsafe, then, on Ryle's theory, the explanation turns out to be empty. For when we look at the Rylean account of this belief it includes a disposition to say that the ice is unsafe when asked. And now it looks as though we are explaining why someone said the ice is unsafe when asked by saying that she is disposed to say the ice is unsafe when asked. This looks empty. By contrast, if the belief that the ice is unsafe is identical with a brain state, identical with something that can be understood quite independently of the effects to which it gives rise, then it looks as if we have a genuine cause. This argument depends, of course, on a certain understanding of explanation and causation, of which there will be more to say later (chapter 3). I shall not take the issue further here, other than to note that Ryle himself was quite aware that his view entailed that beliefs and desires could not count as causes of our behaviour and was not embarrassed by this. But he did not doubt that citing mental states, understood as complex dispositions, could be explanatory. Roughly, they are explanatory in that they reveal something about a person's character, something about the sort of person they are, and the sort of things they would do in a range of similar circumstances (cf. *ER*, 136–7).

For all these perceived merits, the textbook narrative finds the identity theory wanting. The central objection is that the theory is chauvinistic. This is to say that it excludes, on illegitimate grounds, some members of the class of conscious rational agents. Suppose that the identity theory concludes that a certain kind of pain is identical with a particular kind of brain state, say the firing of neurons j37 through to k19 in sequence beta-9. Call that brain state X. Now, runs the objection, imagine a creature, most often a Martian, that behaves in ways very similar to humans, and to all appearances has pains when it stubs its toe, but whose brain has a different structure. In this brain we can find no neurons to correspond to j37 through to k19.

According to the identity theory it would seem that the Martian could never be in pain because she could never be in brain state X. And, closer to home, other kinds of animals, such as octopuses or, say, cats and dogs, could not have pains either, their brains being too different from our own. Surely, argue the opponents of the identity theory, all this is absurd. Surely, Martians, octopuses, cats, and dogs can all have pains. It is just that these pains would be 'realized' by different brain states in these cases. More generally, goes the objection, we expect mental states to be multiply realizable: that is, in different agents, or perhaps even the same agent on different occasions, the physical states that are identical with mental states could be different.

By contrast with the identity theory, behaviourism is liberal and not chauvinistic. It cares not a jot for the insides, so long as something has the right kind of behavioural capacities, abilities, and dispositions. The something can be a Martian, a left-hander, a robot like Cogit-8, or whatever. The concern about chauvinism is a serious one. But in the textbook philosophy of mind narrative the concern does not lead to a resurgence of behaviourism. Rather, it leads to a new doctrine that seeks to take the best of the identity theory and the best of behaviourism. This is the doctrine of functionalism.

Functionalism

The central idea of functionalism is that for a creature to be in a given mental state is for its brain – or the equivalent of its brain – to be in a given functional state. Suppose that in the Martian brain, toe-stubbing is followed by the firing of neurons r15 through to p24 in sequence gamma-12. And suppose that such firing typically causes whining and complaining. Given this, we can say that the Martian is in pain. And what realizes the pain is not the brain state that realizes our human pain, but the brain state that is the firing of neurons r15 through to p24 in sequence gamma-12. This state, the functionalist says, plays the same functional role as – it does the same job as – our brain state, and by virtue of this it realizes the same mental state.

All varieties of functionalism share this basic idea. This said, the doctrine comes in a wide variety of forms. The kind of functionalism I am concerned with here has the following characteristics. It begins with a comprehensive theory of a person's psychology. The comprehensive theory specifies explicitly the causal relationship between stimuli, inner mental states, and behaviours, for example, toe-stubbing, pain, and whining. Of course, for every kind of stimulus, inner state, and behaviour, there will be very many different causal connections. So the theory will be complex and, indeed, very large. But functionalism is a philosophical doctrine, rather than a practical proposal. All that matters is that the comprehensive theory could be constructed in principle. In order to construct the comprehensive theory we need to make use of intentional concepts. But once it is constructed, these can be discarded, as any given mental state can be defined in terms of its causal relations to other inner states, to stimuli, and to behaviours. In this way, functionalism reconciles science and our self-conception. It does so by, in effect, reducing intentional states of the mind to causal states of an inner mechanism.

For functionalism, what makes it true that something is a conscious rational agent is that its internal mechanism conforms to an abstract causal blueprint derived from a comprehensive psychology. The blueprint specifies all the causal relationships between inputs, internal states, and outputs. What it is to have a particular thought or a particular experience is for the mechanism to occupy a state that plays a given causal role. For example, if the mechanism is in the state that is caused by toe-stubbing and causes whining, then the agent is in pain.

A key attraction of functionalism is that it is more liberal than the identity theory. But it is too liberal for some. For it is clear that functionalism makes it possible that, say, our imaginary robot Cogit-8 has thoughts and feelings. If Cogit-8's internal mechanism has the same abstract causal blueprint as ours, then Cogit-8 thinks and feels. Moreover, if we could somehow arrange for the population of China to conform to that same abstract causal blueprint, then the population of China would think and feel. For some this is just absurd. The serious functionalist, however, will bite the bullet and argue that any view that is less liberal than hers will be fatally chauvinistic. Dennett, who is a committed liberal, will endorse this move. Indeed, he must, because for Dennett a key flaw in functionalism is that it is not liberal enough.

We can see why Dennett takes this line by thinking more about Cogit-8. For although it is clear that functionalism entails that Cogit-8 could be a conscious rational agent, it does not guarantee this. At least it does not if Dennett is correct when he writes:

> There really is no more reason to believe you and I "have the same program" in *any* relaxed abstract sense, considering the difference in our nature and nurture, than that our brains have identical physicochemical descriptions. (*BS*, xvi)

If the abstract causal blueprint of the mechanism inside Cogit-8's head is different from the abstract causal blueprint of our brains, then, according to functionalism, Cogit-8 is not a conscious rational agent. Or, to use the language of computer science, if Cogit-8's program is distinct from the program inside us, then Cogit-8 does not really have thoughts and feelings. This result should be very worrying for functionalism. For although functionalism is clearly much more liberal than the identity theory – it does not mind what our internal mechanisms are built out of, so long as they conform to the same abstract causal blueprint – it turns out to look chauvinistic in another way.

This much said, a great deal turns on whether or not you agree with Dennett that there could be things with very different insides, say Cogit-8 and a person, that behave in very similar ways. If you think that the only way such behaviour could be causally underpinned is by means of a fairly specific abstract causal blueprint, then Dennett's worry will have little bite. For, in response to the idea that Cogit-8 might have a distinct program, you will insist that if the program is distinct then the relevant behaviour will not be forthcoming.

The functionalist can attempt to meet this kind of worry by allowing that there is not just one abstract causal blueprint for conscious rational agency, but a whole set of blueprints that can do the job, each differing in detail, but each describing a plausible psychology. Could we then say that to be a person, and to have mental states such as our own, an entity must conform to a comprehensive theory that is a member of this special set? This might work. And it might also help with octopus, cat, and dog pains; the alert reader may have noticed that these have been left unaccounted for by the formulation of functionalism given so far. But the suggestion raises the question of what is required for a comprehensive theory to belong to the special set in the first place.

One of the attractions of functionalism is that it clearly meets the demands of naturalism by showing us that we can discard intentional concepts once we have established a comprehensive theory. Intentional states come to be defined in terms of causal relations to other inner states, to stimuli, and to behaviours. But in the response just outlined, it turns out that intentional concepts are not abandoned at all. For we will constantly need to go back to our intentional concepts to check to see whether any given internal mechanism implements a plausible psychology or not. And now what is doing the real work in our theory is our judgement about what is and what is not a plausible psychology, that is, something to do with outward appearances, and not something to do with the insides.

A detailed look at how functionalists can respond to these criticisms is beyond the scope of this book. I would concede that some functionalists may be able to find good responses. But the functionalist who seeks to show what it is to be a person – a creature with mental states like our own, in terms of a fixed blueprint, a description of the basic causal structure of all persons – looks as though she is in serious trouble. For it seems, at least so Dennett presses, that no single specification of a blueprint could capture all the causal structures that would be sufficient to underpin a person. And shifting to a special set of fixed blueprints does not seem to help. Unless, that is, the membership of that set can be specified without appeal to intentional concepts.

I should stress again that the view I am discussing here is not the only kind of functionalism there is. Some though not all of the criticisms rehearsed here also affect other forms. One point is worth making, however. On occasion Dennett has himself described his own view as functionalist (*BC*, 359). To the extent that Dennett is relaxed about multiple-realizability, and emphasizes the importance of what you can do as opposed to what you are made of, this self-ascription makes sense. But given that Dennett's view is so very different from many of the canonical statements of functionalism the tag strikes me as unhelpful. So, throughout, I will portray Dennett as a critic of functionalism. And he is, as we shall see, a critic of the kind of functionalism just described.[3]

Who holds the trumps?

Cartesian Dualism, the identity theory, and functionalism are all examples of what I have called Cartesian Theories. Unlike Rylean Theories, of which behaviourism is an example, they require that what makes it true that something is a person, and what makes it true that someone has a given thought or a given feeling, is a set of facts about their insides. A critical consequence of this is that ordinary judgements, judgements based on outward appearances, can be trumped by judgements about what is going on inside. In some contexts this is just what we want. We are content to let a biologist 'trump' our ordinary judgements – she may tell us that for all the creature before us looks like a wolf, it is in fact a thylacine, a marsupial rather than a placental mammal.

Dennett, however, is not persuaded that our ordinary judgements about persons could be 'trumped' in a similar way. While it is true that subtle behavioural observations – such as those made by a psychotherapist – might trump the appearance of more superficial ones, such trumping takes place squarely within the realm of intentional concepts. What we cannot imagine, or so Dennett would contend, are facts of a different kind – say, about the configurations of neurons – being used as evidence to tell us that someone who to all outward appearances is a rational conscious agent is not, after all, an agent at all. Consider this passage from Dennett:

> Suppose, for the sake of drama, that it turns out that [the brain wiring] of some people turns out to be dramatically different from that of others. One can imagine the newspaper headlines: "Scientists Prove Most Left-handers Incapable of Belief" or "Startling Discovery – Diabetics Have No Desires." But this is not what we would say, no matter how the science turns out. (*IS*, 235; cf. *CE*, 405–6)

Dennett thinks that we should take very seriously the moral of this story. But in doing so Dennett runs against a significant tide in contemporary philosophy of mind. Functionalists see it as a virtue of their account that facts about internal organization can trump facts about behaviour. A pain will typically cause a person to whine and complain. But for the functionalist you can be in pain even if, for some reason or another, it fails to manifest its effect. Of course, behaviourism also allows that. For, along with the pain, you might believe that whining is inappropriate in the present circumstances. But the functionalist is after a bolder claim. She argues that it is possible to have the pain, and for there to be no circumstances in which behaviour would reveal the presence of that pain.[4] Someone, for example, might train herself to withstand pain, to never complain, to never acknowledge to anyone that she was in pain. But the functionalist argues that the behaviourist must accept that such a person feels no pain. And this, she presses, is absurd. If the person's innards are going through the relevant motions, then she feels pain regardless of how she behaves. According to the theory, a brain scanner, or a functional organization scanner, could show a person was in pain, trumping any denial she might make and any lack of behavioural disturbance she might manifest.

If this functionalist argument is sound, then it would show that any broadly behaviourist account of experience, and that will include Dennett's account, seriously misses the mark. But there is a clear line of reply available to Dennett and to any behaviourist. The behaviourist can say that someone who has trained herself to be as stoical about pain as the functionalist suggests is someone who has trained herself not to feel pain. The functionalist only seems to have an edge here because she underdescribes the case. To distinguish herself from the behaviourist, the functionalist must admit that, even in her most private moments, the person does not complain to herself about her pain. And, once this is admitted, the behaviourist can press, it begins to look as though it is the functionalist's view that is absurd.

Once again we have a stand-off. The functionalist insists that the behaviourist is not taking consciousness seriously enough because she denies that what inner experience a person has can detach itself from her behavioural inclinations. The behaviourist insists that the functionalist notion of consciousness here makes no sense: a pain that does not even slightly incline someone to complain, even in circumstances when complaint would be perfectly acceptable, is, by her lights, just not a pain.

The representational theory of mind

The representational theory of mind, the final phase of the textbook narrative, does not really proceed as a logical step from functionalism. That said, by modifying functionalism in a certain way, it does go some way towards addressing the problem of chauvinism just outlined. What is most distinctive about the representational theory is that it aims to connect the purely metaphysical doctrine of functionalism with an actual theory about how the relevant functional structure might be constructed. The theory suggests that there are core brain mechanisms that are responsible for thought, perception, and action. Sometimes the target is *actual* brain mechanisms, and the data this version of the theory draws on will include not only studies of behaviour but also studies of the brain. On other occasions the target is *possible* brain mechanisms. Here the version of the theory will draw on research into artificial intelligence, the art of reproducing cognitive capacities by means of complex computer programs. Either way, a basic assumption of the representational theory is that brains have a core mechanism – an inference engine – that processes internal symbols or representations.

Functionalism, as just described, insists on a comprehensive psychological theory, a theory that describes the whole of someone's psychology. The representational theory insists only on a core psychological theory, the aspect that deals with thinking, perceiving, acting, and so forth. The details of someone's psychology, the particular ideas and inclinations that they have, are not part of the core theory. They are free to change. All that the representational theory insists is that each and every person has a part of their brain – or the equivalent of their brain – that is correctly described by the core theory. The rest, which accommodates a set of internal symbols or representations, is free to vary from species to species, and is free to vary with age and experience.

What is meant here by representation? A representation is a physical object, and hence one that can be readily accommodated by naturalism. As a physical object it has causal powers. It can cause things to occur and it can be caused to occur. But a representation also has intentional properties. It is about something or stands in for something, where that something is an actual or a possible entity in the world. So, for example, a bust of Socrates is a representation. For it is both a physical object and it is also, in a suitable sense, *about* Socrates. Or, then again, it can *stand in for* Socrates. Representations not only stand in for, or are about, objects. They can also stand in for or be about claims. The sentence 'Juli drives fast' is a physical object – a set of marks on the page – that represents a claim, namely the claim that Juli drives fast.

The representational theory of mind claims that representations of claims exist inside the brain, and it is by manipulating such representations that the brain is able to underpin the process of thinking. What the brain cannot do, what no merely mechanistic process can do, is respond directly to the meanings of a representation. A mechanism can be directly affected by the physical structure of a representation, such as the pattern of light and dark made by printed letters on a page, but it has no way of being directly affected by the meaning. But the physical properties of representations, be they patterns of light and dark on paper or patterns of neural signals in the brain, can drive a mechanism in such a way that the mechanism appears to be sensitive to the meanings of the representations.

Think about a mechanical cash register. It has sets of wheels and keys that are painted with the digits zero to nine. The machine is arranged so that the manipulations of the wheels and keys, which are of course representations, follow the rules of addition. To be sure, the cash register does not understand what numbers are or what addition is. But by responding to the physical features of the representations that form part of its mechanism, it can operate just as if it did understand the meaning of the representations. Computers work in much the same way as mechanical cash registers, though they can deal with many more and more diverse representations. Just as the cash register can manipulate representations about numbers to produce the right answers to addition sums, so a computer can manipulate representations about claims. For example, it can string a series of claims into an argument, and derive whatever conclusions logically follow from those claims. The idea, as Jerry Fodor explains, is taken from the mathematician Alan Turing (1912–1954):

> Having noticed [a parallel] between thoughts and symbols [i.e. representations], Turing went on to having the following perfectly stunning idea: "I'll bet", Turing (more or less) said, "that one could build a *symbol manipulating machine* whose changes of state are driven by the material properties of the symbols on which they operate . . . And I'll bet one could so arrange things that these state changes are rational in the sense that, given a true symbol to play with, the machine will reliably convert it into other symbols that are also true." (Fodor, 1992)

Computers are just such representation-manipulating machines. We can equip a machine with a set of representations and a set of rules for manipulating representations. And we can arrange things so that if the initial set of representations only made true claims about the world then so will the new set. This is done by setting up rules for manipulating representations that correspond to rules for drawing valid inferences. And all this can be done simply by the application of mechanical processes, processes that are not sensitive to the meaning of the representations, but just to their physical form. This is, in outline, how Fodor explains the process of thinking. Deciding what to do is explained in the same sort of way, only here the inputs into the process include not just claims that capture what the person believes to be the case, but also claims that she would like to be the case.

According to the representational theory of mind, what makes it true that something is a conscious rational agent is that they have inside an inference engine, that is a mechanism, that can be specified by an abstract causal blueprint, that processes representations in an appropriate way. And what makes it true that someone has a thought or experience is that, in their head, there is a representation corresponding to that thought or experience. Perhaps, as Fodor argues, these internal representations are arranged like sentences, that is, with various component parts that can be reordered in a variety of ways. The core mechanism, the inference engine, processes these representations, generating new thoughts from old, generating thoughts from external stimuli, and generating behaviour from thoughts.

The representational theory appears to have many advantages. It gives us a clear picture of how our self-conception can be reconciled with science. It does so in a way that makes sense of the intuition that thoughts and experiences can be causes of our behaviour. It avoids the clear chauvinism of the identity theory and is more liberal than (at least some forms of) functionalism. It is also a Cartesian Theory. It regards behaviour as mere evidence for what someone is thinking and feeling: the facts that determine what someone is thinking and feeling are ultimately facts about what goes on in the inside.

What does the representational theory say about our imaginary robot Cogit-8? Although more liberal than functionalism, the representational theory, once again, cannot guarantee that Cogit-8 is a conscious rational agent. It cannot because, at least if Dennett is right, there are ways to produce Cogit-8's behaviour that do not require that Cogit-8 contains, inside its head, an inference engine of the kind specified by the representational theory. And so, by Dennett's lights, the representational theory is not liberal enough. Its failure to include a Cogit-8 that happens to have a different kind of internal mechanism is, for Dennett, indication that the representational theory has not hooked on to what matters about being an agent, about having thoughts and experiences.

1.3   Investigating our concepts

In looking at Dennett's view in relation to other views in the textbook philosophy of mind narrative, we have identified a number of stand-offs. These are common in philosophy and arise because different protagonists have importantly different understandings of certain problematic concepts. In this section I want to outline three different temperaments or ideologies that can come into play when investigating problematic concepts. By making these temperaments explicit, we can better understand how to respond to the stand-offs that arise in philosophical debate, and, further, better understand why Dennett takes the various positions that he does.

The first temperament favours what I shall call common-sense analysis. The common-sense analyst is impressed by our concepts as we find them. While not opposed to clarification, refinement, and, on occasion, careful revision in the light of philosophical reflection, she is basically conservative.[5] In particular, she sees no role for empirical inquiry in contributing to the investigation of concepts such as person, belief, consciousness, and freedom. As a result she tends to favour Rylean over Cartesian Theories.

The second temperament favours what I shall call scientific analysis. The scientific analyst is impressed by the power of science to reform our concepts. She sees many of our concepts as rough-and-ready attempts to pick out significant fault-lines in nature. She will tend to favour Cartesian Theories of concepts, theories that allow facts about inner essences to trump common-sense intuitions about outward appearances. Empirical inquiry is the key tool in picking out the fault lines made by such inner essences, and so can help bring our rough-and-ready concepts into line, teaching us that, after all, whales are not fish, and that jade is not one kind of substance, but two distinct substances that share a superficial appearance. For the scientific analyst concepts such as person, belief, consciousness, and (probably) freedom work in the same way. That is, Cartesian Theories are favoured. And, given this, empirical investigation can lead to fairly radical revisions of these concepts and even outright elimination.

Common-sense and scientific analyses both share the assumption that there is a correct way to understand a problematic concept. If we keep investigating the concept of, say, 'belief' then we shall eventually come to a definitive understanding. Moreover, as our investigation proceeds, both these methods understand the process as one that aims to uncover more about the very same topic, with later research correcting earlier mistakes if all goes well. That is, both common-sense and scientific analyses take the attitude that conceptual investigation is a matter of discovery rather than decision.

So, for example, both common-sense and scientific analysts may be inclined to say that when earlier generations said that whales were fish, they were simply making a mistake. And, similarly, they may both be inclined to say that when Aristotle was talking about people and gold he was talking about exactly the same kinds of thing we moderns talk about. And they may say this despite the fact that culture has changed, including deep-seated beliefs about the nature of the self, and despite the fact that neither Aristotle nor any of his contemporaries understood chemistry in the way we or some of our contemporaries do.

The third kind of philosophical temperament differs here. This temperament favours what I shall call consensual analysis. Perhaps, consensual analysts may point out, modern biology has actually changed our concept of fish, so that those earlier generations were not mistaken but just applying a different concept. Their concept of fish might have applied to any water-dwelling creature with a backbone, of which the whale is clearly an example. Perhaps Aristotle really did mean something different by gold, and perhaps, even, people in Aristotle's day were not quite the same kind of entity as people today.

This third kind of philosophical temperament, that of the consensual analyst, is marked by the idea that there are no eternal and immutable facts to be discovered about the correct applications of some of our problematic concepts. For example, someone like Richard Rorty seems to go as far as to say that the issue of whether or not an animal feels pain could never amount to anything more than the issue of whether or not we, a community of speakers, can reach a common agreement about whether to grant the animal a certain kind of moral status, roughly a moral status that will lead us to think twice about doing things to the animal that if done to us would cause us pain (Rorty, 1979, 182–92). Whether the concept of pain applies to an animal, then, is determined by whether or not the community of speakers elects to deploy the concept in that context. Dennett has sympathy with much of Rorty's thought, but, like so many others, he finds this sort of suggestion deeply shocking.

Rorty's thought shocks because something that seems as though it should be a matter of discovery and not decision is made out to be the opposite. Rorty and his defenders may quite legitimately point out that it is hardly as if such decisions could float free of what we, the community of speakers, could consider reasonable in the light of evidence and argument. But what Rorty and his defenders will not do is to admit that there could be some fact of the matter quite independent of what we, the community of speakers, can come to agree is correct. It is the commitment to such facts – in core cases if not penumbral ones – that makes Dennett's view importantly different from Rorty's. We might express the difference like this: Rorty is merely looking for ways to achieve consensus in our application of concepts, whereas Dennett is looking for the truth. Rorty, of course, would express the difference in quite another way, and in particular would attack the notion of truth understood independently of consensus agreement.

Tackling cases

I have described the common-sense, scientific, and consensual approaches as temperaments or ideologies. They are not universal policies. Each temperament recognizes concepts that are best analysed by one or other of the alternative methods. Some concepts are clearly answerable only to our predilections – concepts such as chair, sofa, and fashion. Others are clearly answerable only to the results of scientific experiments – concepts such as gene and uranium. And for others again, the consensual case can be made attractive: consider, for example, whether unmarried men living in long-term partnerships are well described as 'bachelors'. Plausibly, our concept of a bachelor has changed in response to new social mores.

The temperaments come into play with problematic concepts – beauty, truth, justice, belief, person, freedom, and rationality. Take the concept of belief. A representational theorist, such as Jerry Fodor, favours scientific analyses. Common-sense ascriptions of belief are a rough-and-ready way of picking out beliefs, but the best way of picking out beliefs is to look at the mechanisms of believers. Once these mechanisms are well understood, the scientific analysis can come to replace the common-sense analysis. And, moreover, it becomes possible for the scientific analysis to trump the judgements of the common-sense analysis. By contrast Gilbert Ryle favours common-sense analyses; indeed, he is fiercely opposed to scientific analysis. So he is sceptical about finding some deeper understanding of what beliefs are, other than what is provided by reflection on our ordinary practice of ascribing beliefs to one another.

How can we settle a dispute about a particular case, when the participants begin with a different temperament or ideology? The main working method of philosophy in this area is to test out analyses of concepts in a range of different circumstances, both imaginary and real. An imaginary situation might try to encourage us to believe that it is conceptually possible that a person has, say, only one belief (Stich, 1983, 54–6). A real situation might involve a psychology experiment that encourages us to believe that, say, that a person can be influenced by a stimulus in the absence of any conscious awareness. But the way in which a theorist responds to this 'data' is very much dependent on her philosophical temperament.

Imagine, for example, that brain scientists learn how to 'decode' brain representations – written in the language of thought. They discover a high correlation between belief ascriptions and what these brain sentences say. Does this 'data' support the scientific analyst? One might think so. But, in fact, the common-sense analyst may argue that this shows not that beliefs really are 'sentences in the head', but merely that beliefs can, in certain circumstances, be accompanied by 'sentences in the head'. Indeed, this is more or less what Dennett says in just this case (*BS*, chapters 3 and 6).

So it seems that theorists with different temperaments, or different ideologies, can reasonably take different attitudes to the same cases. And this means that direct argumentation between different adherents of the different ideologies is not always productive. It is not productive because the arguments concentrate on the case in hand, whereas it is the background ideologies that are actually doing the work in the dispute. Moreover, it is far from clear that direct argument that addresses the principles of the ideologies is very productive. The ideologies run so deep that it can be hard to find a shared perspective from which to discuss the merits of their principles.

What, then, can we do? The best way, I think, and perhaps the only way, to settle disputes of this kind is to see which ideology offers the best overall understanding of ourselves and our place in nature. And so we need to explore the kind of theory each ideology will give rise to, and to explore it in some detail. Faced with a range of problems and a range of puzzling cases, which ideology yields the most satisfying overall package? It will turn out – it always does – that each ideology will require that we give up some cherished beliefs or intuitions, but that each will offer exciting new ways of thinking about ourselves and our place in nature.

Dennett's temperament

Dennett's temperament is closest to that of a common-sense analyst. But his approach is different in one very important respect. Unlike Ryle, who is a flag-bearer for common-sense analysis, Dennett thinks that science does have a contribution to make to conceptual investigation. But what sort of contribution can science make if we do not embrace scientific analysis? Surely, one might think, to give science a significant role is simply to switch sides and embrace scientific analysis?

This is not the case. Dennett's approach is to allow science to *constrain* his common-sense analysis, but not to *subsume* it. Pure

common-sense analysis insists that science has nothing to contribute to its work. It does not assume that the world is round, that
humans evolved, and so forth. But Dennett's approach does include
a very important and non-negotiable empirical premise. The premise is that human beings and all objects to which any intentional
language can be correctly applied are made up of entirely mechanical parts and have come into being solely through mechanistic
processes. Supernature is not needed to account for what we are,
nor is it needed to account for how we came to be.

Dennett does not especially defend this premise. Other things
being equal, he thinks that we have overwhelming reasons
to accept it. The only serious threat to the premise would be if it
forced us to abandon basic elements of our self-understanding. If
it forced us to revise beyond recognition, or even eliminate,
concepts such as person, rationality, freedom, and consciousness,
then we might want to think again. Dennett assumes the premise
and then sets out to show that our self-conception, while needing
some revision, can be retained intact and, even, strengthened.
Our self-conception is not, he argues, unduly threatened by the
premise.

But does adopting the naturalistic premise make a difference?
Dennett's work shows us that it does. It makes a tremendous difference. Throughout the book we shall see in detail how he thinks
it makes a difference in understanding intentionality, agency, consciousness, the self, and freedom of the will. We can get a sense of
how it makes a difference by considering one example here. Adopting the premise means that we have to accept that human rationality will always be flawed. Why? Because an ideal rationality, one
that considered all possible alternatives, could not be underpinned
by a finite mechanism. The mechanism would either have to be
indefinitely large or operate at an indefinitely high speed. Given
that we have finite brains that operate at a finite speed, the best
rationality that we could possibly have will be less effective than
the best rationality we can imagine.

On balance, I think Dennett's version of common-sense analysis,
a scientifically constrained version, is the approach that offers the
best compromise between preserving existing insights and understandings and reconciling them with new ideas about ourselves and
our world, and in particular new ideas stemming from scientific
investigation. But, as noted above, to show this we need to explore
the overall package that is on offer from Dennett, so that we can
assess its strengths and weaknesses in the round.

Further reading

For the work of Wittgenstein that has influenced Dennett, see his *Philosophical Investigations*. There is a vast secondary literature on Wittgenstein. An approachable introduction is McGinn (1997). On Quine, see his article 'The Two Dogmas of Empiricism' (Quine, 1953), and his book *Word and Object* (Quine, 1960). Both are hard-going, even for specialists. A helpful introduction to Quine's work, which includes a detailed guide to 'Two Dogmas . . .', is Hookway (1988). For Ryle, see his *The Concept of Mind*. Chapters 1–3 are essential reading for any student of Dennett or indeed for anyone interested in philosophy at all. On Dennett's move from the armchair to the field, see *IS*, 272ff, and *BC*, chapter 20. For a description of the COG project, see Dennett, *BC*, chapter 9, and also Dennett (2000). A sophisticated take on this sort of example, and one that is amenable to Dennett's view, is Davidson (1973). For someone who expresses doubts as to whether something like Cogit-8 could be a thinker, see Searle (1980; 1992). On Descartes, see his *Meditations on First Philosophy*, and also his *Discourse on Method* (in particular section V). Churchland (1988) provides a clear and concise version of the textbook philosophy of mind narrative. Kim (1996) provides a more detailed survey of the textbook narrative and a detailed discussion of the notion of reduction. A more sceptical view of the textbook narrative is presented by Burwood et al. (1999). Fodor's (1992) newspaper article 'The Big Idea' is a brief and accessible introduction to the representational theory of mind and to Fodor's idea of the language of thought. Follow this up with chapter 1 and the appendix of his *Psychosemantics* (Fodor, 1987). Crane (1995) provides a useful account of the idea of representation and of the representational theory. For Richard Rorty's ideas, see his *Philosophy and the Mirror of Nature* (Rorty, 1979). On Dennett's temperament, Symons (2001) gives a rather different reading, insisting that Dennett does more than pay lip-service to Quine, but is fully committed to science and philosophy being continuous. Finally, the broader background of this chapter, the tension between the apparent demands of naturalism and of our self-conception is brilliantly explored by Taylor (1989, chapter 3).

2

Adopting a Stance

In pursuing his naturalism – his attempt to reconcile a rejection of the supernatural with our common-sense understanding of ourselves – Dennett needs a naturalistic explanation of phenomena such as thought, free will, consciousness, dreaming, creativity, mental imagery, and so forth. His strategy works in two stages (see *CE*, 457; *BC*, 355).

The first stage is to develop an account of agency. For Dennett, agency comes in many varieties: persons, elephants, and spiders all count, on his understanding of the notion, as agents. And so, more controversially, do chess machines and robots. They all count by virtue of being systems that respond to meanings, that act for reasons, and that pursue goals. When we explain their behaviour, we do so by reference to what they 'think' and what they 'value'. In the philosophical jargon, these features are called intentional states, that is, states that involve some reference to a claim about how the world is ('I think the cat is on the mat') or how the world might be ('I'm afraid the cat is out of the bag'). The key question here is how agents, with their intentional states, can be built out of mechanistic devices.

The second stage is to show how all other 'mental treasures' – that is, phenomena such as consciousness, rational deliberation, free will – can be derived from Dennett's account of agency and intentional states. How, as Dennett puts it, can these treasures be purchased with 'intentional coin' (*BS*, xiv)? In this chapter, and chapters 3 and 4, I shall be examining his account of agency and intentional states. In subsequent chapters I turn to the second stage and try to show how he can successfully explain other features of our ordinary self-conception solely in terms of intentionality.

2.1　Intentional systems theory

Dennett's conception of agency goes something like this. Agents act for reasons. A reason is a consideration that speaks in favour of a certain course of action. As such reasons are necessarily tied to interests. If an entity has no interests, that is, if there is nothing that is good or worth pursuing for an agent, then there are no reasons for that agent to pursue any course of action. Indeed, if there are no things that are good or worthwhile for some entity, it is not clear that we can make any sense of that entity being an agent at all. Agency, at least as it is understood by Dennett, is the pursuit of what is, or what is considered to be, worthwhile.[1] Agency, reason, interest, and so forth, are a tightly interrelated set of concepts.

If we are committed to naturalism, how can we accommodate interests in our understanding of the world? In a world of mechanism, surely there is no scope for interests. Why? Well nobody thinks an atom has a stake or an interest in jumping this way or that. There is nothing that is good or bad for the atom. Nor, indeed, does it have any preferences that it aims to satisfy. But, given all this, how can it be that aggregates of atoms have interests? How, that is, by adding together very many small units, none of which have interests, can one have a larger unit that does?

But if there is no scope for interests, then there is no scope for reasons. And if no scope for reasons, then no scope for agents either (*ER*, 20–34). But, unless we are prepared to countenance eliminativism, we can be sure that there are agents. So we need some way of understanding interests, reasons, and agency that is compatible with naturalism. The most common approach is some kind of reduction. This involves defining or identifying agency and its associated intentional phenomena in terms of non-intentional phenomena. (Reduction is explored at length in 2.4.) This, however, is not Dennett's approach. He wants to offer a theory of agency that neither defines agency in terms of something non-intentional nor identifies agency with something non-intentional. To this end he gives us intentional systems theory.

Intentional systems theory is very general in its scope. It does not have persons as its focus, but a very general class of agents. For Dennett, anything that pursues its interests by reliably behaving in ways it has good reason to, is an agent. So the class of agents is, right from the off, very broad. It unproblematically includes persons, but also clearly includes complex animals, and, according to Dennett, can even include robots and computer systems. Lest this suggestion sound quite absurd, we need to note straight away that for Dennett there is no requirement that an agent recognize the reasons it has, and the reasons that, by virtue of being an agent, it reliably acts in accordance with. We persons aspire to be 'completely savvy, to be able to notice *all* the reasons that concern us' (*ER*, 24–5). We do not achieve such heady heights, but we are aware of many of our interests and the reasons to which they give rise. By contrast, for Dennett, many agents have no awareness of any of their reasons. But so long as we can make good sense of their having interests we can make good sense of their having reasons.

So the concepts 'agent', 'reason', and 'interest' are to be understood in a weaker or thinner sense than they are in some contexts. Many moral philosophers, for example, would find such use of these concepts very thin indeed, as, for them, agency is synonymous with moral agency, and reasons and interests are synonymous with considerations that can, at least in principle, be brought to mind. But Dennett's paradigm of an agent is not a person. His basic theory of agency does not aspire to be an account of persons, but of a more general class of agent. Dennett does not ignore the serious and substantial differences between different kinds of agent. But he does begin with an account of agents that are paradigmatically much simpler than persons. The task of building up an account of persons, then, is deferred to the later stages of his theory.

Three stances

Dennett's account of his theory begins with a story about how we engage in the prediction of various 'systems'. The term 'system' refers to any entity the activity of which we are attempting to predict. So a system could be something as simple as a rock or as complex as a person. Dennett asks us to consider three different stances we might take on any given system. When first introducing these stances, Dennett picks a system of intermediate complexity: a chess machine.

When faced with a chess machine, a computer with a dedicated chess-playing program, and asked to predict its behaviour, there is a range of different approaches we can take. First, we could adopt what Dennett calls the physical stance and treat the device as a collection of physical parts. 'From this stance our predictions are based on the actual physical state of the particular object, and are worked out by applying whatever knowledge we have of the laws of nature' (ISY, 4). The physical stance will, in principle, always yield accurate predictions, but applying it to a chess computer would be 'a pointless and Herculean labour' (ISY, 5). To work out the machine's next move using the physical stance would require millions upon millions of calculations. So, second, we could adopt the design stance.

> If one knows exactly how the computer is designed (including the impermanent part of its design: its program) one can predict its designed response to any move one makes by following the computation instructions in the program. One's predictions will come out true provided only that the computer performs as designed: that is, without breakdown. (ISY, 4)

A computer program is just one way in which we can have knowledge of a system's design. The design stance can be pitched at different levels of detail. We could look at a level below that of the program, say the level of the computer hardware. This is a lower level, but still a much higher level than that of the physical materials. Knowing the design details of a given circuit allows for much quicker predictions than the physical stance approach of following the flow of electrons through each individual part. But it would be much slower than making predictions based on the program.

Whatever the level at which we pitch the design stance it allows us to make predictions more 'economically', i.e. with less effort, than the physical stance. The price we have to pay for this economy is to assume that the device is working properly. When this assumption fails then our predictions will become unreliable. If an electricity spike alters the chess machine's stored program, then the design stance pitched at the program level will cease to yield reliable predictions. However, the design stance pitched at the level of the computer hardware will not be affected. If, on the other hand, one of the computer's circuits breaks down, then both the program-level and the hardware-level design stances will cease to yield good predictions. By contrast, on either scenario, the predictions of the physical stance would be unaffected.

Though much 'cheaper' than the physical stance, applying the design stance to the chess machine is still 'very expensive'. If you were attempting to play chess with the machine and were interested to work out what sort of moves it was likely to make, the design stance would be close to hopeless. Even pitched at the relatively high level of the computer program, to work out the chess machine's next move would take hours, perhaps days or weeks, of hard effort. This is because for each given move, the computer executes thousands upon thousands of program instructions. So for practical prediction, the design stance is no use. When playing chess, you need to predict your opponent's play in real time. And so, practically, the design stance will not help us play against the chess machine.

But Dennett has a third stance: the intentional stance. When adopting this stance you:

> first . . . decide to treat the object whose behaviour is to be predicted as a rational agent; then you figure out what beliefs the agent ought to have, given its place in the world and its purpose. Then you figure out what desires it ought to have, on the same considerations, and finally you predict that this rational agent will act to further its own goals in the light of its beliefs. A little practical reasoning from the chosen set of beliefs and desires will in many – but not all – instances yield a decision about what the agent ought to do; that is what you predict the agent *will* do. (TB, 17)

In adopting the intentional stance, you need to adopt much stronger assumptions about the system. You assume that the chess machine has some overarching goals (to win at chess), that it is capable of gathering and comprehending information about the state of play, and that it is, to a suitable degree, rational. Being rational here does not simply mean being good at logic, at deriving valid conclusions from a set of premises. It is not the notion that philosophers call theoretical rationality. Rather, it is what philosophers call practical rationality, something that may involve theoretical rationality, but which is primarily understood as the skill of acting in accordance with reasons, acting in ways that serve to promote what is good or worthwhile for the agent.

In any case, given these assumptions, you can work out the sorts of intentional states the device ought to have. Thus, in response to certain inputs, we can recognize that the device ought to believe this or ought to want that. For example, in a given situation, we might say that it ought to believe its queen is in danger and hence it ought to want to move it to safety. If we have had more experience seeing the chess machine at work, the intentional stance may suggest more sophisticated intentional states, such as the belief that it should vary its openings, the desire to outflank its opponent's bishops, or the hope that its opponent will not notice the ruse it is devising.

It is clearly the case, urges Dennett, that we can and do apply the intentional stance to chess machines, as well as a host of other systems (ISY, 21–2). And that if a system is constructed in a certain sort of way then the stance will yield 'reliable and voluminous' (ISY, 15) predictions. That is, on many occasions over a wide range of different circumstances, the predictions of the stance will often succeed. Dennett labels any system that meets these criteria an 'intentional system'.

What do I mean here by 'constructed in a certain sort of way'? We expect the intentional stance to work well with the chess machine because it is designed and constructed to perform the job of playing chess. Moreover, the design and construction is sufficiently effective to yield a viable commercial product. If the machine were designed badly we would not be inclined to adopt the intentional stance. If, that is, the moves it tended to make were wholly irrational, or even marginally rational, then adopting the stance would not help us understand the machine. But if, as is usually the case, the machine is designed well enough to play a decent game of chess, the stance pays dividends and it is the best 'strategic' choice.

Of course, the intentional stance is even more vulnerable to failure than the design stance. We may have failed to take account of beliefs and desires that the device has acquired, and hence make faulty predictions. Or our estimate of what is most rational may itself be sub-optimal; the machine, that is, might be smarter than we are. Or the device may not be operating very reliably. Or it may be operating according to specification but simply not be ideally rational. Even excellent chess machines will make sub-optimal moves from time to time. If it had all the time and resources in the world to consider its moves, then this might not be so. But, like us, chess machines must operate in real time and with limited resources. And, like us, the problems they are having to solve are complex and difficult. But it is no requirement of employing the stance that the system, be it a chess machine or anything else, is ideally rational. In adopting the stance, Dennett tells us, '[one] starts with the ideal of perfect rationality and revises downward as circumstances dictate' (TB, 21; cf. TK, 53–4). But even as we revise downward Dennett wants to insist that such revisions are 'laid over a funda-mental . . . normative framework' (TK, 54), i.e., a framework based on how things should (ideally, according to the norms of rational-ity) work. What Dennett's theory requires is not that a system be ideally rational, but that we can best understand it in light of that ideal.

As Dennett notes (TB, 17, quoted above), the intentional stance may not be able to predict exactly what move the chess machine will make at every turn. But it will be able to narrow down the range of moves it might make. Assuming that it is functioning properly, it will, by and large, only make a move for which some good reasons can be adduced. The design stance and the physical stance will yield more specific predictions. But they will only do so at a cost. The less specific predictions of the intentional stance, less specific because often there are a range of rational moves that could be made, are much 'cheaper'.

Dennett now makes a radical move. He claims that:

> What it is to be [a genuine agent][2] is to be an *intentional system*, a system whose behaviour is reliably and voluminously predictable via the intentional [stance]. (TB, 15; cf. TB, 29)

So it is not simply the case that we can treat chess machines as if they were agents; Dennett is actually claiming that they are. Or, more carefully, he is claiming that if the intentional stance turns out to be the most appropriate stance to take towards the chess machine, then, in virtue of that, the chess machine has as much claim to be a genuine agent as anything could have.

Baldly stated this claim can sound, as Dennett puts it, 'perverse' (TB, 29). Consider some worries. First, we may find it simply absurd to think that a chess machine is an agent at all. If we are to be tempted by this idea, we shall need more help. Second, we may think Dennett has spectacularly failed to distinguish between treating something as if it is an agent and its actually being an agent: for, surely, we might think, the two cannot come to the same thing? Third, if being an agent is just a matter of being amenable to some kind of interpretation, does that not mean that agency is something that exists only in the eye of the beholder; and, if that is so, is there not a sense in which agency is not a real phenomenon, not part of the natural ordering of the world, an ordering that is 'out there' whether we choose to notice it or not? Fourth, the claim implies that some systems that are clearly not agents, such as rocks and lecterns, actually are agents. For if being an agent is just being an intentional system, and being an intentional system is just being predictable from the intentional stance, then rocks and lecterns must count as agents too. And this, of course, is absurd.

In the next section (2.2) I want to take a closer look at the theory and examine some of its implications. Some of the details of the theory make Dennett's radical move seem less bold, whereas others may make it seem more so. With these details in place I explore a central question for the theory, namely, how can it draw a plausible distinction between systems that really are agents and those that are not (2.3)? For example, how can Dennett make it plausible that we should include devices such as chess machines within the general class of agents, and, on the other hand, how can he make it plausible that his theory excludes rocks and lecterns? In pursuing this issue, more details of the theory are laid out. With the theory placed fairly clearly on the table, I turn to the issue of reduction. What is reduction and why does Dennett reject reduction as his mode of reconciling science and our self-conception (2.4)?

2.2   Clarifications and objections

Clarifying the design stance

To employ the intentional stance we must assume that the system we are dealing with is rational. To employ the design stance we must assume that the system has a particular design and that it is working properly; we must assume, that is, that the system 'performs as designed' (ISY, 4). But 'performs as designed' is an ambiguous expression. Design can be specified in two quite distinct ways, ways which Dennett fails to mark (see, for example, slippage between the two in TB, 17.) To avoid ambiguity we need to distinguish two interpretations of the design stance. On one interpretation, which I shall call the causal blueprint interpretation, we understand 'performs as designed' in terms of the operation of its component parts and the causal connections between them. On the other interpretation, the teleological interpretation, we understand 'performs as designed' in terms of the job the system is designed to do, for example, to play chess, to operate as a word processor, to control the temperature of the room, and so forth.

Consider first the causal blueprint interpretation. We might specify the design of a system in terms of conformity to a computer program. Dennett presents this as one paradigm of.adopting the design stance (ISY, 4; TB, 17). The program is something that imposes a particular causal structure on the system. The critical point here is that we can check whether or not the system conforms to the program without knowing what the program is for, without knowing the job that the system is designed to do. Someone wholly ignorant of chess, say, could still ascertain whether the chess machine was working as it is supposed to, simply by comparing the actual operation of the chess machine with the operation specified by the program. Moreover, someone wholly ignorant of chess could predict what the chess machine would do next, simply by following through the program instructions.

A computer program is only one way of specifying a causal blueprint. Other methods include engineering flow charts, wiring diagrams, and the 'box-and-arrow' diagrams used by psychologists (see *BS*, 155, 200–5 for examples and chapter 4 below for discussion). But for all these methods the same point applies. We can understand whether or not a system is performing as designed, and we can make predictions from the design stance, without having to know what it is the system is designed to do. We do not need, that is, to appeal to the design purpose of the system in order to employ the design stance.

However, that does not mean that talk of purpose need be eliminated altogether. Causal blueprints can be wholly mechanistic, but they need not be. For, often, when we specify a causal blueprint, we appeal to the purpose of a component part in order to work out what it will do in a given situation. Dennett uses the example of a spark plug (TB, 26; cf. the example of the alarm clock, TB, 17). We do not need to know how a spark plug works in any detail to understand what it will do when power is supplied. The same may apply to a procedure, sub-routine, or method in a computer program or a box in a box-and-arrow diagram. A program may have a procedure that retrieves an item from a database. In specifying a causal blueprint, we do not need to fill in the details of how such a procedure works. It is enough that we know what it is supposed to do. Then we simply assume that it is working as it is supposed to, and predict that it will do its job successfully.

This leads us to the teleological interpretation of the design stance. For Dennett, we use the design stance to predict the operation of systems such as spark plugs. But here we make use of the teleological interpretation. We appeal, that is, directly to the job that the spark plug is supposed to do, namely create a spark when power is supplied. We need not know anything about the spark plug's causal blueprint in order to make this prediction. So here we have a different sense of the expression 'performs as designed'. The spark plug 'performs as designed' when it does the job it was designed to do.

Note that one and the same system can be understood with respect to either the teleological or the causal blueprint interpretation. For example, I might conclude that a system is a word processor by noting that it is a computer running a particular program. Given this, I can predict what this system will do next by reference to the program. In this case I do not actually need to know what word processors are supposed to do. I just need to know that this system is supposed to conform to this causal blueprint. However, I can also understand that a system is a word processor by noting that it is a device that is well-suited to the job of processing words. I can note that it fulfils this function well. It lets me create documents, edit them, save them to disc for later use, print them out, check their spelling, and so forth. And I can predict what the system will do by reference to this function. I can, for example, predict that when I hit the 'Print' button the system will, somehow or other, generate a hard copy of the document I have been working on. Here, of course, I am adopting the teleological interpretation of the design stance. And in this case, I do need to know what a word processor is supposed to do in order to confirm that this is one and in order to predict what it will do.

So in the one case, the teleological interpretation, our predictions appeal to what the system as a whole is designed to do. And in the other, the causal blueprint interpretation, our predictions appeal to the operation of and connections between the system's component parts. And, as it happens, some of these component parts may themselves be understood teleologically, that is, understood not in terms of how they work inside, but in terms of what they are designed to do.

All this is hard enough to hold in your head, but there is one more complication that I need to mention. Dennett sometimes suggests that some of the component parts that feature in the causal blueprint of really fancy systems, systems such as persons, may themselves be best understood as intentional systems, i.e. systems that are best predicted from the intentional stance. The thought here is that a causal blueprint for a person might itself feature mini-intentional systems. This gives rise to the position that has been described as 'homuncular functionalism' (*BS*, xx; 123–4; see Lycan, 1981). An intentional system is made up of smaller intentional systems, or homunculi (literally, little people), where each little homunculus is 'more stupid' (*BS*, 124) than the system of which it is a part. Eventually, at the lowest level, the homunculi are so stupid that they can be directly replaced by mere mechanisms.

In discussing this idea Dennett is largely concerned with the claim that causal blueprints can explain how intentional systems have the capacities that they have, such as the capacity to think, even though built out of devices that lack such powers. Defending this claim is a critical part of his naturalistic project. However, Dennett only says that components 'could' (*BS*, 123) be described as intentional systems. On his view it is perfectly possible that some components are mini-intentional systems, but there is no requirement that all or even most of them be so. Indeed, there is no requirement that any of the components be best understood in this way. Perhaps the most perspicuous causal blueprint of a person might include no mini-intentional systems, but rather lots of systems that are closer in character to spark plugs and word processors. And indeed, on occasion, Dennett concurs with just this thought. (See *BC*, 224–5; cf. *BC*, 362.)

I think it is distracting to emphasize the idea that causal blueprints feature mini-intentional systems which are, in turn, composed out of more intentional systems. It is distracting because it encourages a very liberal conception of what can reasonably be counted as an intentional system. As we shall see, although Dennett sometimes finds this idea attractive, it is one that can create problems for him.

Dennett does not distinguish between these two quite distinct ways of understanding the design stance, and will quite often shift from one to another. On occasion, he describes the intentional stance as a sub-species of the design stance (*KM*, 30; *BC*, 312; cf. *IS*, 73). This only makes sense on the teleological interpretation, where the design purpose of an entity is specified as 'being a rational agent'. But, on other occasions, the design stance is used to describe the way in which an agent's internal mechanisms operate, for example, when he talks about predicting the chess machine's moves by reference to its program (ISY, 4, quoted above). This only makes sense on the causal blueprint interpretation. In fact, I think the causal blueprint interpretation is the one that is most often required for Dennett's arguments to make sense, and I shall adopt this interpretation throughout except where there is a special need to appeal to the teleological interpretation.

Choosing a stance?

Dennett talks about which stance we adopt being a matter of which stance is most 'effective' or 'practical' (TB, 16–17). He says that our choice of stance is 'a matter of decision, not discovery' (MR, 239). Or, then again, that the decision of which stance to adopt is 'pragmatic, and is not intrinsically right or wrong' (ISY, 7). But this, I think, is rather misleading. And, indeed, Dennett suggests that some of his comments on this score have been too liberal (TB, 24). In attempting to qualify his view he notes that the 'decision to adopt the intentional stance is free, but the facts about the success or failure of the stance, were one to adopt it, are perfectly objective' (TB, 24). The implication here is that some instances of adopting the stance are, objectively, inappropriate for some purposes (see also MR, 253–4; TB, 27–8; RP).

What is true and what is important for Dennett is that on any given occasion when dealing with a system we can always switch from one stance to another. And we might want to switch stance for pragmatic reasons, because, for example, switching stances will help us explain something or come to understand something. But the idea that which stance we adopt is purely pragmatic cannot be right. On the one hand, sometimes Dennett does want to say that the right stance to adopt is the intentional stance. Or, at least, he wants to say that to fail to adopt the stance is to miss something that is really there. On the other hand, sometimes Dennett wants to say that to adopt the intentional stance is a mistake. He admits, for example, that we can predict the behaviour of a lectern – it does nothing because it wants to be passive and so forth – using the intentional stance (TB, 23). But he does not want to count the lectern as an intentional system. He wants to restrict his use of the term, and applications of the stance, to 'truly interesting and versatile' systems (TB, 29). But we need to work quite hard to cash out what the condition of being 'truly interesting and versatile' amounts to. Such a cashing out is one key task of the remainder of this chapter and of the following one.

But, given what I have just said, why is Dennett prepared to countenance adopting the intentional stance with respect to systems that do not seem particularly interesting or versatile? He is certainly prepared to countenance treating such lowly systems as thermostats as intentional systems (see BC, 327 and 362; but see also his qualifications at TB, 30). Dennett wants to be relaxed on this issue in order to emphasize that in one significant sense 'truly interesting and versatile' intentional systems are not so very different from thermostats. He notes that the 'reasons for regarding a . . . thermostat . . . as an intentional system are unimpressive, but not zero' (*BC*, 362). Here I am suggesting that those reasons, while non-zero, are easily trumped by the reasons against treating the thermostat in that way. The thermostat's operation is not especially interesting or versatile, and we gain nothing by adopting the intentional stance rather than sticking with the design stance. This is enough reason to say that adopting the intentional stance is not appropriate, even though, strictly speaking, it is possible, in this case. I shall say more about this as we proceed (see 2.3 and chapter 3).

Inputs and outputs

When we adopt the different stances we are not merely adopting a stance towards the inner workings of the system. We are also adopting it with respect to our understanding of its inputs and outputs. For example, suppose our chess machine is equipped with a speech recognition device. If we are operating at the physical stance, we need to understand the inputs as physical events. As such, the same instruction 'Knight to King Bishop 3' spoken by different speakers, or even the same speaker on different occasions, will count as completely different inputs. From the intentional stance, however, a vast array of physically quite different noises will all count as the very same instruction. Similarly, if the program can generate its output in different ways, for example, via a robotic arm, on a video screen, via a print-out, and so forth, then each different output will, from the physical stance, be quite distinct. It takes the design or intentional stance to pick out the fact that it is the same move in chess that the machine is performing.

From the perspective of the physical stance, then, a certain pattern in the inputs and outputs is not revealed. That a vast array of diverse physical inputs or outputs all have the same 'meaning' is a fact that is simply invisible from the physical stance. Although this is more contentious, as we shall see below, Dennett must press the same point for the design stance. From the design stance (under the causal blueprint interpretation), the inputs and outputs have nothing to do with chess. The inputs are just particular configurations that have a certain causal effect, as opposed to a rational effect, on the workings of the chess machine. The outputs are just the causal consequences of the preceding inputs combined with the effect of the current internal state. So, arguably, it takes a further act of interpretation – that is, the adoption of the intentional stance – in order to understand the inputs and outputs as chess moves. The thought here is that for something to be a chess move is for it to be something that has significance for a rational agent. And, according to Dennett's theory, we can discern no rational agents if we are restricted solely to the design stance.

Intrinsic, as if, and derived intentionality

When we adopt the intentional stance, we view the chess machine as an intentional system. And we ascribe to it beliefs, desires, and the ability to reason. Well, that is the loose way we talk about it that I have been using up to this point. But if we want to be more careful we will talk about belief-like states, desire-like states, and the ability to conform to what is reasonable. We may want to do this to make space for very substantial differences between the intentional states of systems such as chess machines and the intentional states of systems such as people.

Dennett in no way wants to deny the vast differences between the intentional states such agents possess and the intentional states of persons. When we say a person has this or that belief, our so saying carries all sorts of implications that simply do not hold in the case of the chess machine. People can reflect upon their beliefs and their desires, they can report them, self-consciously adopt or discard them, and so forth. And nobody, Dennett included, thinks that the average chess machine has any of these capabilities.

But, nonetheless, Dennett does claim that as far as intentionality is concerned, the way in which the chess machine's states have intentionality is exactly the same as the way in which a person's states have intentionality (ISY, 6–7; IS, chapter 8; KM, chapter 2). Even if we do not want to call the chess machine's states beliefs and desires, they are genuinely intentional states. They are about things, such as the position of the chess machine's rook, just as much as a person's beliefs and desires are about things.

Intentionality has been one of the key focal points for locating the tension between the mechanistic conception of ourselves and our common-sense conception. In particular, Dennett has often been criticized for failing to give a clear account of the difference between genuine and non-genuine intentional states. John Searle is a key proponent of this criticism. Searle begins his critique with a discussion of the intentionality of signs, pictures, and sentences. Such intentionality is, he claims, real enough, but it is 'derived intentionality'. Signs, pictures, and senses really are about things, but they only get to be about things because of the people who use them and create them. They derive their intentionality from the thoughts and intentions of people. Searle (1992, 78) contrasts derived intentionality with what he calls 'as if' intentionality. He might say that his lawn is thirsty, because it has not been watered for a week. But it is not literally true that the lawn has a desire for water, an intentional state about alleviating its thirst. By contrast if Searle says that he is thirsty because he hasn't had anything to drink all day, then he is reporting a real intentional state, one accompanied by an inner conscious feeling. Real intentionality is what 'as if' intentionality is a pale imitation of, and 'derived' intentionality is derived from. Hence it is often dubbed original intentionality or, sometimes, intrinsic intentionality (*IS*, 288).

Searle sees a clear connection between consciousness and intrinsic intentionality, a connection he wants to make much of. But what is important here is not so much Searle's particular criterion for intrinsic intentionality, but his claim that there is a sharp and categorical difference between 'as if' intentionality and intrinsic intentionality. Other theorists offer different criteria for the difference between 'as if' and intrinsic intentionality, such as history of learning (Fred Dretske), history of selection (Ruth Millikan), and the presence of subtle counterfactual conditions giving rise to an 'asymmetric dependence' (Fodor).

Searle and others are at pains to point out that 'as if' intentionality is not a kind of intentionality, any more than fake fur is a kind of fur. Attributions of 'as if' intentionality do not imply any genuine mental phenomena:

> [Any] attempt to deny the distinction between intrinsic and *as if* intentionality faces a general reductio ad absurdum. If you deny the distinction, it turns out that everything in the universe has intentionality. Everything in the universe follows laws of nature, and for that reason everything behaves with a certain degree of regularity, and for that reason everything behaves *as if* it were following a rule, trying to carry out a certain project, acting in accordance with a set of desires, etc. (Searle 1992, 81)

Doing without intrinsic intentionality

In one sense Dennett does reject the distinction between 'as if' and intrinsic intentionality and in another he does not. As we have already seen, Dennett is committed to distinguishing between cases where adoption of the intentional stance is appropriate and cases where it is not. And hence he is committed to a distinction between mere 'as if' intentionality and some more kosher kind of intentionality. If he can defend this distinction, he will be able to avoid the reductio ad absurdum that Searle presents. However Dennett does not want to embrace the idea of intrinsic intentionality at all. The starting point for that idea typically involves the idea that the meaning of one's thoughts is immediately transparent to the mind, and, even if it is not, the meaning of one's thoughts is wholly determinate.[3] Dennett rejects both of these claims. They are, he thinks, a product of an over-inflated concept of intentionality (*IS*, 301ff; cf. *KM*, 50–5).

We can illustrate this by looking at the case of a drinks machine that is designed to detect the difference between fake and genuine coins. Dennett reports Fodor's response to the introduction of such an example into a discussion of intentionality:

> 'That sort of case is irrelevant,' Fodor retorted instantly, 'because after all, John Searle is right about one thing; he's right about artefacts like that. They don't have any intrinsic or original intentionality – only derived intentionality.' (*IS*, 288)

Dennett's contention is that discussing this sort of case is in no way irrelevant. He asks us to imagine a sequence of ever more subtle artefacts, starting with something as simple as a drinks machine, and progressing to an autonomous robot that can achieve its goals across a wide range of changing and potential hostile circumstances (*IS*, 295–8). For Dennett, there is no particular point along this sequence of increasing complexity at which we would have a definitive reason for saying that now, and only now, we are required to adopt the intentional stance. Rather, it is simply that as the artefact increases in sophistication, we have more and more to gain by adopting the stance, and more and more to lose by not. When the stance becomes practically indispensable, then, as far as Dennett is concerned, the intentionality we ascribe to the artefact is as genuine a kind of intentionality as we could ask for. By contrast, it seems that Fodor, and others, believe that there must be something more than the mere degree to which the application of the intentional stance is attractive that separates drinks machine from human. There must be some difference that makes the difference, be it consciousness, a particular style of functional organization, a history of learning, a history of selection, and so forth. As we shall see later in the chapter, Dennett attempts to apply a general argument against the possibility of there being any such difference that can play this role.

In discussing this issue, Dennett sometimes appeals to 'what Mother Nature has in mind' (*IS*, 314) or, without the metaphor, to the power of natural selection to impose good design upon organisms. Our intentionality, he suggests, is derived, 'and in just the same way that the intentionality of our robots (and even our books and maps) is derived' (*IS*, 318). This move is useful to the extent that it illustrates Dennett's point that there is no special line that needs to be crossed, no special set of necessary conditions that need to be met, in order to generate a system that has as kosher a set of intentional states as he thinks it is possible to have. But as it stands the move puts far too much pressure on the metaphorical 'Mother Nature'. It immediately forces the question of whether her intentionality, or the intentionality that can be discerned in the process of natural selection, is itself derived, 'as if', or intrinsic. Elsewhere Dennett argues that we are often better off ignoring history and appealing to the 'discernible prowesses of the objects in question' (*IS*, 319). Despite lapses, I suspect this is the view he ought to stick with consistently, i.e. here-and-now behavioural capacities should trump historical considerations. For in all the key presentations of his theory the success or failure of the adoption of the intentional stance does not depend on the system in question having any particular history. It depends only on it being capable of sustaining certain patterns of behaviour.

Holism vs. atomism

Intentional systems theory shows us how to ascribe a whole set of intentional states to an agent, the set of states that figure in the best interpretation of her behaviour at, and around, a given time. As such, the theory is deeply committed to the doctrine of holism, the view that what any given intentional state is about is critically dependent on other intentional states possessed by the agent. Holism contrasts with atomism. In its extreme form, atomism holds that the possession of any given intentional state is wholly independent of the possession of any other. As such, it would be possible for a person to have just one belief, or for all of a person's beliefs to be contradictory. Dennett rejects such possibilities (cf. Stich, 1983,

54–6). If having a belief were, say, simply to have a sentence or an image before one's mind, then a very extreme atomism could be sustained. Fodor's language of thought theory permits a fairly strong form of atomism. For, according to that theory, what sentences in the language of thought mean is only weakly determined by their interconnections with other sentences in the language of thought. For Fodor, to believe that the cat is on the mat is to stand in a certain relation to the language-of-thought sentence 'the cat is on the mat'. Each symbol in the sentence 'cat', 'mat', 'on', etc. means what it does either because it is an innate concept or because it stands in a certain causal relation to things in the world, such as cats or mats. And these causal relations can stand whatever else the agent believes.

Critics of holism, such as Fodor (Fodor and Lepore, 1992), often argue that holists cannot make sense of how two different people can share one and the same belief. The case is this: holists insist that what a belief means (or is about) is partly determined by what all the other beliefs of the agent mean (or are about). We never expect that two people share all of their beliefs. Hence, we can never expect two people to ever share any of their beliefs. Yet this is clearly absurd, for different people very often share one and the same belief. By contrast, holists tend to think that this argument turns on an overly narrow conception of what it must be for two people to share the 'same' belief. However, I shall not explore the issue further here other than to say that, while holism remains a contested issue amongst contemporary philosophers, Dennett is by no means unusual in endorsing the doctrine. Moreover, if there are unpalatable consequences of the doctrine that will not be finessed, Dennett is more than prepared to bite the bullet on those issues.

Stances and identity

Earlier, I noted that at times Dennett promotes the idea that our choice of stance is simply a matter of strategic choice. He sometimes portrays the intentional stance as simply providing an easier way of making predictions that could otherwise be made using the physical or design stance. On other occasions, however, Dennett insists on something that is at odds with this. That is, he insists that the failure to adopt the intentional stance can result in missing features of the world that are really there, whether we care to take notice of them or not. And, further, that these features can only be revealed by the intentional stance.

It is interesting that this latter view is very close to Dennett's first treatment of intentional states, as developed in *Content and Consciousness*. There Dennett makes great play of the idea that talk of intentional states – beliefs, desires, and the like – is akin to talk of voices or sakes (*CC*, chapter 1; cf. the discussion of 'fatigues' *BS*, xix–xx).[4] We can say true things about the voice: she lost her voice, her voice was tired, she has a good voice, and so forth. But no theory of the voice would seek to identify it with any kind of physical entity or property. To attempt such an identity would simply be to misunderstand the nature of our talk about voices. In Dennett's first account of intentional states, formulated before he came up with the idea of different stances, he insisted that there was no need, and indeed every reason not, to identify intentional states with physical entities (*CC*, chapter 1). This point, made so clearly in *Content and Consciousness*, tends to get lost during the early development of Dennett's intentional stance. But in later work (TB; RP) the point is recovered. For Dennett, intentional states are not really something else, they are not to be identified with instances of the kinds or properties of the physical sciences nor, as we shall see in 2.4, of the kinds or properties of any sciences.

In the same way, though Dennett does not advance this point himself, his view must commit him to thinking that the systems which the different stances describe cannot be identical to one another. The striking implication, then, is that just as a voice is not identical to any physical entity or property, neither is an intentional system. This point is obscured by Dennett's talk about stances. For the very idea of adopting different stances invites the idea that we are taking different attitudes to one and the same system. But if we can genuinely locate the intentional system from the physical or design stance, then the autonomy of the intentional stance is undermined. If an intentional system just is identical with some entity that can be discerned from, say, the design stance, then the view we are dealing with is not Dennett's, but some sort of functionalist view, a view in which agents are defined as or identified with design stance systems, with systems that are what they are because they have a certain causal blueprint.

To avoid this sort of muddle it is important to block the invitation that different stances target the very same system, a system that is equally discernible using the resources of any of the stances. Dennett insists that without the use of the intentional stance we can neither discern, nor understand what it is to discern, agents. That is, we cannot pick them out from the general flow of ongoing physical activity that makes up the world. The claim here is very strong. Any observer that lacked the intentional stance could not discern agency in the world. In particular, she could not, in a more laborious and long-winded fashion, discern agents by means of either the physical or the design stance. Of course, we find it so easy to pick out agents – or people and animals at any rate – that it is difficult to conceive of not being able to do so. And, moreover, it may seem implausible that we need the fancy assumptions of the intentional stance to do so. Surely, people and animals are just 'out there', objective features of the world. Dennett does not disagree. But he does deny that being 'out there' means that something must be identical with an instance of physical entity or property.

Here is one solution to the muddle.[5] To make sense of Dennett's talk of different stances we insist that whenever we adopt the design or the physical stance, we do not altogether abandon the intentional stance. Rather, we put that stance in the background. We still make use of the intentional stance to discern the agent, to tell which physical structures (physical stance) or which interconnected component parts (design stance) are part of the agent and which are not. But we do not make use of it to explain the doings of the agent. Rather, we step back and explain, not actions and behaviour, but movements and input/output signals. This, then, is how I suggest we understand intentional systems theory. When Dennett speaks of adopting different stances to 'the system', the system at issue is an agent, an intentional system.

Of course, this is not to say that we cannot, or that Dennett does not, speak of causal blueprint systems or of physical systems. Talk about computer systems or lecterns will typically be of this kind. But it does mean that, say, no causal blueprint system can be strictly identical with an intentional system. At best, we can say that an agent is made of the same matter as a causal blueprint system, but is not identical with it.[6]

2.3 Genuine agency

Why should we follow Dennett in thinking that the chess machine, an intentional system, really is a simple kind of agent? We can agree that we treat it as an agent for some purposes. But this, in itself, is not a sufficient reason to believe that it actually is one. If our paradigm of agency is closely tied to our understanding of persons, then we will have a ready answer. The chess machine lacks the kind of capacities that are distinctive of human agency. Of course this is true. But it is not to the point. Dennett is aiming to account, in the first instance, for a much broader class of agents. His claim is only that a chess machine is a simple agent. Pointing out that it is not a complex one is no objection to his view. But, given this broader notion of agency, is there anything important that the chess machine lacks, anything important enough to disqualify it as a genuine agent?

De-differencing agency

To argue that the chess machine lacks nothing that should matter to us when it comes to counting it as an agent, Dennett employs an argumentative strategy that I call 'de-differencing'. I honour the strategy with a special label because Dennett uses it time and time again throughout his work. To see that he does this, and to see how he can defend the strategy, are important steps in understanding how apparently disparate aspects of his philosophy hang together.

In outline, de-differencing works like this. The first phase consists of identifying the difference that is supposed to make the difference between genuine and non-genuine examples of some category. In the case at hand, we are asking what difference is supposed to make the difference between genuine and non-genuine agents, for example between persons and chess machines. The second phase consists of attacking the relevance, role, or nature of that difference. The third phase either concludes that the supposed difference was spurious all along or, as we shall see in the case of agency, offers an altogether different basis for the difference.

Perhaps the difference that makes the difference is that chess machines are made of metal, plastic, and silicon whereas genuine agents, such as anteaters and people, are made out of biological stuff? John Searle (1980; 1992) attempts to defend the importance of biological stuff. Searle advances some interesting arguments about the difficulty we have in understanding the relationship between a formal description of a system – such as a computer program – and the properties of a system. But it remains obscure why he thinks that a system built from biological parts is supposed to be relevantly different from a system built from non-biological ones. From

Dennett's vantage point, Searle's emphasis on biology looks like some sort of metabolic prejudice.

This suggestion often leads on to a second and independent one. Perhaps the difference that makes a difference is consciousness. Again, Searle advances a version of this idea. Roughly, the thought is that genuine agents, including people and anteaters, are conscious, but non-genuine ones, such as chess machines, are not. And perhaps, according to such a view, simple creatures such as ants are not conscious and, hence, not genuine agents either. But as soon as this suggestion is raised, we must ask what difference is supposed to make the difference between being conscious and not? We might appeal to biology again, and argue that being made of gloopy stuff disposes an intentional system towards consciousness in a way that being made of silicon, plastic, and metal does not. But to make this appeal convincing, to make it more than metabolic prejudice, a positive account of consciousness is needed.

As we shall see later, Dennett has a positive account of consciousness. But this account makes consciousness wholly unsuitable as a candidate for the difference that makes the difference. For his account grants all agents, ants included, a very basic form of consciousness, but limits the more exciting form of consciousness to language-using creatures, such as humans. In a sense, then, Dennett thinks that chess machines are quite as conscious as ants and anteaters, and that is, to put it crudely, not very conscious at all. We shall return to these issues in chapters 5 and 6. For now, it is enough to note that it is a fundamental feature of Dennett's project that consciousness, the exciting kind of consciousness, is itself to be accounted for in terms of the special capacities that some but not all agents have. So he cannot allow that this kind of consciousness be a criterion for agency in the first place. Of course, to the extent that a critic is sceptical about Dennett's theory of consciousness, and many are, the point just made will have little force. But to rob it of its force, the critic will need to engage with Dennett's arguments on that topic, arguments which we shall discuss later on.

A third suggestion might be this. The chess machine is disqualified as a genuine agent because of its impoverished environment. The machine is only rational with respect to its chess interests; indeed, it may have only chess interests. It can make no steps to restore its power supply if it is disrupted, nor to flee a burning building. It could be pressed that genuine agents must have a broader range of concerns, and in particular must have some concern for their continued existence. If so, then the chess machine is in trouble. This suggestion has more going for it than the previous two. But it does not threaten Dennett's basic position. If it is pressed, Dennett can change his example from the static chess machine to a mobile chess robot, a device that, as well as playing chess, has survival goals and means for achieving them (cf. TB, 30–2). Changing his example in this way does not affect his basic approach, just the point at which the application of the intentional stance comes to count as successful. It is still the case that, for Dennett, all there is to being a genuine agent is to have your behaviour reliably and voluminously predicted by the intentional stance. Nothing more is needed.

A different approach

There are other criteria for genuine agency that we might explore, other differences we might check out, and ask whether they could really make the difference between a genuine and a non-genuine agent. And, indeed, we shall look at the important challenge from the representational theory later in this chapter and in chapters 3 and 4. But the pattern of Dennett's response has already been established by the examples given. Dennett is hostile to the idea that there are any particular neat and tidy criteria that are necessary and sufficient conditions for agency. The concept of agency cannot be broken down in this way. This is part of what I meant earlier when I said that agency, interest, reason, and so forth are tightly interrelated concepts. For Dennett no one of these concepts is more basic than any other. So for some purposes it does not help us to define agents as systems that have interests and act for reasons. For if we then ask what an interest or a reason is, we cannot but appeal to the notion of agency.

What positive story can Dennett tell about the difference between a system that is a genuine agent and one that we can, for convenience, simply treat as if it were an agent? Think about a continuum. At one end the application of the intentional stance is marginal. We can treat a bit of the world as if there is an agent present, but doing so yields few if any predictive dividends. And, moreover, we continually find we have to adjust our interpretation in ad hoc ways. At this end of the continuum lie the rock and the lectern. Some way further on are macromolecules and then, much further on still, single-celled organisms. At the opposite end of the continuum we have systems such as mice, dolphins, and humans.

Here treating a bit of the world as if an agent is present yields very many predictive benefits, and, moreover, yields benefits that we cannot gain from the physical or design stance. Whereas the application of the intentional stance at the rock and lectern end of the continuum appears ad hoc, at the human end of the continuum it is what we might call self-legitimating (cf. TK, 67). That is to say, the intentional stance more than earns its keep, by providing access to generalizations that cannot be expressed within the design or physical stance (cf. TB, 25). For example, how, other than by employing the intentional stance, can a range of very different movements on different occasions all be described under the common head of 'this mouse searching for food'? And yet, if we cannot employ that common head, and others like it, we are not in a position to account for the mouse as an agent at all (cf. TB, 26).

As with intentionality, Dennett sometimes tries to support this positive story by appeal to evolution by natural selection (*ER*, 21–4; *KM*, 19–34; *DDI*, chapter 7). And again he is not very clear whether being designed by natural selection is supposed to validate a claim about genuine agency or if he is referring to evolution simply to illustrate his point. On the other hand, he is clear that we will not actually encounter agents that lack the right kind of design history, and has little patience with examples that turn on such a possibility (Dennett, 1994 or 1996). But this is no reason to be less than clear whether genuine agency depends upon the right kind of history or simply on here-and-now behavioural capacities. Although he swithers, as noted above, the balance of his remarks seems to favour the latter view. We can grant that it would be miraculous if something had the relevant here-and-now behavioural capacities for the successful application of the intentional stance and yet lacked the relevant design history. But we can still insist that what makes it true that something is an agent is the here-and-now behavioural capacity. The design history simply explains how it got to be here.

In any case, Dennett asks us to imagine the unfolding of evolutionary history. At some early stage in that history there would have been no genuine agents. The use of the intentional stance in the case of self-replicating macromolecules will not clearly yield dividends, will not clearly be self-legitimating. But, at later stages in evolutionary history, it becomes more and more difficult to avoid the intentional stance. Moreover, it becomes unclear why we would want to. Why, for example, would we want to think of mice and dolphins as anything other than organisms, systems that work actively to preserve their boundaries and to pursue intelligently a variety of goals, not least that of reproduction?

At what stage between self-replicating macromolecule and human does the adoption of the intentional stance become self-legitimating? That is, at what stage in history do genuine agents come into being? What we can be sure of is that at an early stage there were no genuine agents and at a later stage there were. And, for Dennett, this shift is a shift from a highly marginal application of the intentional stance to a clearly self-legitimating use of the stance. But there is no precise point that marks the onset of genuine agents.

Dennett's argument seems to come down to this. In some cases it is plausible for us to be neutral about the question of whether or not a bit of the world contains an agent as opposed to, say, a very complex aggregate of chemical parts. The single-celled organism might be one such case. But it is not plausible to be neutral in the case of, say, a mouse or a chimpanzee. To fail to see this bit of the world as containing an agent, and as the locus for intentional states, is to fail to see something that is there. There is, Dennett says, a 'real pattern' that can only be discerned from the intentional stance (see chapter 3). In between those cases where it is plausible to be scep-tical about the appropriateness of adopting the intentional stance and those where it is not, there is a grey area, an area where the facts about genuine agency are simply not that clear.

Note that for Dennett it is the facts that are not clear, not that our access to the facts is in some way limited (*IS*, 40; *RP*, 118). It is not as though there are some deeper facts, perhaps theoretical facts to do with the internal architecture of the system under scrutiny, that could decisively determine whether agency was or was not present in a given case. What matters is not what is on the inside, but what possibilities of interpretation the system offers to the outside. And to the extent that there is uncertainty here, so there is uncertainty about whether agency is present, an uncertainty due to a fuzziness in the world and not fuzziness in our appreciation of it.

A 'sort of anti-essentialism'

This difficulty of drawing a precise dividing line between genuine and non-genuine agency is an illustration of a general theme in Dennett. Dennett describes himself as committed to what he calls a 'sort of anti-essentialism', a view 'that is comfortable with

penumbral cases and a lack of strict dividing lines'. This gives rise
to categories, such as agent and interest, mind and self, such that
'we should expect that the transitions between them and the phenomena that are not them should be gradual, contentious and gerrymandered' (*CE*, 421).

This view allows that there can be difficult cases, cases where,
say, it is not clear that genuine agency is present. In fact, Dennett
does not think that nature provides many such cases (*CE*, 421–2).
For him, as far as I can discern, all living organisms are very clearly
agents. That is, they are well past the grey area on the continuum
between merely 'as if' agents and genuine agents.

What is most central to his 'sort of anti-essentialism' is the idea
that there can be important and categorical differences between
entities, for example, the difference between being an agent and not,
without the need for a criterion of difference that can be unambiguously applied in every case. Surely, he tells us, there is an
important and categorical difference between mammals and non-
mammals. And, just as surely, there was no one animal that we have
any special reason to call 'the first mammal' (*ER*, 84–5). For Dennett,
it is key, and indeed, self-evident, that the second fact in no way
undermines the first. Then, given that the reasoning works in that
case, he is prepared to apply it to other cases, such as the possession of interests, of rationality, of free will, and so forth (see chapter
8).

Dennett's anti-essentialism is closely tied with his idea of different stances. From some stances, the physical stance or design stance
(understood in terms of causal blueprints), the emergence of agency
is not a special event at all. There need be, for Dennett, no necessary or sufficient conditions that can be drawn at the physical or the
design stance that mark the onset of agency. From these stances,
there is no important discontinuity between systems that are
genuine agents and systems that are not. By contrast, from the intentional stance there is an important discontinuity between systems
that are agents and systems that are not. That said, Dennett allows
plenty of room for ambiguous cases, cases where it is quite unclear
whether or not a system is an agent.

Some will find Dennett's anti-essentialism an uncomfortable
metaphysical position. For example, it generates problems concerning causation: the real causal work seems to go on at the level
of physical stance and not at the level of the intentional stance. Does
that mean that when we explain actions by appeal to the intentional
stance, our explanations are not causal? We shall look at this issue

in the next chapter. The fact that anti-essentialism allows penumbral cases generates another serious worry. Some will think it is just absurd that the fact as to whether or not something is an agent could be unclear. And it is, for Dennett, the fact that is unclear, not our knowledge of the fact. Is it an offensive absurdity that the world itself might contain such vagueness? Either there is an agent or there is not, we might say. And this does seem reasonable. Moreover, there are general arguments against genuine concepts, concepts that pick out features that are really 'out there' in the world, being vague in this way. Dennett does not engage with these general arguments. His attitude here is that 'something has to give' if we are to develop a successful account of agency and, for him, the benefits of giving up on certain sharp boundaries is more than worth the costs of keeping them.

2.4 Reduction and reconciliation

In chapter 1, we looked briefly at different ways in which we could respond to the tension between science and our self-conception. We could give up science and embrace the supernatural. This is what Cartesian Dualism recommends. Or we could give up on our self-conception, accepting that it is hopelessly wrong-headed. This view, most notably defended by Paul Churchland, is eliminativism. But if we reject both of these responses, as Dennett does, then we need to seek some way of reconciling science and our self-conception. According to what I shall call the standard naturalistic picture, by which I mean the set of assumptions that are most commonly adopted by naturalistic philosophers, the only way to achieve such a reconciliation is through some kind of reduction. Fodor expresses this commitment in the following passage:

> I suppose that sooner or later the physicists will complete the catalogue they've been compiling of the ultimate and irreducible properties of things. When they do, the likes of *spin*, *charm*, and *charge* will perhaps appear on their list. But *aboutness* surely won't; intentionality simply doesn't go that deep. It's hard to see, in face of this consideration, how one can be a realist about intentionality without also being, to some extent or other, a reductionist. If the semantic [i.e. meaningful] and intentional are real properties of things, it must be in virtue of their identity with ... properties that are themselves *neither* intentional *nor* semantic. If aboutness is real, it must be really something else. (Fodor, 1987, 97)

Think about a parallel claim: if magic is real, it must be really something else. We might want to say this because we think if magic is just as it appears to be, then we could never reconcile its existence with our scientific world view. This is what Fodor thinks about intentionality. However, we can vindicate the reality of magic by reducing it to something else, that is, defining it as or identifying it with something else. And, indeed, this is what we do. What magic really is, we say, is conjuring tricks. Magic is reduced to conjuring, and what magic cannot be so reduced is eliminated. That is, if there is magic that we cannot ever explain in terms of conjuring we simply deny that it exists, deny that it is real. But the magic that we can reduce to conjuring tricks is magic that we can reconcile with our scientific world view.

Our conception of magic is somewhat revised, but not too much. We can see ourselves as explaining magic, rather than just eliminating it. What we are left with might be called the mechanical view of magic; it is a view of magic that shows us how there can be magic without the need for supernature. Returning to agents and intentionality we have the mechanical view of mind, where '[the] central idea of the mechanical view of mind is that the mind is a part of nature, something which has a regular, law-governed causal structure' (Crane, 1995, 131). On the face of it agents do not have a regular, law-governed causal structure. According to Dennett, their behaviour is not made best sense of by appeal to laws, but by appeal to what is or is not rational for them to do. They have, as we might say, a regular, norm-governed behavioural structure. Their behaviour is explained and predicted by appeal to rational norms rather than causal laws.

But on the standard naturalistic picture, nothing in nature is directly sensitive to rational norms. However, as we have seen in chapter 1, we can build machines that manipulate representations and we can arrange things such that mechanical operations over those representations yield rational transitions over what the representations stand for. A mechanical cash register is a simple example of this. The mechanism does not have any grasp of number, of addition, and so forth. It is the material properties of the representations that move the mechanism. But the movements of the mechanism echo rational transitions such that, by the sheer movement of cogs and wheels, addition is reliably performed. And this, for the representational theorist, is how the mind works, only the representations are thoughts and values and the mechanism echoes not the process of addition but the process of practical reasoning.

What is reduction? – the first round

A reduction is, most generally, a way in which we can redescribe entities that are part of problematic phenomena, such as astronomical entities, in terms that, as far as the scientific world view is concerned, are non-problematic. When we stopped thinking of stars and planets as utterly unlike any object that we encounter on earth, and started to think of them as massive bodies floating in space, we were engaged in a reduction.

More specifically, a reduction is usually understood as a relationship between two different theories. By theory we need mean no more than a systematic attempt to describe a phenomenon. So we can have a theory of lightning, of the movements of the stars and planets, of water, of tables, and so forth. In some cases a theory will be more systematic and interesting than in others. But every theory will talk about basic kinds of stuff and basic kinds of entities, and the basic properties they may have. And every theory will aim to include rules or principles that describe the behaviour and interaction of those stuffs and entities. Some theories will yield more and more interesting laws and regularities than others. A theory about what happens on Tuesdays will not, as Fodor (1992) has wittily pointed out, yield very many interesting laws or regularities. But theories of many natural phenomena do. Hence the success of geology, oceanography, astronomy, chemistry, and so forth.

The classic formulation of reduction requires that there are 'bridge laws' that show how entities, stuffs, or properties in one theory are in fact the very same as some set of entities, stuffs, or properties in the other. In some cases, bridge laws are easy to find. The stuff water can be identified with aggregates of H_2O molecules. The event of a lightning strike can be identified with the event of electrical discharge. The property temperature can be identified with mean kinetic energy. And in all these cases, it turns out that once these bridge laws have been established, we can go on to derive the laws of the less basic theory (the theory of water, of lightning, of temperature) from the laws of the more basic theory (of chemistry, of electricity, of physics).

For the most committed reductionist, all good scientific theories can ultimately be reduced to physics. If they cannot, this shows that either the theory needs more work, or that it should be eliminated, that is, discarded in favour of a theory that will meet the test of

Adopting a Stance

reduction. Reductions to physics may take place in a single step, as in the case of astronomy. Or they may go via intermediate stages. For example, a theory of water may first be reduced to a theory of chemistry. And then the theory of chemistry may further be reduced to physics. And when it is, it becomes clear how the phenomenon of water is wholly accommodated within our scientific world view.

Autonomy

The kind of reductionism just described is a very demanding doctrine. For although there are some very successful reductions in the history of science, there are also many examples of what look to be good scientific theories that cannot be reduced in the way that classic formulation requires. For example, it is not clear that the basic kinds of geology or meteorology can be related to any complex expression in the language of physics and chemistry to yield a bridge law. Nor is it clear that classical genetics can be reduced to molecular genetics. And, most significantly for us, there is widespread agreement that there is no serious prospect of finding bridge laws between intentional kinds, such as belief, agent, and so forth, and complex expressions in the language of physics or of any science that can be reduced to physics. One reason for this is that in many sciences there appears to be scope for kinds and properties that are 'multiply realized' (cf. chapter 1).

The gene for blue eyes, say, may have a number of quite disparate realizations at the level of DNA. The property of 'resistance', important to the science of weathering, may have a number of quite disparate realizations at the level of chemistry. The strict reductionist will reject as good scientific theory any theory that allows for the possibility of such open-ended realizations. However, according to an influential argument by Fodor (1974), naturalism can accommodate 'special sciences'. Special sciences cannot be reduced to any basic science in the way that classic formulation prescribes. That is, they cannot be reduced to physics or to some other science that can be reduced to physics. But, nonetheless, we can see clearly how they can be reconciled with the scientific world view.

The classic formulation of reduction requires that for every kind in the theory to be reduced, there must be a bridge law that identifies that kind with some complex expression involving only the kinds of the reducing theory. For example, water (a kind in the theory to be reduced) is identical with H_2O (a complex expression of the reducing theory). Fodor's suggestion is that this requirement is relaxed. He insists only that for each occasion we refer to an instance of a special science kind, that instance can be identified with some complex expression involving only the kinds of the reducing theory. Inselbergs, isolated hills of rock rising out of a plain, are the result of a resistant rock being subjected to onion-skin weathering. The expression 'resistant rock' is basic to the special science of geology. But on any given occasion, resistant rock might be identical with aggregates of quite different chemical compositions. If we insisted on a classic bridge law, we would not be able to see what was common to different inselbergs. We would miss out an important regularity that is out there in the world.

At the same time, however, adopting a special science exposes the theorist to the possibility of exceptions:

> Exceptions to the generalisations of a special science are typically inexplicable from the point of view of (that is, in the vocabulary of) that science. That's one of the things that makes it a special science. But, of course, it may nevertheless be perfectly possible to explain the exceptions *in the vocabulary of some other science*. In the most familiar case, you go 'down' one or more levels and use the vocabulary of a more 'basic' science. (Fodor, 1987, 6)

For Fodor, the kinds described by the special sciences are genuinely part of the fabric of the natural world. To use his metaphor, the kinds of geology and meteorology do not 'cut as deep into the fabric of reality' (Fodor, 1992) as the kinds of physics and chemistry, but they do nonetheless cut some way into that fabric. Kinds such as Tuesday and chair, on the other hand, if they cut at all, barely dent that fabric.

Fodor wants to defend special sciences, despite their failure to reduce, because such sciences clearly have a great deal of explanatory power. The laws and generalizations of special sciences are genuinely helpful – they help us to predict and explain things. Moreover, they appear to reveal regularities in the world, such as what is common between inselbergs, that are not obviously visible from the vantage point of physics or any other reducible science. As such, to refuse to adopt a special science is, it would seem, to refuse to acknowledge features of the world that are really there, whether we care to acknowledge them or not. All in all the special sciences are, in Dennett's phrase, self-legitimating (TK, 67; and see above).

Special sciences are sometimes said to be autonomous because they cannot be reduced to basic sciences. They exhibit a certain kind of independence from the basic sciences. At first glance, autonomy appears to be the enemy of the project of reconciliation. If a theory is autonomous, if it is independent of physics, then does this not threaten the completeness of our scientific world view? For Fodor the answer is a clear 'no'. For him, there is no threat to our scientific world view because he thinks that every instance of a special science property, such as the 'resistance' of a rock, can be identified with a property of physics or some other reducible science. In this way, the special science introduces no new ontological features into the world, it just describes features that are already there.

What is reduction? – the second round

Because Fodor is committed to the autonomy of the special sciences, he can be described as an anti-reductionist. However, it is important to understand what kind of autonomy Fodor is prepared to countenance and what he is not. For Fodor, it is critical that the special sciences are formulated by appealing only to descriptive laws and descriptive regularities. The kinds of special sciences are defined with respect to the causal role they play in that science. Some physical state or property can be identified with a gene because of the causal effect it has, because of the causal relations in which it stands to other physical states or properties. These roles are purely descriptive. That is to say, there is no point at which we ever need to appeal to a function or a purpose in specifying these roles.

Agents appear to be directly sensitive to rational norms: their behaviour appears to track what it is reasonable to do, other things being equal. But a mechanism cannot, so the standard naturalistic picture insists, be moved by whether something is reasonable or not. No mechanism could be directly sensitive to that. So, according to Fodor, if such a sensitivity is real, it must be reduced to a sensitivity to something else.

We can now return to the question of what difference might mark the difference between genuine and non-genuine agency. On the standard naturalistic picture, if agents are real, then they must really be objects of some special science. The difference, then, between genuine and non-genuine agents will be discernible either using the resources of the special science or of some lower-level science. For Fodor, in particular, the science of computation can be used to say just what all and every agent has in common, namely the capacity to process representations in a certain way. Translating Fodor's point into Dennett's terminology, we can say that Fodor thinks that the difference between genuine and non-genuine agency can be specified using the resources of the design stance *under the causal blueprint interpretation.* For causal blueprints are, in effect, fragments of special science theory.

Dennett's argument against reduction

With a clearer picture of what reductionism has to offer, we can re-examine Dennett's argument against reduction. The key argument is one we identified in chapter 1. Reductionist theories insist that there is something in common between all and only systems that are agents, and that something can be specified without appeal to intentional concepts. The most liberal versions of reductionism, such as the representational theory, are still, by Dennett's lights, too chauvinistic. This is because for Dennett there is always the possibility of a system that behaves just like a genuine agent, but which, because of the nature of its inner workings, is excluded from the class of genuine agents by the reductionist theory. To recall our imaginary robot from chapter 1, there is always the possibility of a Cogit-8 whose inner 'program' is nothing like our own. Yet, for Dennett, it is clear that we would regard that supposedly fake agent as a genuine agent. And what this reveals is that what we take agents to be is concerned with what they do and not with what goes on inside.

The difficulty with this argument, however, is that we can expect the representational theorist to dig in her heels. She can simply challenge Dennett's intuitions, arguing both that there is no good reason to think that a different inner program could actually underpin an agent, and, that if something did do it in a very different way, then precisely for that reason we would actually have good grounds to be sceptical as to whether we were faced with a genuine agent. So can we find something more principled behind Dennett's argument? I think perhaps we can, though we have to rely on what is tacit rather than what is explicit in Dennett. The considerations on offer here are certainly amenable to what is explicitly present.

Consider first a slightly different use of the example of clocks raised in chapter 1. Imagine developing a reductionist theory of clocks. If clocks, Fodor might say, are real, they are really something else. But is this quite right? Any given clock, to be sure, is made out of mechanical parts. But what can we say, without appeal to the purpose of the clock, all and only clocks have in common? Surely, we can say nothing. Simply by reflection we can see that the concept of clock is open-ended. Any device that tells the time reliably can, in the right circumstances, be counted as a clock.

We can understand this feature of the clock concept in the following way. The clock concept groups together a class of artefacts according to the end they can (or plausibly aim to) achieve, namely being good for telling the time. And, simply by reflection, we can see that there is no limit on the different means that can be taken to achieve this end. But any reductive account of the clock concept, that is any account that eschews the language of ends, can only draw on the language of means. And even the most liberal of reductive accounts can only spell out a limited set of means. There will, then, always be some means to the same end that the reductive account will miss out.

Another illustration may help bring this point across. Suppose that we have a causal blueprint specification for an agent, let us say an agent that speaks English with a soft Edinburgh brogue. And we build a system according to this specification and, lo and behold, we create an agent that talks as if she has lived and breathed the city talk all her life. Now, after a time, one of the components that figures in the causal blueprint specification fails. That is to say that the behaviour of this component no longer corresponds to the set of law-like causal regularities laid down by the system's blueprint. How, in this circumstance, are we supposed to tell whether this failure is serious or trivial?

According to Dennett's account we cannot tell whether the failure is serious or trivial except by appeal to the intentional stance. Suppose we try to restrict ourselves exclusively to (the causal blueprint interpretation of) the design stance, taking special care to ensure we are not making even tacit appeals to distinctions that are only discernible from the intentional stance. Imagine that the failure of our component turns the system's vocal utterances into utter gobbledegook. How can we determine that this has happened if we are restricted to the set of concepts available at the design stance? An observer, using just the design stance, could tell that the system was still uttering noises, just as it did before. And she could tell that the noises had changed in overall character. But how could she tell that the system was now producing gobbledegook as opposed to, say, English with a thick Glaswegian accent. In the gobbledegook case it very much seems as if the component failure has effectively destroyed the agent. (I am, of course, assuming that the failure here is more than merely superficial, i.e., it is not analogous to acquiring a mere vocal deficit.) In the Glaswegian accent case the agent is fully intact. Indeed, it is doing just what it did before, speaking English, only it is achieving this end via slightly different means. But how can we tell whether any given component failure leads to a change that wholly undermines the proper functioning of the agent as opposed to marginally affecting the way in which it achieves its proper functioning? Dennett's response will be that we can only tell by appeal to the intentional stance.

I do not for a moment want to insist that the clock example or the Edinburgh agent example represent decisive arguments. In the first case the premise which draws on what we can know simply by reflection is clearly contestable. In the second case, the reductionist will argue that there are features of the design stance account that can be called upon to distinguish between a change into a gobbledegook speaker and a mere change in style of vocal delivery. She may well suggest that my examples beg the question against her view. Nonetheless, I think the examples do take the argument forward. They do because they bring out a principled reason for thinking that intentional concepts cannot be reduced, namely, that intentional concepts fundamentally involve a certain set of normative standards which non-intentional concepts lack. Intentional concepts, as it were, dwell in the realm of ends, whereas non-intentional language can deal only with means.

Of course, whether the argument seems initially attractive or initially question-begging is something that almost certainly depends on your philosophical temperament (chapter 1). To defend this kind of argument, Dennett may need to appeal to his wider picture and its advantages, and to highlight some of the less palatable consequences of his rival's picture.

However, according to the standard naturalistic picture, if Dennett's argument against reduction is successful, he must accept that in some important sense agents and their intentional states are not real, are not properly part of nature. After all, if the anti-reductionist argument is right, then the mind is not something that 'has a regular, law-governed causal structure' (Crane, 1995, 131). Dennett is generally (though not consistently) reluctant to concede that agents and intentional states are not real. After all, he does not think they have the same status as fairies or Sherlock Holmes. Nor does he think they are simply a product of human convention, such as Tuesdays or chairs. Indeed, it turns out that to defend the reality (or at least the lack of unreality) of agents and their intentional states, Dennett must present a major challenge to what the standard naturalistic picture is prepared to countenance as real. We shall see how he sets about this challenge in the next chapter.

Further reading

Two primary sources for Dennett on intentional systems theory are 'True Believers' (TB) and 'Intentional Systems Theory' (ISY). Aspects of the theory are discussed at length in Part I of *BS* and throughout *IS*. Dennett makes most use of the 'economic metaphor', and talks of costs vs. benefits of the use of different stances, in 'Real Patterns' (RP). Dennett discusses 'homuncular functionalism', the strategy of decomposing an intentional system into simpler intentional systems, in a number of places, including: *BS*, 80–1; ISY, 12–13; *IS*, 73–4; *BC*, 253, 312–16, 362.

Naturalistic philosophers of mind who emphasize intentionality as a starting point, rather than agency, include Searle, Fodor, Millikan, Dretske, and Stich. A helpful introduction to this approach can be found in Crane (1995). Holism of the mental is notably defended by Quine (1960) and by Davidson (1980). It is critically discussed by Fodor and Lepore (1992). Their introduction provides a useful survey of the key issues and detailed references.

For a detailed defence of the idea that the difference between an electronic brain and a biological brain might make the difference between consciousness and its absence (and hence agency and its absence), see Searle (1992). A particularly clear expression of Dennett's anti-reductionism and his argument for it can be found in 'Three Kinds of Intentionality' (TK). See also the example of Mary and Ruth at *BS*, 105, and of rival face-recognizers at *BS*, 23–6. See Glossary and chapter 7 for more on Dennett's use of the term 'reduction'. For an introduction and pointers to literature on vagueness, see Michael Tye's article 'Vagueness' in *The Routledge Encyclopaedia of Philosophy* (Craig, 1998).

See Churchland (1981) for a classic statement of eliminativism. The idea is further explored in the paper in Churchland (1989). For a different version of eliminativism, see Stich (1983). Kim (1996, chapter 9) outlines the classic formulation of reduction as well as discussing its relevance to the philosophy of mind. For discussion of the claim that classic genetics cannot be reduced to molecular genetics, see Sterelny and Griffiths (1999, chapter 7) and Dupré

(1993, chapter 6). On special sciences, see Fodor's seminal paper 'Special Sciences' (Fodor, 1974). A brief but useful discussion that places Fodor's work in context can be found in Burwood, Gilbert, and Lennon (1999, chapter 2). Papineau provides an interesting critical discussion (see either his 1993, chapter 2, or his 1992). For more on reduction in general, see Kim (1996, chapter 9), Papineau (1993, chapters 1 and 2), Burwood et al. (1999, chapters 2 and 3). More advanced material can be found in Charles and Lennon (1992). Footnotes aside, I do not attempt to address the relationships between Donald Davidson's and Dennett's view. On Davidson, see Davidson (1980) and Evnine (1991). Child (1994) is an excellent study of this topic; a briefer account is given in Burwood et al. (1999, chapter 5).

3

Real Patterns

In the last chapter we saw how Dennett's picture failed to fit into what I called 'the standard naturalistic picture'. According to that picture, for agents and their intentional states to be part of nature they must be things which have a regular, law-governed causal structure (cf. Crane, 1995, 131). Reductionists aim to show how agents and their states do have such a structure. For example, representational theorists, such as Fodor, argue that intentional states are simply representational states and that being an agent is simply a matter of conforming to a certain design stance specification (where, as I have emphasized, we understand the design stance in terms of a causal blueprint). Reductions can take different forms. For example, there is the attempt to reduce intentional states to abstractly specified states of a neural network, as is proposed by some connectionist theorists, or there is the attempt to reduce intentional states to brain states, as is proposed by the identity theory. The point is that something intentional is reduced to something non-intentional, and hence something that can be understood as part of nature, or as something that is readily reconciled with the mechanistic conception.

Under the standard naturalistic picture, it is only by being vindicated via some kind of reduction to the special or basic sciences that agents and their intentional states can get to count as real. Because Dennett rejects that reduction, proponents of the standard naturalistic picture argue that he cannot also claim that agents and intentional states are real, cannot, that is, claim that they should be included in a serious count of what there is in the world.

How does this sense of 'real', the sense adopted by the standard naturalistic picture, play out across a range of cases? It turns out that the crystalline spheres, in which our ancestors thought the stars and planets were suspended, are not real. And they are not because they are entities postulated by a theory that is now defunct. The best current theory of stars and planets simply leaves no room for crystalline spheres. The same can be said of phlogiston, the stuff that people used to think was given off in combustion. Modern chemistry, a much better theory, suggests that some stuff, oxygen, is taken on board in combustion. And that is why we think that oxygen is real but phlogiston is not. Eliminativists, such as Churchland, share Dennett's scepticism about reduction. But, cleaving to the standard naturalistic picture, the eliminativist takes the failure of reduction to indicate that agents and intentional states are not 'real' or 'natural' kinds. A serious study of what there is in the world will leave them out, just as a serious study of what there is in the astronomical realm will leave out the crystalline spheres. But just as Dennett rejects reductions, so too he rejects eliminativism. For him, it would be a serious error to suggest that agents and their intentional states had a status that was on a par with crystalline spheres or phlogiston.

Sherlock Holmes, unicorns, fairies, and time-machines are not real. They are fictions. While we talk about them we do not expect to gather evidence for or against their existence or to undertake an empirical investigation into their nature. Again, for Dennett it would be a serious error to suggest that agents and their intentional states had the same status as Sherlock Holmes and fairies. That said, he often, and unhelpfully, does use the word 'fiction' in describing agents and intentional states.

Finally, Tuesdays and chairs are not, in the relevant sense, real. But Tuesdays and chairs are not entities that figure in defunct theories, ones that have since been superseded. And nor are Tuesdays and chairs fictions, like Sherlock Holmes and the unicorns. We can say true and false things about Tuesdays and chairs. But there are no regular, law-governed causal structures that are affected by whether or not the day is a Tuesday or a physical object is a chair. When chairs do things, such as break windows by being thrown through them, it is not in virtue of being a chair that they do what they do, but simply by being physical objects with such-and-such a mass and such-and-such a shape. The chair-ness, if you like, of the physical object is not part of reality so much as a label, a convenient but parochial categorization, that we impose upon the world. Or, putting the point in another way, Tuesdays and chairs are in the eye of the beholder. Dennett wants more for agents and their intentional states. He wants to insist that they are part of the world. Unlike Tuesdays and chairs, to fail to see them, is to miss something that is really there. When a belief leads you to throw a chair through the window, it *is* in virtue of being a belief, and not anything else, such as a physical state of your brain, that it does this.

So Dennett wants to resist the idea that agents and their intentional states fail to be real in the manner of crystalline spheres, unicorns, or Tuesdays. And yet, by rejecting reduction he also resists the idea that they are real in the manner of viruses, oxygen, or planets. But, according to the standard naturalistic picture, there is just no room for such a position. Because Dennett himself feels the tug of the standard naturalistic picture, he finds it very difficult to articulate his distinctive view. Indeed, he has veered from insisting that agents and their intentional states are robustly real to saying that they are merely useful fictions. All this can be very confusing, but I shall argue here that his actual view is stable, even if the way in which he presents it is subject to wide variation. Once we see that Dennett has to reject the standard naturalistic picture, we can also see a way of expressing his view clearly and unambiguously. We can see, that is, how Dennett can defend the claim that agents and intentional states are real, but are not real by virtue of being part of a regular, law-governed structure.

3.1 The standard naturalistic picture

What's real is what does pushing and pulling in the world. This slogan points to a key feature of a very common view about what can properly count as 'real'. When science and philosophical reflection about science meet this slogan its content becomes more precise and it leads more or less directly to the standard naturalistic picture. The story goes like this. Pushing and pulling is a matter of causation. And causation, it is commonly insisted, requires regular, law-governed patterns of activity. But this specific understanding of pushing and pulling and, indeed, of the more technical notion of causation, can be contested and, if I am right, must be contested by Dennett if he is to defend intentional systems theory.

It is important to preface any discussion of causation by noting that the issue raises a great number of controversies within the philosophical literature. It is far from clear that there is any such thing as a standard view. Here I shall give a brief sketch of an account of causation, a sketch that pulls out features that must be emphasized by Dennett's critics on the topic of the reality of intentional states. So, while some features of my sketch may be highly contestable, the features that matter for the arguments to follow are held by the relevant critics of Dennett.

For an event of type A to cause an event of type B, two key conditions are required. First, the two events must be independent of one another. Second, the fact that events of type A lead to events of type B, in certain conditions, must be a non-accidental regularity. I do not want to defend these two conditions in any detail – they are much discussed in the philosophical literature and by no means accepted by all – but it will be useful to make a brief comment in defence of each of them.

First let us consider the claim that the events of type A must be independent of events of type B. Here is the kind of worry that the condition is intended to avoid: suppose we were to say that conception is the cause of pregnancy (*CC*, 35 and *CE*, 386; see also *CE*, 63–4). And suppose, further, that we were to define conception as that which, other things being equal, leads to pregnancy. If this is our definition then the claim that conception causes pregnancy can be spelled out more fully as: 'That which leads, other things being equal, to pregnancy is the cause of pregnancy.' And it seems as though this claim is not saying anything at all. It is akin to our asking who stole the money, and being told that it was the thief. What we are citing as the cause is not sufficiently distinct from the effect. It is as if, at root, we are saying that the cause of the type B event is just whatever it is that is the cause of the type B event.

Of course, if we have an independent cause, the situation is very different. Suppose we define conception in terms of certain physiological processes. Now when we spell out the causal claim it would read 'Such-and-such a physiological process is the cause of pregnancy'. This is akin to saying that Frank committed the robbery. Frank is the thief, but here we are picking him out independently of his role as thief.

Second, let us consider the claim that events of type A leading to events of type B must be non-accidental. We come to think that events of type A might cause events of type B when we observe that type B events regularly follow type A events. But we need more than regularity. As it happens, everyone who walked into Alice's office last week had brown hair. But this regularity is just a coincidence. There is no reason why this pattern should be sustained.

Were a man with red hair to attempt to walk into her office, nothing would stop him, nor would his hair turn brown. For us to say that events of type A *caused* events of type B we need to appeal to something that makes the regularity non-accidental. And we can do this by appealing to the idea of a law, a fact about the way the world actually works, such as facts about how matter interacts with matter. Think about Newton's law of gravitation, or the laws that govern the interaction between electrons and protons and neutrons. Always allowing that the science may lead us to change our mind, we accept these laws as basic facts about the way the world works.

When bricks are thrown at windows the windows regularly break. We can characterize the brick-throwing independently of the window-breaking. Bricks can be thrown without windows breaking, and windows can break without bricks being thrown. So the first condition is met. And the regularity is not accidental. Rather, the regularity reflects a law, a fact about how the world actually works. Of course, there are very hard questions that can be asked about what exactly a law is and also about how we can be sure we have discovered a genuine law. Fortunately those questions need not detain us here, for different answers to them will not affect the main line of argument. What matters is just this. To vindicate the claim that bricks thrown at windows *cause* the windows to break, we must at least say that brick-throwing and window-breaking meet the independence condition, and that the connection between one and the other is law-like and not accidental.

Laws that describe causal connections, causal laws, take the following form. If an event of type A occurs then, other things being equal, an event of type B will occur. They describe what *will* happen in certain circumstances. I have added the clause 'other things being equal' because many causal laws have exceptions. (Though, again, it should be noted that this issue is hotly disputed amongst specialists.) Sometimes when a brick is thrown at a window it does not break it, but just bounces off. Perhaps the brick was thrown with very little force, or perhaps the glass is extra tough. Such exceptions do not show that the law is false, just that it is restricted in its application. And, critically for the scientific project, wherever a law is found to have exceptions, the exceptions can be explained in terms of other more general laws, such as laws which take into account the precise momentum of the brick and just how brittle the glass is (see Fodor, 1987, 6, quoted in chapter 2, p. 61).

We can now see more clearly how the standard naturalistic picture comes to admit atoms and electrons as well as bricks and windows into its account of what's real. Atoms and bricks do pushing and pulling, where pushing and pulling is understood in terms of participation in causal laws. Atoms are real because there are causal laws that correctly describe their interaction with one another and other fundamental particles. Bricks and windows are also real, and for the same reason: there are causal laws that correctly describe the interaction between the two types of object. Of course, it is true that brick-and-window laws admit of more exceptions than atom-and-electron laws. The former are more restricted in their application than the latter. But, within their limits, brick-and-window laws are just as robust as the atom-and-electron laws.

The reality of Dennett's intentional states

How, then, does all this talk of causal laws relate to Dennett's intentional systems theory? If we adopt the physical stance then we make direct use of causal laws, and, indeed, causal laws of a very general kind. If we are making predictions about what a chess machine will do next, and we adopt the physical stance, then we will advert to laws that describe the behaviour of the atoms and electrons that make up the circuitry of the device. And atoms and electrons are, on the standard naturalistic picture, unproblematically real.

What about the design stance? If we adopt the interpretation of the design stance that I argued for in chapter 2, then, as with the physical stance, we will make direct use of causal laws in formulating our predictions. The laws which apply to the chess machine will describe the effects of inputs on internal states, and the effect of internal states on one another, and on outputs. And, given the criteria of reality on the table, the inputs, outputs, and internal states will count as real. They are real, because there are causal laws that correctly describe how they affect one another.

Of course, the success of the design stance depends upon the device in question working properly, that is, conforming to its causal blueprint. If we interfere with the chess machine's power supply, it may develop an intermittent fault. In such a circumstance – depending how serious the disruption is – we may be able to say that the same causal laws apply, but that exceptions will occur. These exceptions can be explained by more general laws, such as the laws available at the physical stance. On the other hand, if we place the chess machine in a hot oven, and all its parts begin to melt, then we will no longer expect the same set of laws to apply. Once the device ceases to conform to the causal blueprint in a serious way, then those laws are of no help to us.

Finally, we can turn to the intentional stance. Again, we can follow through the example of the chess machine. Consider the intentional states we ascribe when we view the chess machine from the intentional stance. Do these states count as real according to the standard naturalistic picture? It would seem that they do not. We ascribe intentional states to the chess machine and we use them to predict its behaviour by means of the `norms of rationality. We predict that the machine will do what the norms of rationality say is appropriate. But this seems quite at odds with the standard naturalistic picture. And we can see this more clearly by checking the two conditions required for causation just set out.

First, are intentional states (the putative causes) independent of the behaviours (the putative effects) which they predict? At first blush it would seem that they are not. Suppose that the chess machine 'believes' that unless it moves its queen forward three squares it will lose the game and suppose it has a standing 'desire' to win the game. On the basis of this, we can confidently predict that the machine will move its queen three squares forward. But here there seems to be a logical connection between the putative cause and the putative effect. It is like the case where conception, understood as that which, other things being equal, leads to pregnancy, was suggested as a cause of pregnancy. Consider what it is, according to Dennett's account, to have a belief that unless you move your queen forward three squares you will lose the game, and to have a desire to win the game. It seems to be just this: if you have these two together, you will, other things being equal, move your queen forward three squares. So the suggestion that the 'belief' and the 'desire' cause the chess machine to move its queen forward three squares could just as well be expressed as 'that the chess machine will, other things being equal, move its queen forward three squares is the cause of the chess machine moving its queen forward three squares'. And this seems to say nothing at all.

Second, are there intentional laws, laws that relate some beliefs and desires to actions, or beliefs and desires to new sets of beliefs and desires? Is it a causal law, say, that if you want something X, and believe that you can get something X by doing something A, then, other things being equal you will do A? In the philosophy of mind literature, it is often suggested that this is a law. But, on closer examination, this generalization seems to be quite different from the generalizations that have so far been counted as causal laws.

Clearly, it will often describe what goes on correctly. If I want a cup of tea, and if I can have a cup of tea by going to the kitchen and making one, then, other things being equal, I will go to the kitchen and make one. The trouble comes, however, with the 'other things being equal' clause. For the way that clause works here is rather different from the way it works with the causal laws discussed so far.

Take the case of the causal laws that describe the operation of the chess machine when viewed from the design stance. In this case, we can get a good handle on the work the 'other things being equal' clause is supposed to do. Things are not equal when the causal structure specified in the chess machine's blueprint ceases to exist. If, say, a wire is cut on a circuit board, then the chess machine will no longer correspond to its causal blueprint. Other things are not equal, and to be sure of predictive accuracy we will need either to appeal to some more general laws, either at the physical stance, or at the design stance but pitched at a lower and more general level. We might, for example, switch from a design stance based on a computer program to a design stance based on the specifications of the component parts.

But, in the case of the intentional stance, it seems as though the ways in which 'other things' can fail to 'be equal' is utterly open-ended. For example, there may be many other ways in which I can get the tea. I could ask Helen to make me a cup, instead of doing it myself. I could just sit and wait, knowing that Gavin will make some tea soon anyway, because he always does. Or something might trump my desire for tea. Extreme laziness, and the knowledge that if I make tea for myself Helen and Gavin will want some too, may overcome my desire for tea. All of these circumstances would make the operation of the supposed law fail. But none of these circumstances are explained by the system 'deviating from its design' or 'not working as it should', as is always the case with the design stance. Nothing has gone wrong here at all. And there would be no merit in switching to the design or even physical stance in order to explain the deviation from the supposed intentional law (again, see Fodor, 1987, 6; chapter 2, p. 61).

Reductionists must argue that these problems can be overcome. Intentional states, they will have to insist, can be identified with design stance states, where the design stance is construed in the manner of a causal blueprint. And so, according to the standard naturalistic picture, the intentional states get to count as real by being governed by causal laws. Dennett is sceptical of such attempts. And, in any case, as we have seen in chapter 2, he has independent reasons for rejecting such reduction. As such, he does not see any point in trying to overcome the problems that may arise here. His response, then, is to shift the ground and argue against the standard naturalistic picture.

3.2　Dennett's early responses

Dennett's writing on the issue of the reality and causal powers of intentional states is one of the least consistent parts of his work. In *Content and Consciousness* he was clear that intentional explanation was not a species of causal explanation (*CC*, 35). He insisted that talk about beliefs and desires was perfectly legitimate in the right contexts, but that the terms did not literally refer to an entity or state that could be picked out in some other way. Intentional terms, he told us, were not 'referring terms'. They were akin to terms such as 'sake' and 'voice' in the expressions 'she did it for his sake' and 'she has lost her voice' (*CC*, chapter 1).

In subsequent work he made use of the idea of 'instrumentalism', a doctrine developed in the philosophy of science. He allowed that his attitude towards beliefs and desires was an 'instrumental' one (*IS*, 71; *BDB*, 210). This is to say that the ascription of intentional states is simply part of a theoretical 'instrument' for predicting behaviour, but the question of whether these features of the 'instrument' are real or not is not a subject for proper debate. But he found that endorsing instrumentalism seemed to invite criticisms which, as far as he could see, missed the point of his position. He repudiated instrumentalism, putting his endorsement of it down to a well-intentioned but ultimately unhelpful tactic of his expository strategy (again, see *IS*, 71; *BDB*, 210).

There followed a phase in which he described intentional states in a variety of ways which suggested that they were less than robustly real. They were 'abstracta but not illata', he said, drawing on an idea from the philosophy of science. They were 'useful fictions' (*CE*, 459; *RP*, 96; cf. *BC*, 311) or 'real only if we exempt them from a certain familiar standards literality' (*IS*, 72). Or, then again, he said that intentional ascriptions made true claims, but that they were only 'true with a grain of salt' (*IS*, 72–3). All these moves show Dennett refusing to engage with the realist critics by, in effect, denying that the question is an important one. This kind of move persists in Dennett's work. But, while he continues to press that the issue is not as important as his critics make out, he has also adopted a different strategy. This is the strategy of trying to reclaim the concept of 'the real' and to show how intentional states, as he understands them, can be considered to be as real as anything else. This move is made in the important paper 'Real Patterns'. There he defends a view which he calls 'mild realism' (RP, 98). Before looking more closely at the 'mild realism' proposal, it is important to see why some of Dennett's earlier responses were false starts. In particular, we need to see why Dennett's view has very little in common with the doctrine of instrumentalism, a doctrine that comes out of debates within the philosophy of science. And we also need to see why Dennett's appeal to another idea from the philosophy of science, the distinction between 'abstracta' and 'illata', fails to pick out one critical feature of his view.

Abstracta and illata

In 'Three Kinds of Intentional Psychology' (*IS*, chapter 3) Dennett draws attention to a distinction between abstracta and illata. Illata are concrete whereas abstracta are 'calculation-bound entities or logical constructs' (*IS*, 53). We can gain a clearer sense of the terms by thinking about examples. Atoms, electrons, and planets are illata. These entities have a definite place in a scientific theory. For example, planets are understood by us moderns as massive material objects under the sway of gravitational forces, and not, as many pre-moderns thought, objects made from quintessence and embedded in crystalline spheres. And we can fairly readily understand the claim that they are concrete, even if we might be hard-pressed to spell out exactly what that amounts to. On the other hand, centres of gravity and the Equator are abstracta. They are not concrete – we do not expect to trip over or bump into either of these sorts of entities. And we can work out their properties, such as where they are located, by making calculations based on facts that we know about illata.

In 'Three Kinds of Intentional Psychology' Dennett advances the suggestion that intentional states are abstracta but not illata. In one respect this move is useful, but in another it is misleading. The distinction is helpful in this respect. It draws our attention to the fact that Dennett does not think that beliefs and desires are objects that live inside people's heads. This is in contrast to, say, someone like Descartes, who thinks that thoughts are objects in our minds, objects that appear before us in consciousness. And it is also in contrast to Fodor, who thinks that beliefs and desires are (partly made up of) objects inside the head, sentences in the language of thought.

Electrons are illata. We think of them as objects that live inside larger material objects. We can contrast electrons with magnetic states. A small block of steel has been magnetized. And so now we can say that the block is magnetic. But its magnetism is not an object inside it. For all this we can quite happily talk about the block's magnetic condition. This is an abstractum. The condition can be north–south or south–north, for example. Or the condition can be 'unmagnetized'. But it is not the case that there is an object, the magnetic condition, that is literally present, absent, or oriented in a certain way. There are just very many iron atoms, which are aligned one way or another. And if they happen all to be aligned in the same way, then the block is magnetic.

For Dennett, having a belief or a desire is akin to the block having a magnetic condition in the following sense: it is a property or attribute of you, and not some object inside your head. Of course, we do talk about having this or that thought 'in our heads' or 'before our minds', but, for Dennett, this carries no ontological weight. It is simply a manner of speaking, one which indicates that we are preoccupied by something without necessarily talking about it or acting upon it. In this sense, then, it is helpful to think of beliefs as abstracta rather than illata.

But the abstracta/illata distinction is not helpful beyond this first point. In their home territory both abstracta and illata are understood with respect to a scientific theory. Now some theorists may prefer to deny that abstracta are real entities and insist that only illata are. Such a preference might stem from a deep-seated commitment to illata being the fundamental units of reality. But, regardless of such a preference, abstracta and illata are equally good candidates to figure in causal laws. A causal law might appeal to an atom's having a certain number of electrons or a block's being magnetic: it does not matter that electrons are illata and the magnetic conditions are abstracta. This means that whether we actually call them real or not, the standard naturalistic picture has no reason to deny the legitimacy of abstracta; it has no reason to line them up alongside fictional entities or the crystalline spheres which hold the stars.

So if intentional states were abstracta in this sense, Dennett would be right to dismiss the challenge concerning realism. He would be right, that is, to say that nothing of great importance turned on the label 'real' in such a dispute. But on Dennett's account intentional states simply cannot be abstracta in the sense so far discussed. They cannot, because it is a central part of Dennett's account that explanations involving intentional states cannot be reduced to causal law explanations whether they involve illata or abstracta. And so, for him, intentional explanations cannot be causal explanations in the same way that, say, explanations that appeal to magnetic states or centres of gravity are. It is this issue that Dennett's critics are really concerned with. The abstracta versus illata issue is peripheral. From the perspective of the standard naturalistic picture, what's wrong with Dennett's theory is that intentional states cannot figure in causal explanations.

So it is no good Dennett saying that intentional states are as real as abstracta, such as centres of gravity, and that that should be real enough for anyone. It is no good because the adherent of the standard naturalistic picture is going to take a quite different attitude to abstracta that figure in causal laws and abstracta that don't. And she is going to think that abstracta which do not, which for Dennett will include agents, beliefs, and desires, are not to be taken any more seriously than fictions and crystalline spheres.

Instrumentalism

Instrumentalism is a view in the philosophy of science about the ontological status of the hidden entities that are invoked by a scientific theory. A hidden entity is one that cannot be directly observed, but whose presence or absence is inferred on the basis of other observations.[1]

A good example of a hidden entity is the electron. We cannot directly observe electrons, but we make statements about their absence or presence on the basis of other observations. It turns out that a theory that postulates electrons can explain all manner of physical happenings. For example, it can explain how television sets and computers work. Realists about electrons say that the success of the theory is evidence that electrons are real entities. That is, they are real just like rocks and rivers, but, as it happens, they cannot be observed directly. On the other hand, instrumentalists argue that there is no need and, more critically, no reason to suppose that hidden entities are real. The electron theory is treated as a mere 'instrument' for prediction of those phenomena that we can readily observe. It is useful to talk as if electrons exist but, when it comes right down to it, we have no good reason to think that they do.

Dennett squirms uncomfortably with the term 'instrumentalism' in the 'Three Kinds of Intentional Psychology' paper, and commits himself to no stronger a claim than that ascriptions of intentional states are 'instrumentalistic'. He cannot quite bring himself to say that they are merely 'instrumental' or mere 'instruments'. He notes in the commentary to the paper (*IS*, 69–81) that he had let intentional systems theory be described as a variety of 'instrumentalism' (*IS*, 71; *BDB*, 210), although he had not actively promoted that description himself.

Dennett tells us that he was drawn to the idea of instrumentalism because he wanted to describe the different attitudes his theory took to 'brains and their neurophysiological parts, states, and processes' and to 'belief-states that appear as *abstracta* when one attempts to interpret all those real phenomena by adopting the intentional stance' (*IS*, 71–2). But he regrets this tactic because it has led critics to suggest that he thinks belief-states and the like are not real where 'not real' is understood as having a status akin either to fictions or to crystalline spheres. Quite why it should have is a bit of mystery, but in any case the upshot has been unhelpful to Dennett.

In fact, the issue of concern to Dennett and his critics really has nothing to do with instrumentalism at all. For what is at dispute is not whether, as a general rule, we should hold back from saying hidden entities are real, but whether the case of agents and their intentional states is importantly different from the case of electrons or computational states. An instrumentalist will say that none of these entities are real. But she can still distinguish between those that figure in successful theories and those that do not. Dennett's point is that although agents and their intentional states do not figure in successful causal law theories, that is not a reason for classing them along with crystalline spheres and phlogiston.

3.3   Reconciliation without reduction

The standard naturalistic picture insists that to be part of nature something must have a regular, law-governed causal structure. Dennett sees this picture as too conservative. For him, one way, and a very important way, in which something can be part of nature is to have a regular, law-governed causal structure. But he also thinks that something can be part of nature if it has a regular, norm-governed behavioural structure. In both cases, law-governed causal structure and norm-governed behavioural structure, we have what Dennett describes as a *real pattern*. The pattern of brick-throwing followed by window-breaking is a predictable regularity, a real pattern. You can, as Dennett puts it, 'get rich' by betting on it (RP, 103–4). The pattern of wanting a beer followed by going to the fridge to get a beer is another predictable regularity, another real pattern. Of course, Dennett agrees, indeed insists, that these two kinds of real pattern are different. But they are not different as far as their right to be taken seriously is concerned, they are not different in so far as they have the capacity to pick up on features that are in the world whether we care to discern them or not, features that in some way or other do pushing and pulling in the world.

To make this challenge to the standard naturalistic picture plausible, Dennett must give us a reason to think that there really are norm-governed behavioural structures out there, as opposed to things which look a bit like them but, as it happens, can be either eliminated or reduced to law-governed causal structures. And, further, he must give us a reason to think that the existence of such norm-governed structures is compatible with naturalism. Dennett's approach is, at root, very simple. When we look at fancy mechanisms that we have designed, such as chess machines, it turns out that they exhibit a simple kind of agency even though they only have mechanical parts inside. And when we look at more subtle agents, such as people and animals, we find that they only have and only need to have mechanical parts inside. And so, if – and it is by no means a small 'if' – Dennett's anti-reductionist arguments are successful, it is just a brute fact about the way things can be that there are norm-governed behavioural structures in the world, made out of, but not identical with, law-governed causal structures.

If we accept this first move, another challenge immediately arises. It is not enough to say that in a world like ours, it is possible for agents, that is norm-governed behavioural structures, to exist; we also need a story about how they come to exist. For in the case of the chess machine and other artefacts there is no great mystery as to how an agent – something sensitive to reasons – has come into existence. For we artificers have cunningly arranged mechanical parts in such a way that they give rise to norm-governed behavioural patterns. We have applied foresight and insight, we have tinkered and adjusted, and, as it turns out, the world is made in such a way that this sort of design work can give rise to norm-governed behavioural structures. But there is still a challenge of accounting for how, in a world without supernature, persons and animals could come into being. And here Dennett appeals to the power of natural selection. Natural selection has designed plants, animals, and persons to be, in various degrees and in various ways, sensitive to reasons (see chapter 7).

For adherents of the standard naturalistic picture, the existence of norm-governed behavioural structures that are neither supernatural nor reducible to law-governed causal structures can seem very weird. So Dennett has quite a lot of work to do to show how this proposal can make sense. This is the work he undertakes in the 'Real Patterns' paper. A central element of the story is the insistence that the real patterns in question are 'real but noisy'. This is to say that the observed pattern can deviate from the predicted pattern in a variety of ways. When science encounters such deviations, it (usually) seeks to find further causal laws that can improve prediction. That is, it takes the failure of precise prediction as a demand to refine the account of what lies behind the pattern, a failure to pick up on the real processes that generate it. But Dennett argues that, for some patterns, when the best available means of prediction fails, we need not presume that there is a deeper or more fundamental method of prediction that could do better.

In particular, he argues that when we predict what agents do by means of the intentional stance, and their behaviour fails to match our prediction, sometimes there is no way of improving our predictions by appeal to 'deeper' or 'more fundamental' features. Rather, we must simply accept that the pattern here is 'real but noisy'. This is because what sustains real patterns in these cases is not so much an inner mechanism but the successful interaction of the inner mechanism with environmental factors. This, as Dennett makes much of, is what happens with natural selection: if they do not go extinct, then populations will make 'reasonable' adjustments to their traits in the face of environmental change. Or, then again, consider agents that can engage in trial-and-error learning. By hook or by crook they will, if they do not die trying, come to adopt 'reasonable' behavioural policies. They do so by rejecting the failed policies and sticking with the ones that reap rewards. In these ways 'reasonableness' imposes itself on the unfolding of a lineage or the development of an agent's behavioural policies. But the imposition is far from perfect. The real pattern of 'reasonableness' is there all right, but the cobbled-together mechanisms that result from natural selection, or trial-and-error learning, only approximate to the ideal.

Having given a brief outline of the work Dennett needs to do to challenge the standard naturalistic picture, let me try to fill in some details. I shall look first at Dennett's defence of the very existence of norm-governed behavioural structures – patterns that are irreducible to law-governed causal structures but are nonetheless compatible with naturalism. And then I look more closely at the details of what these norm-governed behavioural structures are and how it can be that they are compatible with the mechanistic world view. In the following section I turn to two lines of objection: the first is concerned with the issue of whether there is always a clear fact as to what an agent's intentional states are, something Dennett is happy to deny; the second is concerned with the powerful intuition that intentional states are themselves causes.

Norm-governed behavioural structures

Why should we believe that there really are norm-governed behavioural structures out there as opposed to things which look a bit like them but, as it happens, can be either eliminated or reduced to law-governed causal structures? And, if we have a reason to believe in such things, is it compatible with a rejection of supernature? That is, could such norm-governed behavioural structures be made out of merely mechanistic bits and pieces?

Dennett rarely talks about his methodology, so the following description is based on an analysis of the way he actually makes his case. It is helpful to try to make his methodology explicit so that we can critically assess it. This, then, is how Dennett makes his case. He tells us a set of stories about actual and imagined systems. So, for example, he tells us about a thermostat to which the designer adds more and more features, such that, by the end of the story, 'it chooses the boiler fuel, purchases it from the cheapest and most reliable dealer, checks the weather stripping, and so forth' (TB, 30). Or he tells us about a robot designed to house and protect your frozen body until science can advance enough to revive you and cure your ills (*IS*, 295–8). Through these stories he aims to show us two things. The first is that, as it happens, cunningly constructed mechanistic devices just can exhibit the powers of agents, such as sensitivity to reasons. Albeit they do this in a partial and limited way. But, nonetheless, it is a brute fact that, by close examination of cases, we can come to see. The second is that, as it happens, we can relieve ourselves of all puzzlement about how this is possible by means of 'flipping' between the intentional stance and the design or physical stance.

Dennett's method relies on him persuading you that what might have seemed to be intractable puzzles are, in fact, dissoluble. But what you are left with at the end is not a new scientific theory, one in which the (supposedly) puzzling intentional terms are replaced with (supposedly) non-puzzling non-intentional terms. Indeed, what you are left with is not something that is easy to explain to someone who is still deeply troubled by the existence of norm-governed behavioural structures that are neither reducible nor supernatural. All that can be done, if Dennett persuades you, is that you in turn aim to persuade others in a similar way, that is, by telling various stories that shift your interlocutor's understanding of the issues at hand.

Of course, this sort of approach will strike many as deeply suspect. Is Dennett not just avoiding a hard problem by means of some fancy rhetoric? Is he not turning his back on proper standards of rigour and clarity, of argument and explanation? I do not think he is. Rather, he is trying to find a way to break out of, and to help his readers break out of, certain deeply entrenched patterns of thought, and in particular he is trying to break the grip of the standard naturalistic picture. He is, in effect, engaging in what might be called a 'therapeutic approach' to philosophy. This approach, which is closely associated with Wittgenstein, and to a lesser extent Ryle, works by talking an audience around by means of repeated examples and by demonstrations of how existing assumptions lead to absurdity. The influence of Ryle is always clear in Dennett's doctrines (see chapter 1). The influence of Wittgenstein, which Dennett occasionally draws attention to (for example, *CE*, 462–3), is less explicit. But his use of stories that aim to shift our understanding, to dissolve problems rather than find a solution that fits into a pre-existing template, is very much in the spirit of Wittgenstein.

In any case, let us work through the application of this method more closely. Dennett's stories feature a range of actual and imagined devices. He may tell us about chess machines or the latest robots created by artificial intelligence researchers. Or he may ask us to imagine machines that have not been built now, but could be, or that could not be built now, but may be in the future. In the case of such artefacts it is simply stipulated that they are made up only of mechanistic parts. He then asks us to think about different stances that we may be able to take towards these systems, and, in particular, the intentional stance. He aims to show, that is, that such artefacts can come to be seen as intentional systems. And, by switching from the physical or design stance and back to the intentional stance, we come to see how an intentional system, an agent, can be made out of nothing more than correctly arranged mechanistic parts.

Working from the other direction, Dennett tells stories about natural agents: ants, bears, cats, and people. We naturally employ the intentional stance in understanding all these systems. But, as modern science has shown us, we can also come to understand these systems from the design or physical stance. Put very crudely, if you open up such agents and look inside, all you find are mechanistic parts. And, once again, Dennett aims to persuade us, by asking us to 'flip' between the intentional stance and the design or physical stances, that nothing more than the mechanistic parts need be inside.

In the course of this process of 'flipping' between stances we can, for example, follow through patterns at the design stance and then, returning to the intentional stance, see what sort of effect they have.[2] We can also label features of the system as viewed from the design stance with 'intentionalistic labels' (see chapter 4 for more on 'intentional labels' and also *IS*, 63, 92, 95; *BS*, 26–7). And this further aids the task of making it intelligible how the mechanism we view at the design stance underpins the agent that we view at the intentional stance.

Of course, as Dennett is happy to concede, his approach does require a modest deflation of our understanding of what it is to be a rational agent. A tradition which goes back at least as far as Plato has it that the human mind has something of the divine about it. Aristotle famously thought that there was no thought the intellectual soul could not think, a belief which was a key premise in his argument that the intellectual soul could not be material. But Dennett insists that human minds, and the cognitive capacities of simpler agents, could never be so grand. Actual rational agents, the ones that are built out of mechanistic bits and pieces, are limited in what they can grasp, in how fully they can appreciate meanings, in how wide a range of perspectives they can adopt. Actual agents cannot take account of every possible side-effect of their actions (*BC*, chapter 11 and chapter 12; *ER*, 26–31). Why do they fall short in this way? They do because thinking, or more generally cognition, requires that the bits inside you tick over in a certain way. More thinking requires more bits, more time, or both. And actual agents are limited in the size of their brains and limited in the time they have to make decisions and arrive at conclusions. So, for all that they are rational, they are imperfectly rational. They approximate the ideal. And while capable of improvement, perhaps indefinite improvement, they can never consistently achieve that ideal.

Faced with the standard naturalistic picture, Dennett calls for a shift in our vision. In our world there is room for the existence of norm-governed behavioural structures which are neither reducible to law-governed causal structures nor dependent on supernature. But to recognize this we need to see, first, how sophisticated mechanisms can be and, second, how our conception of agency can be modestly deflated without serious damage. Once we see these two things we can, by flipping back and forth between the intentional and the design stance, come to see actual agents as constructed from no more than mechanistic parts. We achieve, then, reconciliation without reduction. Of course, Dennett's answer is highly contestable. It is contestable on grounds of his method, which to the sceptic may seem like so much hand-waving. And it is contestable because reductionists will argue that all and every successful intentional system does share some non-intentional description. With all this in mind, we can turn to the details of what these norm-governed behavioural structures actually are.

Real but noisy patterns

In the 'Real Patterns' paper Dennett begins by noting that we can reliably predict certain systems by means of the intentional stance. To make these predictions we need to ascribe intentional states. For example, faced with the same stimulus – the last bagel – Ruth and Tam behave in different ways. One goes for the last bagel, the other waits for it to be offered. These ways reflect, let us say, their beliefs about how important their own hunger is and how important it is to be polite. While the type of agent ('person') and the situation ('the last bagel') remain the same, something varies. We assign different beliefs and desires to Ruth and to Tam, and we use these predictive variables, combined with the norms of rationality, to make our predictions.

On this much, Dennett and reductionists can agree. But when it comes to explaining further what intentional states are, and how they relate to scientific modes of explanation, there is a sharp divergence. The way Dennett and the way reductionist theorists explain the success of the predictive strategy, indeed the way they think it is possible to explain the success, is very different. We shall look at both ways in turn, beginning with the reductionist way.

Explaining the patterns: the causal law way

Fodor is once again a good representative for reductionism, the attempt to reduce the intentional to the non-intentional. Dennett tells us that Fodor thinks that the only way we could vindicate an ascription of a real pattern would be if, by and large, the pattern was caused by a mechanism whose inner states corresponded to our predictive variables (RP, 111). In the case of agents, then, the condition would be that the inner states of the mechanism must correspond to intentional states. Only if the outward pattern was also discernible in the inner mechanism, would the reality of the intentional ascriptions be vindicated.

Fodor's thought is that intentional states, along with a set of general principles, yield good predictions because, hidden within the brain, there are physical states – such as the representations within a computational system – corresponding to them and a mechanism that ensures that the causal powers of these physical states correspond to the connections laid out in the general principles. On this story what intentional states 'really are' are internal representations.

As outlined in chapter 1, a representation is a physical object which also exhibits intentionality. It is a physical object that is also about something. A word, 'lunch', say, is both a set of ink marks on a piece of paper and also something that carries a meaning. No mere mechanism is sensitive to the meaning of the word. Indeed it is a basic principle of naturalism, one that Dennett signs up to, that mechanisms cannot be so sensitive. But a mechanism can be sensitive to the mechanistic properties of a representation, its physical shape and structure. These are often called syntactic features. The big idea of the representational theory is to arrange for the syntactic features to have causal powers that are appropriate to their semantic features, that is, to what they stand for. If a representation is about bagels, then it should in the right circumstances be caused by the presence of bagels, cause the production of further bagel representations, cause appropriate bagel behaviour, and so forth.

If, argues the adherent of the representational theory of mind, there were not internal states corresponding to beliefs and desires, then how could we explain the persistence of the pattern of rational agency? Just as we need to write down, as it were, these variables if we are to predict what a person is going to do, so too they must, in a suitable sense, be written down in the person's head so that they can cause her to do what we predict that she will do.

Explaining the patterns: Dennett's alternative

Dennett's alternative to the causal law explanation of a real pattern is subtle. But it is also absolutely central to understanding what is distinctive about his overall view. We shall approach the position by stages. The first move Dennett makes is this. The presence of the pattern: 'could be there thanks to the statistical effect of very many concrete minutiae producing, as if by a hidden hand, an approximation of the "ideal" order' (RP, 111). A 'hidden-hand' theory is one in which the appearance of a hidden but conscious planner or coordinator is explained by other means. The forces of the market maintain a coordinated balance of production and consumption. One might think any process that worked so smoothly must be a result of deliberate oversight. But this is not the case. Someone who is predicting the behaviour of the market must keep track of a range of variables, just as someone who is predicting the behaviour of a person. And we might think that the process that sustains the economic real pattern must itself feature states that correspond to those variables. But this is not the case. The variables that we use to make our economic predictions in no way correspond to any elements in the process that maintains the balance. For that process is simply the outcome of 'very many concrete' market transactions, each no more than a 'minutiae'. The variables that feature in the best description of that process, the description that allows us to get a firm grip on the patterns, do not correspond to any of the specific causal elements that drive that process.

There are, then, some hidden-hand theories that do not work in the same manner as the representational theory, that do not require that the process that sustains them carries some echo of the variables required for successful prediction. Economics here is, of course, just a model. And I would not want to make any bold claims about the reality of economic entities or even the predictive powers of economic theory. The example simply shows that there could be a hidden-hand theory of rational agency which worked in a different way from the suggestion of the representation theory. But how could many 'concrete minutiae', that is, a range of causal forces, come to be arranged to generate the patterns of interest?

Dennett notes that the patterns of interest, the patterns revealed by the intentional stance are:

> those that are preserved under selection pressure: the regularities dictated by principles of good design and hence homed in on by self-designing systems. That is, a "rule of thought" may be much more than a mere regularity; it may be a *wise* rule, a rule one would design a system by if one were a system designer, and hence a rule one would expect self-designing systems to "discover" in the course of settling into their patterns of activity. Such rules no more need be explicitly represented than do the principles of aerodynamics honoured in the design of birds' wings. (RP, 112)

In the biological realm the patterns that are 'preserved under selection pressure' are those that it is better or more rational to pursue given the aim of surviving long enough to reproduce. By the expression 'self-designing system', I think Dennett intends to include not only systems that are designed as a result of the process of natural selection but also those that can achieve a degree of lifetime learning, i.e., agents that can try out a range of different behavioural tactics, and fix upon those that yield the best results. Such agents can learn from their mistakes and perhaps also try out options 'in their heads', letting, in Karl Popper's memorable phrase, some of their hypotheses die in their stead. (See *DDI*, chapter 13, or *KM*, chapter 4, for Dennett's discussion of the different kinds of 'self-designing systems', from hard-wired systems to sophisticated lifetime learners.) Such agents will fix on more rational patterns of behaviour, that is, better rather than worse patterns of behaviour. And this is why Dennett expects them to discover 'wise rules', what I have been calling norms, norms that are sensible or rational guides to behaviour.

Some behavioural strategies just are better than others. This is an objective fact. But it is not a fact that can *directly* move any mechanism. For self-designing systems, however, those strategies which fail to conform to what is reasonable will tend to be abandoned in favour of those strategies that do. And so a repeated process of trial-and-error can come to shape the workings of a mechanism in line with rational norms in an *indirect* manner. Natural selection (for species) and various forms of 'generate-and-test' learning (for individuals), tend to converge on objectively good solutions to problems. Where systems are shaped by natural selection, and/or by generate-and-test learning, their behaviour will come to conform to rational norms.

That we and other agents are lifetime learners is important. Were we to have all our behavioural patterns innately programmed, then it might be plausible that, where two of us had the same thought, the same sorts of processes were going on in our brains. But a great deal of our behavioural patterns are acquired, even if that acquisition is heavily supported by innate learning mechanisms. Given this, there is plenty of scope for differences in our internal mechanisms. Two agents who have, from the perspective of the intentional stance, the same beliefs and desires, the same reasoning ability, can, on this account, look very different from one another when we adopt the design and physical stances.

For example, on Dennett's picture we positively expect that every person has a slightly different set of brain connections that govern her response to the word 'lunch'. But what is *reasonable* to do with the word 'lunch' is what determines what it is the word 'lunch' eventually does. The details may be different in each case. We may all have a slightly different grasp of the word 'lunch', and our usage may diverge from each other in some peripheral circumstances. But this is simply noise that slightly obscures the underlying pattern. By and large, any two English speakers will share the same real but noisy pattern of behaviour with respect to the use of the word 'lunch', and with respect to most of our other words and concepts.[3] They will do so because self-designing systems in our kind of habitat, a habitat dominated by words and ideas, will adjust themselves to conform (cf. *CE*, 417).

Dennett usefully draws attention to a passage from Quine, which helps to illustrate this point:

> Different persons growing up in the same language are like different bushes trimmed and trained to take the shape of identical elephants. The anatomical details of twigs and branches will fulfil the elephantine form differently from bush to bush, but the overall outward results are the same. (RP, 115, n. 15; see Quine, 1960, 8)

In terms of Quine's analogy, it is as if Fodor is, and adherents of the representational theory in general are, looking for specific patterns in the twigs and branches, patterns that will account for the elephant shape that the bush makes. Dennett, by contrast, is looking at the power of the environment to shape the twigs and branches so that, some way or other, they come reliably to sustain the pattern of the elephant.

There are often two ways to account for commonalities in different entities. We can, as Fodor does, appeal to an internal common-ality. Two entities appear the same from the outside because, at root, they are the same on the inside, for example they share the same abstract causal blueprint. Or we can, as Dennett does, appeal to the presence of external pressures and a capacity to be moulded by those pressures. Two entities appear the same from the outside because, give or take, they have been exposed to the same external pressures. Self-designing systems, either across generations or in the lifetime of individuals, mould and remould themselves in the face of pressure from their environment. The shape of this pressure depends on what it is 'good for' an organism to do, most critically on the 'goods' of survival and reproduction. What makes the behaviour of organisms rational, regardless of how their insides work, is that behaving in rational ways just is the best way to survive and reproduce. Arguably, and as we shall see in later chapters, especially 7 and 8, a person's environment is rather different. It is an environment dominated by language and, most critically, by the pressure to give an account of yourself to both yourself and others. Human beings try out various ways of responding to linguistic features, to arguments, to criticism, and so forth, and they tune and retune their approach until they acquire reasonable competency. For Dennett, then, what makes humans conform to the patterns of the intentional stance is (a) the fact that they are highly effective lifetime learners and (b) they are all exposed to a relevantly similar environment, an environment in which the appreciation of rational norms is what is required to get by successfully.

For Fodor, the only explanation of a real but noisy pattern seems to be this. In ideal conditions the pattern exists in its pure unsullied form. But various interfering factors sully the pattern, undermining its purity. The pattern, in its pure form, must arise out of causal laws. And Fodor's suggestion for how this is done is the representational theory of the mind. Dennett's explanation of real but noisy patterns is quite different. For him, there are no ideal conditions under which the pattern would be pure and unsullied. Rather, self-designing systems can modify themselves, either across generations or within their own lifetimes, to produce behaviour that better converges with what it is rational for that system to do, given what is 'good for' that system. A system, then, may reliably converge towards the behaviour described by the pure pattern, but it is always approaching this purity from impurity, and not, as with Fodor, the other way around.

Dennett's view is obviously right for elephant-shaped bushes. But is it right for agents? One advantage Dennett seems to have over

Fodor is this: Dennett need not deny that many of the patterns in human behaviour will be explained in the way that Fodor suggests. What he does deny is that we should think that this, at root, is what intentional states really are. So what does he think beliefs and desires are? The short answer here is that they simply are what they are. They are what we talk about when we predict the behaviour of agents using the intentional stance. And, as against Fodor, they are not really anything else (cf. chapter 2; Fodor, 1987, 97).

The longer answer must go something like this. Beliefs and desires are part of what we must, as it were, write down if, having assumed that we are faced with a real pattern of agency, we want to make successful predictions. Beliefs and desires are features of our interpretation of the pattern. Are such features real? Well, they are abstracta rather than illata. They do not qualify as real in the same way that other abstracta do, such as centres of gravity, because they are not part of any law-governed causal structure. But they do not fail to be real in the way that fictions do (unicorns and Sherlock Holmes), or the entities in defunct theories do (phlogiston and crystalline spheres). And they do not fail to be real in the way that Tuesdays and chairs do, i.e., they do not fail to be real because they are simply 'in the eye of the beholder'. And this gives Dennett a reason for insisting that they are real enough.

3.4   Two challenges

Indeterminacy

This image of approaching purity from impurity can help to explain Dennett's tolerance of what philosophers call 'indeterminacy'. Dennett thinks it is not always clear, or determinate, what particular intentional states of an agent are about. Being 'clear' or 'determinate' here is not merely a matter of there being some clear fact that we cannot access effectively, but there being no clear fact of the matter at all. Similarly, and relatedly, Dennett thinks that it is not always clear, or determinate, which overall interpretation, that is complete set of intentional state attributions, correctly apply to an agent. Again, this is not merely the idea that we may be ignorant of the correct interpretation, but the stronger claim that there may be no fact of the matter which interpretation is correct.

Consider first indeterminacy with regard to particular intentional states. Suppose Kate tells us that 'capitalism is evil'. Must it be the case that what she believes when she says this is wholly determinate? Does, for example, this form of words determinately fix her beliefs? They do fix something. By saying 'capitalism is evil', Kate places herself under an obligation to defend a view that is compatible with that form of words. But, as a moment's reflection reveals, there are plenty of different ways to understand such a form of words. What does Kate mean by 'capitalism' and by 'evil'? Does she have precise definitions in mind? In the course of an argument, would we be able to wring any qualifications out of Kate, such as, 'Capitalism can be rendered morally neutral if fettered by effective state controls but, since that is next to impossible, on the whole it is true to say that capitalism is evil, which is what I meant all along'? Must it be the case that Kate meant something definite all along? Must it be the case that she goes through a series of discrete changes of mind, where what she believes could be precisely determined at each stage? Dennett thinks we have no reason to think this. Rather, the form of words, for both us and for Kate, was never any more than a rough-and-ready indicator of one aspect of her behavioural profile, a profile that only approximately exhibits rationality and, hence, can only approximately be accurately described by means of intentional states. For practical purposes, indeterminacy presents us with few problems. This is because, by and large, we approximate well to the ideal of rationality and so our behavioural profile is well described by intentional states. But the idea of an underlying precision that is occasionally blurred by noise is, for Dennett, getting things back to front.

Dennett's view follows naturally from the idea that agents are self-designing systems, systems that, through various trial-and-error processes, better bring their behaviour into line with rational norms. Actual agents fall short of the ideal. There are considerations we might appeal to in an attempt to make intentional ascriptions more precise. For example, we can appeal to the agent's history. But, given Dennett's line that historical factors can be defeated by contemporary capacity (*IS*, 319; see chapter 2, p. 47), even such an appeal will not always be decisive. Thus, any conclusion we come to may be somewhat arbitrary. But this is just how it is with real but noisy patterns as Dennett understands them. There is no pure and wholly unsullied pattern that lies behind what we observe, a pure pattern which would make all intentional ascriptions wholly determinate. The real but noisy pattern is all we have to go on. And if that pattern does not settle the issue of what someone thinks, then nothing will.

The second kind of indeterminacy involves the whole set of intentional states ascribed to an agent. According to Dennett, if two or more distinct sets of intentional states are just as good at yielding 'reliable and voluminous' predictions of the agent, then there is nothing to choose between them (for example RP, 115–17). Dennett gives the example of Sam the art critic who 'extols, buys, and promotes mediocre paintings by his son' (*BS*, 39). Does Sam think that the paintings are bad, but support his son out of loyalty? Or is he so blinded by love that he actually thinks the paintings are good? Of course, in such a case we would expect there to be a determinate answer. We would expect that in the right circumstances we could get Sam to say or do something that made it quite clear which of the two hypotheses is correct. Dennett's point is only this: there is no necessity that this be the case. Or, put the other way, it is perfectly possible that there just is no fact of the matter which hypothesis about Sam is correct.

Which hypothesis we go for will affect the other intentional states we ascribe to Sam, such as whether Sam thinks loyalty is ever more important than honesty, and so forth. But such differences will not make the predictions based on one set of intentional states any less 'reliable and voluminous' than predictions based on the other. (If, as we would generally expect to be the case, one set of predictions is more reliable and more voluminous, then, of course, we would have a reason to favour that interpretation of Sam.)

For some critics to accept that intentional states (either individually or as a whole package) are indeterminate entails that they are not real. After all, how can something that is not clearly this, or clearly that, be real? But Dennett does not feel the tug of these claims at all. Or, at least, if the sense of not being real here is supposed to correspond with the sense in which Sherlock Holmes, Tuesdays, and crystalline spheres are not real, he feels no tug. If the sense of not being real is something more subtle then Dennett can concede, and repeatedly has conceded, that agents and their intentional states are not real in some more refined sense of the term. Dennett is aware that in embracing indeterminacy he is asking us to give up a certain conception of what our intentional states are. His view is clearly incompatible with the idea that our own mental states are somehow utterly transparent to us. But, he might add, wasn't that idea, lifted straight from Descartes, a pretty bad one anyway? For Dennett, giving up on determinacy is no more than another instance of a modest deflation of our self-conception. For some, such a deflation may be uncomfortable or even intolerable. But Dennett cannot give up on indeterminacy without giving up all the central features of his view. Something has to give. Dennett's case is that however precious determinacy may seem, especially when in the grip of a certain philosophical outlook, it can be sacrificed without undue damage to our self-conception.

Causation

It is commonly claimed that beliefs and desires are the causes of our actions. But how can mere 'features of an interpretation' cause something? Surely, what is doing the real work is whatever it is that is the source of the pattern, i.e. the mechanistic goings-on in the brain. It is these goings-on, after all, that can be described in terms of causal laws. And, if we subscribe to something like the conception of causation set out at the start of this chapter, this would seem to be the only way that something could be causally efficacious.

Dennett has written less about the issue of causation than the issue of the reality – or otherwise – of intentional states. And what he says about causation varies quite a lot from text to text (for example *CC*, 35–8; *BS*, 234–6; *IS*, chapter 3; *RP*; *DDI*, 412–22). Although I have argued, and will continue to argue, that many of Dennett's apparent changes of mind can be put down to different ways of expressing the same basic view, this cannot be said of his writing on causation. Here, I think, his views really are unstable.

In *Content and Consciousness*, published in 1969, he argues that intentional explanation cannot be causal explanation (*CC*, 35). The argument here seems to be that it cannot because it does not conform to the two conditions set out in 3.1. However in 'Real Patterns', published in 1991, he argues that to deny beliefs and desires have causal powers is a mistake 'traceable to a simplistic notion of causation', and adds that '[if] one finds a predictive pattern [of a certain sort] one has ipso facto discovered a causal power – a difference in the world that makes a subsequent differ-ence testable by standard empirical methods of variable manipula-tion' (*RP*, 112, n. 11). He continues to push this message in more recent work, such as *Darwin's Dangerous Idea* (*DDI*, 412–22).

If, Dennett tells us, we place a sign with the inscription 'Free Lunch' outside a restaurant, we can reliably predict the conse-quences. Putting the sign there, he says, will cause those consequences. What licences the prediction here, however, is our grasp of the meaning of the inscription. The details of the typography, the precise syntactic features, do not matter. And, indeed, if we try to start from those syntactic features and the way in which syntax-processing mechanisms in our heads process them, we will leave behind agents and their behaviour, and thus miss out on the real pattern of interest.

> The fact that the regularities on which these successful predictions are based are efficiently capturable (only) in intentional terms and are not derived from "covering laws" does not show that the regularities are not "causal"; it just shows that philosophers have often relied on pinched notions of causality derived from exclusive attention to a few examples drawn from physics and chemistry. (RP, 112, n. 11)

Many theorists insist that the idea that beliefs and desires combine together to cause behaviour is a central part of our self-conception. Fodor is one such, and would seemingly go to the wall for that view. But it is by no means a universally held intuition. As it strikes me, the strategy of Dennett's earlier self is best here, that is, going on the offensive and denying that intuition altogether. Dennett can, I think, deny the intuition without losing anything from our self-conception that is really worth wanting. The denial might be softened by the following claim: what really seems to matter here is that citing intentional states plays a role in predicting and explaining our actions. The way in which they do this need not be causal.

It is already clear that the intentional stance is a powerful albeit imperfect predictive tool. Explanation can be more problematic. Suppose I predict that you will be in the café at eleven on the basis that you believe you were due to meet me there at that time. And my prediction is right. You are in the café at eleven. Must it be your belief that you were due to meet me that explains your presence? Clearly not. You may well have forgotten all about our appointment when Hayley asked you to meet her for coffee at the same place and time. Or you may have been dragged there, against your will, by secret service agents. How, then, can we tell when the belief that you were due to meet me is the real explanation? One answer is to say it is the real explanation when and only when that belief has caused your arrival. And, in general, the beliefs and desires that genuinely explain action are those that cause it.

Dennett might say a number of things here. First, he might argue that if he is allowed to operate with an 'un-pinched' notion of causality, then he is entitled to this move as much as anyone else. Second, he might offer some account of which intentional states are genuinely explanatory that makes no appeal to causation. So, he might appeal to the idea of explanation as revealing character (*ER*, 136–7). Or he might try a variation on the line that the Hayley-invite explanation is the correct explanation because had Hayley arranged coffee for 11.30 that's when you would have turned up. The Hayley-invite belief is one that is, as it were, in charge of the behaviour, the one to which your behaviour tends to conform. This latter kind of defence is going to be tricky. It may also be vulnerable to the criticism that it illicitly imports various causal notions in via the back door.

Finally, he might also muddy the waters by insisting that there are occasions when the search for a precise explanation is confused. Perhaps the Hayley-invite was uppermost in your mind, but had you not also been invited by me, you would have failed to turn up. So beliefs about both appointments played a role. On Dennett's view this is perfectly acceptable. It need not be determinate whether this or that belief was decisive. Perhaps neither one nor the other is a precise way of capturing the current state of your behavioural profile. If you are falling somewhat short of ideal rationality – and if you are forgetful you certainly are – then maybe there is no precise fact as to whether one belief or the other is the correct explanation. The ascribing of a set of distinct, stable, and efficacious beliefs simply is not possible in such circumstances.

This causation worry may be very serious and may even be the unravelling of Dennett's view. But I do not think that this is obviously the case. Very many theories of mind find the question of how intentional states play a causal role a serious challenge, and Dennett is not obviously so much worse off than many rivals. To the extent that, say, the representational theory can handle this issue well – which is open to dispute – Dennett will counter that it fails on so many other accounts that, when taken in the round, his own view is still to be preferred.

Indeed, on both the indeterminacy and the causation issues, if Dennett's critics dig in their heels, there is little he has to say to them. As elsewhere, his best argument will be that, while the standard naturalistic picture is in place, the phenomenon of agency can either not be accommodated at all or can only be accommodated at the cost of a great distortion. If our aim is accommodation then, Dennett's work urges, something has to give. If the critic is not prepared to give up what Dennett gives up, then she must show how she can achieve accommodation in some other way.

3.5   Where things stand

If the standard naturalistic picture is used to set the standard for what is real and what is not, then Dennett's account of intentional states, of actions, and of agents, leaves them all quite unreal. But Dennett aims to challenge the standard naturalistic picture. In doing so he does not deny that the standard naturalistic picture can give us a complete description of the world, where 'complete' is defined in terms of spatio-temporal extent and causal power (Rorty, 1979, 204–5, cf. chapter 1). Beliefs, desires, actions, and agents do not depend on anything supernatural for their existence. But they figure in a different kind of description of the world, a description made possible by adoption of the intentional stance.

That kind of description gives rise to categories and classifications, some of which yield effective generalizations, predictions, and explanations, and some of which do not. And, of the useful categories and classifications, some of these can reasonably be said to be independent of narrow human concerns. The category 'Tuesday' can do some explanatory and predictive work, as can the categories 'beautiful' and 'corkscrew', but they are all highly parochial. For Dennett, the categories 'belief', 'desire', 'action', and so forth, do both explanatory and predictive work and, further, do so in a way that has nothing to do with our narrow interests. Even if we were not here to adopt the intentional stance to frogs and chimpanzees, this would still be the best way, indeed the only way, to get a grip on what these creatures are and what they do.

When Dennett talks of 'useful fictions' or of 'truth with a grain of salt', he encourages misinterpretation. For Dennett does take intentional states seriously. They are nothing like Sherlock Holmes or fairies. Nor do they have the status of the crystalline spheres of the now defunct astronomical theory. Given this, tactically at least, I think it is helpful for Dennett to insist that his account of intentional states, of actions, and of agents, is a realist account. And, as part of that insistence, to attack adherents of the standard naturalistic picture for having a pinched account of reality.

Further reading

I have used Fodor's version of the representational theory as my reductionist stalking-horse in this chapter. As noted at the start of the chapter, however, reductions can take different forms. The connectionist or parallel-distributed processing paradigm, at least in some versions, aims to reduce an account of agency to an account of causal blueprint specified in terms of networks of interconnected nodes, networks that are roughly isomorphic to the structures found in our brains. Connectionists need not be reductionists – Clark (1989; 1993) is a notable and articulate anti-reductionist whose account of agency is highly Dennettian. For more on connectionism, see Crane (1995) for a basic introduction, then Clark (1989; 1993) and Churchland (1995) for more depth.

Aristotle's argument that the soul must be immaterial since there is no thought it cannot entertain is found in *De Anima*, in particular III.4 to III.8. A crisper version of the argument is found in Aquinas, *Summa Theologica*, First Part, Question 75. While moderns are inclined to scoff at such arguments because they underestimate what cunningly arranged matter can achieve, it is interesting to note that Dennett's approach emphasizes both that mere matter can do more and also that minds do less.

On instrumentalism in the philosophy of science, see Bird (1998). Theorists who are deeply committed to beliefs and desires being the causes of our actions, and also committed to something like the account of causation outlined at the head of the chapter, would include not only supporters of the representational theory (see Crane, 1995), but also eliminativists (such as Churchland, 1981), and anti-reductionists (such as Davidson, 1980).

4

Different Kinds of Psychology

To this point I have been presenting a fairly tidy picture of Dennett's intentional systems theory. Agents, according to the theory, are intentional systems. We predict and explain their behaviour not by reference to causal laws but by reference to rational norms. It does not much matter what is inside them – though what is inside must be mere mechanism and rely on no miracles to do its work – so long as it ensures that a real, if somewhat noisy, pattern of rational agency is sustained. No particular distinction has been drawn between persons and agents who are not persons. For Dennett, both fall squarely into the class of intentional systems.

In this chapter that tidy picture will be disturbed by looking more closely at actual agents, both persons and others, and actual practices of prediction and explanation. While Dennett need not and does not turn his back on the tidy picture there is a great deal to be said about the 'noise' in the 'real patterns'. And Dennett has some important claims to make about how we can make sense of the ways in which an inner mechanism underpins the intentional capacities of the agent. Finally, we shall also look at how Dennett's account deals with the differences between persons and other agents.

I shall begin by looking at how intentional systems theory is related to psychology, where psychology is understood broadly as the empirical inquiry into the principles of behaviour of natural agents. Our everyday methods of predicting and explaining one another, sometimes dubbed 'folk psychology' or 'common-sense psychology', incorporate aspects of the intentional stance, but are not exhausted by it. Scientific psychology, the discovery of principles of behaviour through experimental testing, seems, on the face of it, even further removed from intentional systems theory.

A highly distinctive feature of Dennett's approach here is that he argues that psychology, both folk and scientific, should be regarded as a 'mixed bag'. That is to say different psychological principles often turn out to have a quite different logical character. Thus, any attempt to form a wholly homogeneous psychological theory is bound to cause trouble. But picking out the different elements of the 'mixed bag' is far from straightforward. A whole host of issues crowd in. For example, we shall need to distinguish:

- Rationalizing explanation as opposed to causal law explanation.
- Rationalizing explanation that justifies action as opposed to rationalizing explanation that does not.
- Explanation of why an agent did something as opposed to explanation of how an agent has the capacity to do that thing.
- Explanation of the macro-scale trends in action as opposed to explanation of the micro-scale features.

I shall attempt to steer a way through these issues, though the path cannot but be a winding one. For the terrain is complex. Along the way I shall discuss the differences between the intentional stance as applied to persons and as applied to agents other than persons. And I shall also discuss what Dennett calls sub-personal explanation, namely a kind of explanation that bridges the gap between the purely mechanistic and the intentional. This mode of explanation will be critical when, in the following two chapters, we come to discuss Dennett's account of consciousness. That the terrain here is complex should be no surprise. Our discussion of intentional systems theory to this point has been relatively abstract. When we come face to face with actual agents, and with our actual explanatory and predictive needs, the concrete details start to matter. I aim to show that intentional systems theory holds up well in the face of real world needs and details.

4.1 Psychology and intentional systems theory

Folk psychology or common-sense psychology is the set of methods which we ordinarily use to make sense of our own behaviour and of the behaviour of those around us. These methods and techniques include making use of the intentional stance. But they are not

limited to the intentional stance. Consider, for example, the following folk psychological generalization: people think less clearly
when they are tired or hungry. I take it that this is true. And, moreover, that it is something that pretty much everyone knows and
relies on from time to time in predicting how others, and themselves, will behave. This sort of generalization, along with 'drink-
ing lowers inhibitions' and 'when falling in love people often
neglect other duties and commitments', is very much part of folk
psychology.

In addition to the principles of folk psychology, principles that
pretty much everyone knows, we have also discovered many predictive principles about how agents behave by conducting carefully
controlled experiments. These principles are part of scientific psychology. Some of its principles may be common knowledge, and,
indeed, on their way to becoming part of folk psychology. The principle that a person is less likely to respond to a call for help if she
is in a crowd than if she is alone is an example of a principle that
once fell only into the scientific psychology camp, but is now
making its way into the folk psychological arena. On the other
hand, the following principle remains firmly within scientific
psychology:

> when a person makes judgements about probability, information
> about 'representativeness' tends to outweigh information about pre-
> vailing 'base rates'.

This obscure-sounding principle is best understood with reference to concrete examples. Suppose a person is asked to judge
whether a serious-looking person with a furrowed brow is a
philosopher or a hairdresser. People tend to say 'philosopher'. This
is because 'serious-looking' and 'furrowed brow' are, for most
people, 'representative' of what philosophers look like. But a
moment's reflection will tell us that there are far more hairdressers
in the average population than there are philosophers. That is, the
'base rate' is higher for hairdressers. And so, even given the information about appearance, the right hypothesis to favour ought
really to be 'hairdresser'. One striking aspect of this result is that it
seems to show that people are committed to an irrational procedure
for making probability judgements.

It is worth noting that this experiment, and many others like it,
have been the subject of fierce criticism and heated discussion.
Many critics argue that the way in which the questions are asked
encourages subjects to answer in a particular way. If this is so, it

may show that people are not, after all, committed to irrational procedures. But what also seems clear is that many of these results are
surprising and would not have been predicted by either folk psychology or the intentional stance. There are principles of psychology that only careful experiment can uncover.

A mixed bag

How is folk psychology related to scientific psychology? The fact that
some principles of scientific psychology seem to be able to cross-over
to folk psychology suggests that, fundamentally, the two are in the
same business. And, indeed, this is a view shared by many philosophers of mind and theoretical psychologists. For example, Fodor and
Churchland both agree that folk psychology and scientific psychology are in the same business, even though they differ as to whether
it is a good business to be in. (Fodor thinks it is, and Churchland
thinks it is not.) In explaining this idea – the idea that folk psychology and scientific psychology are in the same business – Dennett calls
on an analogy with what has been called 'folk physics' (*IS*, 7–9, 47–8).
Folk physics is the set of principles that pretty much all of us hold,
either tacitly or explicitly, about the everyday behaviour of physical
bodies. Folk physics is committed to such principles as 'what goes up
must come down'. This bit of folk physics, it turns out, is not universally applicable. But what physics tells us about gravity, combined
with local conditions, largely vindicates it.

Scientific physics is the senior partner to folk physics. Its more
general principles explain all that is true in folk physics, but also
force the outright rejection of some of the folk principles, principles
that while useful in some circumstances turn out to be too confused
to be worth saving. So scientific physics *reduces* some principles of
folk physics and *eliminates* others. Theorists who argue that folk
psychology is fundamentally in the same business as scientific psychology endorse this parallel. They see scientific psychology as the
senior partner to folk psychology, and they expect that it *will*
(Fodor) or *should* if it is to avoid elimination (Churchland) reduce
some folk psychological principles to more general scientific psychological principles, and that other folk psychological principles
will simply be rejected outright.

There are two important consequences of seeing the relationship
between folk psychology and scientific psychology in the way just
described, and Dennett rejects both of them. The first consequence

is that psychology – both folk and scientific – comes to be seen as homogeneous. What I mean here is that all the principles are taken to have the same logical status. In effect they are all attempts at formulating causal laws. Whether these attempts are successful or not is another matter. But having the same logical status means here that what determines the truth or falsity of any psychological principle will involve the same kinds of fact.

This brings us to the second consequence. Given this way of seeing the relationship between folk psychology and scientific psychology, the way in which we determine the truth or falsity of folk psychological principles is by means of empirical inquiry. For, given their logical status, we must look to the world to see whether they are true or false.

Why do I say this? Recall from chapter 3 that with causal laws it is generally agreed that the causes must be independent from their effects. But given this, for all that we can tell before we undertake empirical inquiry, the law may hold or it may not. Independence means that no incoherence or even outright contradiction will result if we deny the truth of a causal law. Hence, we need to look at the world to see whether or not the connection is there.

Dennett cannot accept either of these consequences, and so he cannot accept the picture of the relationship between folk psychology and scientific psychology that leads to them. Folk psychology he tells us is a 'hodge-podge' (*BS*, xiv) or a 'mixed bag' (*IS*, 55). Some of its principles are attempts to formulate causal laws. Hence no incoherence or contradiction would arise were we to say that these principles were false. But other principles are not like this. In particular this is not true of the principles that can be derived from the intentional stance, such as the principle that if you want X and believe you can get X by doing P, then, other things being equal, you do P.

For Dennett, principles derived from the intentional stance are not approximations to causal laws. They are not empirical claims at all. This is shown, he thinks, by the incoherence of denying such principles. Consider again the principle: if you want X and believe you can get X by doing P, then, other things being equal, you do P. Far from being an empirical claim, this is a conceptual claim about the agency. Were anything to fail to conform to such a generalization for at least a good deal of the time we would not conclude that the generalization did not say something true about this agent. Rather, we would conclude that we were not actually dealing with an agent on this occasion.

On the other hand, claims such as 'you think less clearly when you are tired or hungry' could quite easily turn out to be false. If we discovered a person who never got tired, whose urge to help was unaffected by crowds, and whose probability adjustments always took due account of base rates, this would not put in question whether we were dealing with a person. Rather, it would merely tell us something about the (rather impressive) features that person happened to have.

At first blush folk psychology can appear homogeneous. That is, on the surface it can appear that all of its principles have the same logical status. And after reflection some theorists insist that it actually is homogeneous. If we accept that folk psychology is homogeneous we have two options: either its principles are conceptual claims or its principles are empirical claims. The first option is unacceptable: it would make folk psychology too narrow. There are many true principles that we want to count as part of folk psychology that could have been false. Moreover, it divorces folk psychology from scientific psychology in a way that does not make sense of how we can, sometimes, readily recognize scientific psychology as codifying, confirming, or correcting folk psychology.

For Dennett the second option is also unacceptable. This is because he thinks that there are a number of true principles that we want to count as part of folk psychology that we have not discovered by looking at the world and that could not have turned out to be false. And so Dennett thinks that what the folk all lump together, the subject matter of folk psychology, must be separated out into different categories.

Four *kinds of intentional psychology*

In the 1981 paper, 'Three Kinds of Intentional Psychology' (TK), folk psychology (the first kind of intentional psychology) is separated into intentional systems theory (the second) and sub-personal cognitive psychology (the third). This distinction captures two key Dennettian ideas. First, it captures the idea that there is an ineliminable part of folk psychology that appeals to what intentional systems theory codifies, namely the demand for the actions of agents to be reasonable, at least for the most part. Second, it captures the idea that there is a significant part of folk psychology that is fixed by the empirical facts about agents. That is, it allows both an empirical element to folk psychology and for scientific psychology to reveal a range of more subtle empirical principles about particular kinds of agents.

This, however, is only one way that Dennett has broken down folk psychology. In *Content and Consciousness* Dennett introduced a distinction between personal and sub-personal levels of explanation (*CC*, 90–6). Personal level explanation (the *fourth* kind of intentional psychology, as it were) involves what persons do – taking action, having a thought, noticing a difference. By contrast the sub-personal is concerned with what the aggregate of mechanistic parts which make up the person do. The latter might involve a description of neural processes. Or, more abstractly, it might involve a description of the processing within and passing of messages between different sub-systems in the brain, between, say, the speech system and the motor system. The point is that the person does not operate the machinery of her brain. It is not she who sets a sub-system going or arranges for one sub-system to pass a message on to another. (Of course, in doing what she does, such as having a thought, she might indirectly bring such a process about.) The person, as an agent, is wholly absent at the sub-personal level.

When in 'Three Kinds . . .' Dennett refers to sub-personal cognitive psychology, he is drawing on one half of the personal/sub-personal distinction developed in *Content and Consciousness*. As just stated, a typical sub-personal explanation involves different sub-systems, each undertaking their own distinctive processes, passing messages between one another and, at the periphery, attached to perceptual devices (eyes and ears) and motor devices (lips, eyebrows, arms and legs). This kind of sub-personal explanation is often represented by a box-and-arrow diagram (see *BS*, 155, 200–5, for examples), which is a standard expository device in cognitive psychology. The causal structure described by the box-and-arrow diagram can also be represented in the form of a computer program, with various sub-routines and data structures. Whether represented as a box-and-arrow diagram or as a computer program, such sub-personal explanations work just as well as a complement to the personal level explanations of *Content and Consciousness* as they do to the intentional system theory of 'Three Kinds . . .'. And, indeed, sub-personal cognitive psychology corresponds exactly to Dennett's design stance (understood as specifying a causal blueprint).

Why does Dennett describe sub-personal psychology as a kind of *intentional* psychology? It is because the features of the box-and-arrow diagrams or of the computer program are given 'intentionalistic labels' (*BS*, 25–7; *TK*, 63–5; *MSO*, 92–3). A component is described, for example, as a face-recognizer, or a signal passed from one unit to another is described as conveying the meaning 'there is a tree to the left'. These labels, or so I shall argue below, are not to be taken literally. But it is by applying these labels to sub-personal features that we come to understand how it is that mere mechanisms can underpin the intentional capacities of agents.

How do Dennett's two different ways of breaking down folk psychology relate to one another? We might think that he has simply abandoned the earlier contrast in favour of the later. But while the terminology has indeed been largely abandoned, the spirit of the earlier distinction persists. To show this, and to map out the logical geography clearly, will require drawing some new distinctions. As I warned above, the terrain which this chapter surveys is complex, and, unfortunately, that means that the map must be too.

4.2 Rationalizing and non-rationalizing explanation

In the first part of this section I distinguish between the intentional stance as it is applied to persons and the intentional stance as it is applied to other kinds of agents. This leads to a reforming suggestion on my part. We best understand Dennett's position, I argue, if we divide the intentional stance into two. On the one hand we have the basic intentional stance, a stance that can be applied to all agents other than persons. And on the other we have the personal stance, a stance that discerns not only agency, but what is peculiar about the agency of persons.

In the second part of this section I turn to non-rationalizing explanations. Again, I divide these into two broad classes. On the one hand there is sub-personal explanation or, in variant terminology, explanation using the design or physical stance. Such explanations do not explain the actions of agents as such, but rather explain the complex movements of the mechanisms which underpin the agents. I show how Dennett's idea of sub-personal explanation is, in effect, the idea of an annotated design stance explanation. That is, mechanistic components of the agent are described using intentionalistic labels. These labels allow us to bridge the gap between the system discerned at the design stance and the system discerned at the personal or intentional stance. They help us 'flip' (see chapter 3, p. 83) between the intentional stance and the design stance, and hence come to see how an aggregate of parts can work together to bring an agent into the world. On the other hand, there are causal laws that operate at the level of the agent and not at the level of the mechanistic parts which make her up, but which, nonetheless, do not conform to the rational patterns of the intentional or personal stance. These principles yield non-rationalizing explanations, but not sub-personal explanations.

Rationalizing explanation: persons and other kinds of agents

It would be nice if the personal level and intentional system theory were simply terminological variants. But the situation is more complex. In *Content and Consciousness* Dennett's key focus was persons. By the time of 'Three Kinds . . .' Dennett's focus has switched towards agency in general, and away from the contrast between persons and other agents. In this switch the critical differences between persons and other kinds of agents is sometimes left behind.

Dennett first introduced the personal/sub-personal distinction with reference to the example of pain. How is it that a person can tell that she is in pain, can tell what her pain is like, and can tell where it is located? He argues that there is no answer to this question in terms of what a person does. A person does not undertake a series of steps, inspecting her pain, looking at it from different angles, coming to conclusions about its nature. Rather, as a person, she simply can tell that she is in pain and where and what her pain is like. This is a basic capacity persons have.

> When we have said that a person has a sensation of pain, locates it and is prompted to react in a certain way, we have said all there is to say within the scope of this vocabulary. We *can* demand further explanation of how a person happens to withdraw his hand from the hot stove, but we cannot demand further explanation in terms of 'mental processes'. [If] we look for alternative modes of explanation . . . we must abandon the explanatory level of people and their sensations and activities and turn to the *sub-personal* level of brains and events in the nervous system. (CC, 93)

It is not critical that Dennett's example here is the sensation of pain or even a sensation at all. He could equally have written about having a thought or coming to a decision. Of course, the path towards a particular thought or to a particular decision may involve various 'mental processes', various inner actions that the person takes. But for all this, when the final thought or final decision takes place, there is nothing to say about what the person does between the moment before the thought or decision and the moment after. The move from thought to thought or from thought to decision is, as it were, the smallest unit of action a person can undertake. Such actions cannot be broken down into further, smaller, sub-actions. And if we demand further explanation of such a transition, then, it cannot be in terms of 'mental processes'. So 'we must abandon the explanatory level of people' and their thoughts and decisions and 'turn to the sub-personal level of brains and events in the nervous system'.

Dennett tells us that the origins of his personal/sub-personal distinction lie in the philosophy of Ryle and Wittgenstein (*CC*, 95; *BS*, 154, n.). Their approach to the philosophy of mind is very much an analysis of concepts in the personal mode. And: 'the lesson to be learned from Ryle's attacks on "para-mechanical hypotheses" and Wittgenstein's often startling insistence that explanations come to an end rather earlier than had thought is that the personal and sub-personal levels must not be confused' (*CC*, 95). Ryle and Wittgenstein both argued that at some stage you could not explain a mental process by reference to some further more basic mental process. And, as Dennett comments, Wittgenstein in particular emphasized an early end to explanation at the personal level (*CC*, 95). However, both Ryle and Wittgenstein had no concern for the sub-personal level. For them to turn to the sub-personal level would simply be to change the topic. They were concerned with explaining 'people and their sensations and activities' and not with explaining their 'brains and events in their nervous systems'. But for Dennett this is not quite good enough:

> The recognition that there are two levels of explanation gives birth to the burden of relating them, and this is not a task outside the philosopher's province. It cannot be the case that there is *no* relation between pains and neural impulses or between beliefs and neural states, so setting mechanical or physical questions off-limits to the philosopher will not keep the question of what these relations are from arising. (*CC*, 95)

For there to be 'no relation' between beliefs and neural states would be for intentional capacities to be a mystery, to be something underpinned by supernatural and not natural processes. And of course

Dennett rules out this possibility. But at the same time, he also rejects the idea that the relation between the personal and the sub-personal mode is one of reduction.

The distinction between the personal and the sub-personal is central to *Content and Consciousness*. It also recurs more or less intact in the papers collected in *Brainstorms*. But after *Brainstorms* the distinction appears less and less often. Interestingly, Dennett continues to talk about the sub-personal level even after he has more or less abandoned talking about the personal level (TK). And eventually, by the time of *Consciousness Explained*, he has dropped even the sub-personal terminology. Nonetheless, the contrast is still very much at work in his philosophical arguments (see especially chapters 5 and 6).

In my presentation of Dennett's ideas I want to resuscitate the personal/sub-personal distinction. I think it is the most perspicuous way to bring out certain key themes in his work. In particular, it helps us mark the important difference between the personal level and the level revealed by the (unqualified) intentional stance. We have seen that Dennett initially introduces the notion by reference to 'mental processes' – what the person does – and explanations. But we can approach what I think is the very same distinction from a slightly different angle. For example, we gain a fairly good sense of the scope of personal explanation by saying that often what is cited in a personal level explanation is what the person has consciously entertained. Why did you accept the job?, we ask Loretta. She may point to a number of factors – location, colleagues, nature of the work, salary and so forth – and describe how she weighed them all in her mind before deciding.

But as some of Dennett's key influences have argued – and they have persuaded Dennett – there is no need for such reasons to be consciously entertained. (See Ryle, 1949, 130–42; cf. 167–8; Anscombe, 1957; Wittgenstein, 1953.) We may ask Loretta why she watered the plants today. She can offer us reasons right enough. But there is no need for us to think that she consciously entertained those reasons before being moved by them. What matters is that they are the sorts of reasons she might have self-consciously entertained, the sorts of considerations that she can, in the right circumstances, recognize as reasons. And this, I think, means the sorts of reasons that can justify a person's action or, on the other hand, that can be brought up for critical assessment by the person or another person. Reasons offered at the personal level always have this character. The agent can always ask herself or be asked the following sorts of question. Were these good reasons? Should she have been moved by them or not? Should she have considered further?

By contrast, the rationalizing explanations yielded by the (unqualified) intentional stance do not justify the agent's action. They simply make sense of it or show it to be reasonable in the light of what the agent thinks and values. We can explain that the chess machine moved its knight forward to defend its bishop. But the chess machine does not ask itself whether this was a good reason or whether it should have considered further. The chess machine cannot address itself in such a way. It has the capacity to play chess all right, but not, so far as we know, the capacity to participate in the 'question-and-answer game of giving reasons for [its] action' (CP, 283). The plover bird distracts a predator from its nest by 'feigning' a broken wing (CP, 276). But the plover cannot ask itself whether she should have done this or should have opted for an alternative policy. Again, she cannot, because she cannot address herself in such a way.

Consider now the person herself. While asleep Loretta turns over. We understand why she does. She 'feels uncomfortable' and turns to avoid the pain of muscle cramp. But of course she is asleep while all this is going on. She does not put the reasons to herself, nor, in her sleeping state, could she. In the terminology of the 'self' we might that say that the 'self' is just not involved in this action.[1] Hence we do not say, strictly speaking, that turning in her sleep is an action which admits of a personal level explanation. It is not something which Loretta needs to or could justify.

But at the same time, the action admits of a perfectly ordinary rationalizing explanation, the kind of explanation offered by intentional systems theory. It makes sense in terms of what the agent 'thinks' and 'values', only here what she 'thinks' and 'values' is somehow removed from considerations Loretta is capable of being directly aware of. Indeed it is almost as if her body is an animal, with its own thoughts and values, and can take actions independently of her, the person (or the 'self').

Though I have just been making a fuss about the difference between personal level explanation and explanation based on intentional systems theory, for some purposes the distinction can be ignored or, at least, put in the background. Both distinct kinds of explanation are part of the family of rationalizing explanation. In rationalizing explanation there is always a sense-making relation between an agent's antecedent intentional states and her consequent states or consequent actions. The difference between the two modes concerns the nature of that sense-making relation. Indeed, instead of talking about the personal level, we can just as readily talk about the personal stance. (Dennett himself does this in *BS*, 240.)

Here I shall contrast the personal stance and the intentional stance. Whereas in Dennett's writing the intentional stance is often used in contexts where rationalizing explanations are either of the justifying or non-justifying kind, I shall be more circumspect. So when nothing in an argument turns on whether we are dealing with intentional stance (non-justifying) or the personal stance (justifying), I shall speak collectively of 'the rationalizing stances'. But when I want to draw the distinction between the two kinds of rationalizing explanation I shall speak of the intentional stance and the personal stance.

Non-rationalizing explanation

I want to turn now to non-rationalizing explanation. Non-rationalizing explanation does not require that there be a sense-making relation between antecedents and their consequences. Again, it would be a nice result – nice because it would make our theory tidy – if sub-personal explanation mapped neatly onto non-rationalizing explanation. But, again, the situation is more complex. Or, at the very least, it is misleading to describe all non-rational explanations as sub-personal. Non-rationalizing explanatory principles come in a variety of forms, which we can cluster into two groups. The first group is not readily described as 'sub-personal', although it clearly falls outside the scope of Dennett's personal level. This group comprises:

- Causal laws which have intentional antecedents and intentional consequences, for example, 'people are less inclined to respond to calls for help when in a crowd', 'representativeness swamps base rates', and so forth.
- Causal laws which have intentional antecedents and non-intentional consequences, for example, 'excessive worry gives you ulcers', 'thinking certain thoughts lowers your heart rate', and so forth.
- Causal laws which have non-intentional antecedents and intentional consequences, for example, 'eating cheese gives you weird dreams', 'when tired you think less clearly', and so forth.

'Thinking that there are plenty of other people around' and 'noticing that someone needs help' are intentional antecedents. The consequence, 'failing to help where, in the absence of the crowd you would help' is also intentional. But there is no sense-making relationship between the antecedents and the consequence. Rather we have a causal law within the intentional realm.

As an aside it is worth noting that it may be possible to give a sense-making gloss on the help-in-a-crowd generalizations and, indeed, many others. There are a whole host of cottage industries dedicated to developing various kinds of rationales for behaviours that are initially difficult to rationalize. For example, we may be able to provide a sense-making relation in terms of unconscious motivations. Psychoanalytic approaches do this in an interesting way and while they may often take things too far – explaining every slip of the tongue as unconsciously motivated and every failure as unconsciously desired – put genuine pressure on what ought to be included in the scope of rationalizing explanation. But it is clear that even if psychoanalytic explanation moves some generalizations from the non-rationalizing to the rationalizing category, plenty will remain.

Other methods of generating rationales include the philosophical theory of psychological egoism, the claim that everything we do we do to promote our own selfish interests, and hardline sociobiology, the claim that all of what we do comes to make sense only when we interpret it as promoting the interests of our genes. These approaches clearly take things too far, since it is just not true that we are always selfish or always act to promote the interests of our genes. Even if we concede that, on occasion, we are driven by these interests, it still leaves many non-rationalizing generalizations to be explained.

The second group of non-rationalizing explanatory principles is explicitly concerned with the sub-personal. The sub-personal is concerned with intentional systems as they are viewed from the design or physical stance. Of course to speak of the 'sub-personal' implies that the agent at issue is a person. This is, an unwanted implication because we can be interested in that 'level', the level at which we think about the aggregate of mechanistic parts that make up the agent, whether or not we are focused on persons or other kinds of agents. That is, whether we begin with the personal or the intentional stance, we can still be interested in switching to the design stance. The term 'sub-personal' is, however, deeply entrenched in Dennett's writings, and has been taken up elsewhere. So I shall stick with the term with the explicit proviso that sub-personal explanations are not restricted to persons. Where I speak of a sub-personal explanation of, say, a frog, it should simply be understood as a design stance (or physical stance) explanation, that is, an explanation that concerns itself with the various mechanistic parts that make up the frog.

This terminological clarification in place, the first point to note is that the primary role of sub-personal explanations is not to explain what agents do. Rather, their primary aim is to explain how it is that agents that are built out of mechanistic parts can do what they do at all. They aim to explain how it is that agents have the capacities that they have. Note that sub-personal explanations do not discriminate between giving an account of capacities that are the target of rationalizing explanation as opposed to non-rationalizing explanation. Sub-personal explanations cheerfully explain both kinds of case.

Given the primary aim of sub-personal explanations, how can they have a role in explaining a particular action or activity of an agent as opposed to explaining general capacities? We can best see the answer by thinking about cases where something goes wrong. We ask, say, why a person has misspelt the word 'argument' (she spells it 'arguement'), even after she has been instructed very many times. One answer here is that the person suffers from dyslexia. We can fill out this answer by sketching a box-and-arrow diagram of various brain mechanisms involved in reading and writing and then saying that, for this individual, one sub-system or one connection between sub-systems has been disrupted. And, indeed, this is just what cognitive psychologists do. (I set aside how confident we can be that their box-and-arrow diagrams correspond to actual brain mechanisms. All that matters for the argument here is that they could so correspond.) Here we explain a failure by pointing to a difference between our dyslexic subject's sub-personal mechanism in contrast with the normal subject's sub-personal mechanism.

What is going on when we give this sort of explanation is quite subtle. It is worth looking at more closely, not least because this sort of explanation is ubiquitous in cognitive psychology. To put the point provocatively, the sub-personal explanation that I have just sketched is bogus. What is actually doing the explanatory work is a contrast between the capacity of one subject as opposed to capacity of another subject. It just happens that we can use the box-and-arrow diagram to characterize that difference in capacity in a fairly precise way. To see that it is bogus, we need to consider what a thorough-going sub-personal explanation would be. And, indeed, we have already considered this in chapter 2.

A thorough-going sub-personal explanation is exactly the same as an explanation based on the causal blueprint understanding of the design stance. It will take us from sub-personally specified inputs via sub-personally specified internal states to sub-personally specified outputs. But these are not perceptions, intentional states, and actions. The sub-personal inputs, inner states, and outputs can only be understood as underpinning perception, intentional states, and actions if we interpret them using the resources of the intentional or personal stance. Without one of these rationalizing stances we simply have a complicated description of various movements of a mechanism. With the rationalizing stances in play we can come to see how those motions underpin the intentional capacities of the agent.

4.3   Slips in good procedures

Dennett's work places great emphasis on the power of the rationalizing stances. Although he is quite explicit about psychology being a 'mixed bag', a mixture of rationalizing and non-rationalizing explanation, this feature of his account is not always appreciated by his critics. Most notably, Stephen Stich has attacked Dennett's account for its failure to account with our cognitive shortcomings (Stich, 1981; 1983; 1990). As Stich sees it, Dennett's insistence that we assume agents are rational makes it impossible for us to explore empirically ways in which they fail to be rational. Once the 'mixed-bag' idea is in place it is clear how we can block this kind of criticism. But it is worth working through some details, partly because this kind of criticism has been influential and partly because it has forced Dennett to offer important clarifications to his general view.

So, in this and the following two sections, I want to look at some important limitations of the rationalizing stances and what Dennett can say about these limitations. In this section, I examine mistakes or slips. Agents do make mistakes and we can, it would seem, explain this. But the rationalizing stances seem unable to account for them. In the following two sections I look first at ways in which agents can be committed to what seem to be 'bad' or 'irrational' procedures and second at how the rationalizing stances seem unable to predict or explain the fine-grained details of action.

Making mistakes

Consider mistakes or slips. A person may make a mistake in adding a column of figures, or she may trip on a loose paving stone, albeit one that has not caught her out on a hundred previous occasions. Such mistakes, Dennett is clear to tell us, can neither be predicted or explained with one or other of the rationalizing stances (MSO, 84). But such mistakes are not thereby inexplicable. The point is that, while we stick to a rationalizing stance, inquiry into the explanation of an agent's mistake must end early. That is, at some early stage all that can be said is: 'she made a mistake'. Requests for further explanation can, on Dennett's view, only be met by switching away from a rationalizing stance to a non-rationalizing stance, i.e. the design or the physical stance. Or, in the alternate terminology, we switch from the personal or intentional level to the sub-personal level.

When we treat a system as an agent we assume that the system is rational. If that assumption fails, Dennett tells us, we can regain predictive leverage by shifting from a rationalizing stance to a non-rationalizing stance, or, in other terms, to a sub-personal level of explanation. But, as Stich points out in his article 'Dennett on Intentional Systems' (Stich, 1981), this is an extreme step to take. Consider the story introduced by Stich and discussed by Dennett. A boy is selling lemonade for 12 cents a glass. Dennett gives the boy a quarter and receives a glass of lemonade and then 'a dime and a penny change', i.e., 11 cents and not the correct 13 cents. The assumption is that the boy simply made a mistake, not that he is generally incompetent or out to rip Dennett off. Stich points out that when the boy makes a mistake we do not give up on the personal stance. We do not start to treat the boy as a complex designed mechanism. Rather, as Stich says, we simply assume 'that he is not yet very good at doing sums in his head' (Stich, 1981, 175). And yet, Stich argues, Dennett seems to have committed himself to giving up the personal stance in such cases. He cites a passage (IS, 9–10) where Dennett does indeed suggest that whenever predictions based on our presumption of rationality breakdown, we abandon the intentional or personal stance in favour of the design stance. This, as Dennett notes, is the 'fundamentally different attitude we occasionally adopt toward the insane'.

Stich, of course, is quite right to say that we neither do nor should take this attitude to the lemonade-seller. Instead, we do and should do what Stich recommends. But a careful look at the passage Stich quotes reveals that Dennett is only prepared to sanction the abandonment of the intentional or personal stances in 'extreme cases'. Before we do so, Dennett says, 'we cast about for adjustment in the information possession conditions (he must not have heard, he must not know English, he must not have seen x, ...) or goal weightings'. What Dennett did not say on that occasion, but does say in response to Stich's argument (MSO), is that one other thing we can do *before* abandoning the intentional or personal stance is to conclude, as Stich recommends, that the lemonade-seller has simply made a mistake. Stich's criticism forced Dennett to be clear for the first time about the issue of mistakes, and in so doing led Dennett to some important clarifications of his account.

Of course, not everything that we call a mistake fits the pattern of the lemonade-seller. Many mistakes arise because the agent simply has a false belief. Provided there is a story as to how this false belief was acquired in a reasonable way, the personal or intentional stance can readily predict and explain such mistakes. But where mistakes are, as it were, unreasonable, Dennett is forthright that the rationalizing stances really have nothing to say (MSO, 84). Rationalizing stances cannot help when a breakdown of rationality has occurred, however minor and local the breakdown may be.

Moreover, it is revealing what happens when we try to push harder for explanation within the scope of the rationalizing stances, when we refuse, that is, to accept the Wittgensteinian moral that rationalizing explanations end early. When an action or a step in a mental process is puzzling for us, rationalizing explanations attempt to explain it by elucidating sets of beliefs and desires that would make that action or step a reasonable one to undertake in the circumstances. But if a mistake has occurred, this mode of explanation just must breakdown at some stage. For, according to Dennett, 'no account in terms of beliefs and desires will make sense of it completely. At some point our account will have to cope with the sheer senselessness of the transition in any error' (MSO, 87). As we have seen in the previous chapter, when we fail to conform to the ideals of rationality, so it becomes impossible to precisely describe our behavioural profile in terms of beliefs and desires. That is, Dennett has no resistance to the idea that what people believe and desire is sometimes indeterminate.

The desire for precision and the dissatisfaction with an early end to explanation can lead to a rather different kind of move, a move that it is very important for Dennett to resist. The move begins by asking this question: can we not switch from the personal or intentional stance, the stances in which mistakes are things that will occur, but for which there is no scope for precise prediction nor for revealing explanation, and move to the sub-personal level? Dennett agrees, of course, that we can 'descend from the level of beliefs and desires to some other level of theory to describe his mistake' (MSO, 87). We can, that is, switch to the sub-personal level. But it is essential to realize the consequences of the switch. First, the switch does not provide a means for eliminating any indeterminacy that is present at the rationalizing stance. And, second, once we have made the switch, what we are explaining is no longer the action of the agent as such, but a movement of a system. We are explaining something that we discern from a non-rationalizing stance, that is, from the design or physical stance. Of course we, possessed with the resources of the relevant rationalizing stance, can understand these movements (label them, as it were) as if they were actions. But, on Dennett's picture at least, once we make the switch we leave the subject matter of agents and their doings behind. Let us look at these two points in a bit more detail.

Switching to the sub-personal level

According to Dennett '[the] interpretation of a bit of inner, sub-personal cognitivistic machinery must inevitably depend on . . . the whole person's beliefs and desires' (MSO, 92). We can see why he insists on this by thinking about a possible sub-personal explanation of the lemonade-seller's mistake:

> [Once] he is "warmed up," he makes change in a semi-automatic way, while thinking about other things. A temporary change-making "module" is located in his brain, and Nuclear Magnetic Resonance Imaging shows it to have been operating at the time. Moreover, it is established that 350 ms before the change-making module completed its task, the smile of a girl in a passing car caught his eye, indirectly causing the penny-fetching sub-module to Exit after gathering only one penny instead of three. Visual and tactile feedback, which would normally have detected the error, were received but ignored, thanks to the attention shift caused by my noisy slurping of the lemonade and the fact that the module reported back successful completion of its task before shutting down. (*IS*, 104)

Stories in this genre allow us to fully explain the cause of the error. But they need not help us establish precisely what the lemonade-seller believed. If anything, Dennett thinks they tend to reinforce the indeterminacy claim. For nothing at the sub-personal level need settle the question of whether, say, he really believed that '13 = 11' or that he really believed 'a quarter was worth 23 cents'. There might be cases when a sub-personal story could tip the balance between the idea that the boy believed one rather than the other – perhaps a detailed study of other errors he makes might do this. But, even in this case, it would be because the sub-personal story made clear something about how the boy would respond in various scenarios, including perhaps scenarios that we might not have thought of without the prompt of the sub-personal story. This is certainly the case in cognitive psychology. Developing a sub-personal story, using a box-and-arrow diagram or a computer program, can inspire new lines of experimental investigation, and thus make clearer patterns of behaviour of the 'whole person' or the whole agent. For Dennett, all ascription of intentional states is answerable to facts about behaviour. Inner facts, about the state of the brain, for example, cannot trump ascriptions made on the basis of behaviour (see chapter 1).

'Sub-personal intentionality'

But Dennett does want to talk about states with meaning (or content) at the sub-personal level (*BS*, 24–7; TK, 63–5; MSO, 92–3). That is why he thinks that sub-personal explanation is a kind of intentional psychology. But it is crucial to recognize that Dennett does not think that such states could possibly be identified with the intentional states of the whole agent. If they could, then the distinction between the personal and the sub-personal, or the intentional stance and the design stance, would collapse, as, indeed, it does in reductionist theories, such as the representational theory of mind (see chapters 1–3).

So, given this, what can Dennett mean when he talks about the meaning (or content) at the sub-personal level? We should note first that for Dennett the parts that feature at the sub-personal cannot grasp the meanings or contents entertained by the agent. After all, the sub-personal level is another way of referring to the level revealed by the design stance or physical stance. However, Dennett does not always make this clear. We might, for example, be blown off course by the fact that he describes the sub-personal explanation as one kind of *intentional* psychology. Or, then again, we might be confused by Dennett's suggestion that we think of some of the sub-personal components not simply as mechanisms but as functional items or even mini-intentional systems (see chapter 2 and Glossary on 'homuncular functionalism'). We can indeed ascribe intentional states to mini-intentional systems. But the intentional states of parts of a system are not the intentional states of the whole system: after all, the part and the whole have different capacities, interests, and environments. How, then, do sub-personal meanings, meanings that really do relate to the agent's intentional state, get on the scene?

Sub-personal meanings arrive with a certain way of describing or glossing the sub-personal story. When we draw out a box-and-arrow diagram we append 'intentionalistic labels' (*BS*, 26–7; *MSO*, 92, 95; *TK*, 63). These, Dennett tells us, form a 'heuristic overlay' (*CC*, 80; *IS*, 206), a way of making the mechanistic details an intelligible source of the agent level capacities that they underpin. And it is with the use of such labels that the idea of sub-personal meaning (or content) enters Dennett's account. Now, straight away it should be said that Dennett himself does not labour this point, and, indeed, has been less and less explicit about it as his work has progressed. This interpretation receives most textual support from earlier Dennett texts, and in particular *Content and Consciousness*. But the interpretation is given more support by the way in which Dennett actually argues various points.[2]

Let me illustrate Dennett's attitude to sub-personal meanings by means of an analogy. Think about two ways in which we might describe a component of a radio. Consider, say, a potentiometer. It is a device whose electrical resistance varies depending on the position of a slider. It is connected to various other components in particular ways. We can, in this way of talking, refer to the potentiometer without making any reference to the function that it plays in the operation of the radio. Alternatively we might talk about the radio's volume control. We are talking about the same thing, of course. But when we talk of the volume control we are making a reference to the normal operation of the radio. If the radio breaks down, connections are broken, or components fail, then the potentiometer may no longer function as a volume control. And, of course, if we remove the component altogether and place it on the lab bench, then it is no longer a volume control. Similarly, if we remove it from one part of the radio's circuitry and place it in another, it may come to play a different role. Perhaps by relocating it amidst the radio's circuitry it will become a tone control or a fine-tuning control.

Now, with the radio analogy in mind, consider two ways of describing sub-personal processes. Either we describe the processes without reference to the agent which they underpin. This is akin to describing the component as a potentiometer. Or we describe the processes by reference to the contribution they make to the agent's overall behaviour. This is akin to describing the component as a volume control. In this latter case we 'borrow' from the personal or intentional stance in order to describe our sub-personal mechanisms.

This metaphor of 'borrowing' is important for understanding the relationship between the rationalizing stances and the sub-personal (cf. *BS*, 12, 15–16, 61–2). The loan allows us to talk about sub-personal mechanism as contributing to perception, to reasoning, to recollection, and so forth. But the sub-personal mechanisms can only be described in this way to the extent that we can describe the agent from the rationalizing stance as perceiving, reasoning, and recollecting. It is never the case, then, that the rationalizing stance capacity, say, to perceive is the result of a sub-personal mode capacity to perceive. For when we talk about sub-personal perception, the label is appropriate only because we already encounter the capacity for perception at the level of the whole agent. We can only confidently describe the potentiometer as a volume control because we understand what the radio is and how it functions normally. If we did not, the best we could say was that it was a potentiometer connected to other components in this or that fashion. This point is critical for understanding why, for Dennett, the intentional and personal stances cannot be reduced to the design or physical stances, cannot be reduced to the sub-personal level. As he notes, again using pain as his example:

> [when] we abandon the personal level in a very real sense we abandon the subject matter of pains as well. When we abandon mental process talk for physical process talk we cannot say that the mental process analysis of *pain* is wrong, for our alternative analysis cannot be an analysis of pain at all, but rather of something else – the motions of human bodies or the organisation of the nervous system. (*CC*, 94)

Once again it is not critical that he uses pain as his example here. He could just as readily have made the same point with respect to, say, thoughts or decisions. The passage just quoted makes it sound as though the sub-personal mode could never be illuminating, could never contribute to reconciling the mechanistic with the intentional. But when we label sub-personal features with intentionalistic labels then, just as describing the potentiometer as a volume control, we do, or so Dennett presses, come to see how an aggregate of mechanistic parts – or, at any rate, parts which lack the capacities of the intentional system of which they are a part – working together can underpin an intentional system. And we do so by using the 'flipping' strategy described in chapter 3, that is, shifting our perspective from the personal to the sub-personal level and back until we come to grasp how the latter underpins the operation of the former. The labelling scheme, the 'heuristic overlay', is a means of seeing the mechanistic theory in a light that shows how it could underpin an agent, in the same way as labelling the electronic components of a radio by reference to the radio's functional powers.

So it would clearly be a mistake to take the intentionalistic labels literally. No components described at the sub-personal level can grasp the kinds of meanings that people grasp. The sub-personal components are, if you like, too stupid to achieve such a grasp. So while it may be a helpful aid to understanding to speak as if one sub-personal component sends a message that means 'Stich gave me a quarter' to another sub-personal component, this is no more than a manner of talking derived from the general, if not perfect, capacity of the person to recognize entities such as Stich, quarters, lemonade, and so forth.

Because this is the relationship that Dennett sees between the rationalizing stances and the sub-personal level, a certain kind of reduction is completely blocked. In one sense all that is needed for a system to have a perceptual capacity is that it has the correct arrangement of sub-personal components. This is to say only that no supernatural additions are needed. But perceptual capacities themselves arrive on the scene only when we adopt one or other of the rationalizing stances. Abandon the agent level and you abandon the subject matter of the agent level, the subject matter of perception, thought, recollection, sensation, and so forth.

Dennett's trick, and where his view is an advance on those of Ryle and Wittgenstein, is to label the otherwise unintelligible mechanistic parts using terminology borrowed from the agent level and legitimized by the fact that agent level ascriptions can successfully be applied to the system in question. In a sense, then, whenever intentionalistic labels are used at the sub-personal level, we have not wholly abandoned the agent level, but rather simply placed it in the background (cf. the argument from chapter 2, p. 50, about the background role of the intentional stance when using the design or physical stance). Reduction is blocked, then, because if the agent level really were abandoned, then the phenomena at issue would be rendered invisible. But unless we are wholly clear that the status of intentionalistic labels at the sub-personal mode depends on successful agent level ascription, then it can appear that the sub-personal level could indeed reduce the agent level and do so without abandoning its subject matter.

4.4   Rationality and allegiance to bad procedures

The last section took as its focus mistakes that were occasional and unpredictable. Such mistakes cannot be predicted or explained using the intentional or personal stances. In this section the focus is on regular and predictable deviations from rationality. This includes the three kinds of causal laws mentioned in 4.2, i.e., causal laws relating (i) intentional antecedents to intentional consequences; (ii) intentional antecedents to non-intentional consequences; and (iii) non-intentional antecedents to non-intentional consequences. In fact, I shall only deal explicitly with the first of these, which is, I think the hardest case for Dennett. In any case, most of what I say about the first kind of case applies readily to the second and third.

We expect generalizations that take us from intentional antecedents to intentional consequences to be rational. That is certainly what Dennett's theory seems to suggest to Stich:

> If we accept Dennett's [view], we will have no coherent way to describe our cognitive shortcomings nor the processes by which we may learn to overcome them. Equally unwelcome, the thriving scientific study of the strengths and weaknesses of human reasoning would wither and die, its hypotheses ruled literally incoherent. (Stich, 1981, 173)

As we have seen there are cases where we find regular and reliable deviations from the rational, or, at least, from what might most naturally be considered rational. I have illustrated this by reference to the tendency for people to ignore information about base rates in the face of information about representativeness. It is this sort of case and the many others found in the psychological literature that Stich has in mind.

Of course these examples all deal with persons, but it is important to recognize that the point at issue is by no means specific to the personal level. It applies to all kinds of agents. We can illustrate this by reference to one of Dennett's favourite ethological examples: the case of the Sphex wasp (*BS*, 65ff, 245ff; *ER*, 10ff).

> When the time comes for egg laying the wasp *Sphex* builds a burrow for the purpose and seeks out a cricket which she stings in such a way as to paralyse but not kill it . . . the wasp's routine is to bring the paralysed cricket to the burrow, leave it on the threshold, go inside to see that all is well, emerge, and then drag the cricket in. If, while the wasp is inside making her preliminary inspection the cricket is moved a few inches away, the wasp, on emerging from the burrow, will bring the cricket back to the threshold, but not inside, and will then repeat the preparatory procedure of entering the burrow to see that everything is all right. If again the cricket is removed a few inches while the wasp is inside, once again the wasp will move the cricket up to the threshold and re-enter the burrow for a final check. The wasp never thinks of pulling the cricket straight in. On one occasion, this procedure was repeated forty times, always with the same result. (Wooldridge, 1963, 82)

When a Sphex loses her way flying back to her nest site or when she accidentally drops a cricket she makes a mistake. She makes, that is, a slip in an otherwise good procedure. But when she repeatedly rechecks the burrow after realigning the cricket she is locked into a bad procedure. Here the Sphex is in the same sort of position as the person who repeatedly gives too much credence to representativeness while ignoring base-rates. Although, of course, things are worse for the Sphex since no amount of training will lead to an improved performance. Nonetheless the Sphex and the person are both locked into bad procedures.

According to Stich, if Dennett sticks with intentional systems theory, he simply cannot explain the phenomena of being locked into bad procedures. For in assuming that the system is rational, the theory assumes that the agent is not locked into bad procedures. Stich does not see how Dennett can accommodate both the assumption of rationality and the empirical fact that agents are locked into bad (or irrational) procedures. He does not see how because he fails to appreciate Dennett's mixed-bag approach. (As far as I can see it is not the case that Stich does appreciate it and then argues that it is false.) Nonetheless, Stich's criticism is instructive, and, once again, it flushes out some useful points of clarification from Dennett.

In the case of the Sphex, regular deviations from rationality certainly put more pressure on us to abandon the intentional stance than the making of simple mistakes. But the consequences of giving up on the intentional stance and shifting to the design or physical stance, switching, that is, to the sub-personal (the sub-Sphex) level are very serious. For despite her dramatic failure in the artificial circumstances of the experiment described, the Sphex has very many successes. We can observe that the Sphex non-accidentally conforms to rational patterns of behaviour in a wide range of situations. She displays great skill in tracking down the cricket in the first place and in successfully pursuing other goals. The tracking down of the cricket, for example, is not something that is rigidly programmed in the way that the burrow check is. Rather, it requires that the Sphex keep track of many changing circumstances so as to make relevant adjustments as she goes. If we shift to the sub-personal level (the sub-Sphex level), we have to give up on this way of describing the Sphex. At this level we can no longer see her as an agent pursuing her interests, but only as a complex causal mechanism pushed around by internal and external stimuli. The real if noisy patterns that the Sphex maintains cannot be discerned at this level; switching to it means, then, that we miss out on something, and something interesting and valuable to us, and that is 'out there' if only we care to look in the right way.

What is critical about the mixed-bag response is that ad hoc and systematic failures in rationality take place only against a background of success. For Dennett, though not it would seem for Stich, the successes outnumber the failures by a large ratio (cf. TB, 19, n. 1). Of course, saying that successes outnumber failures is not enough on its own, for the truth of such a claim depends on how successes and failures are counted. What does the argumentative work here is the claim that treating the Sphex as a rational agent is the only way to pick up on a real pattern, a pattern that asserts itself again and again in the face of complex and changeable circumstances. Consider Dennett making the same point, though this time directed at human agents:

There are patterns in human affairs that impose themselves, not quite inexorably but with great vigour, absorbing physical perturbations and variations that might as well be considered random; these are the patterns we characterise in terms of the beliefs, desires, and intentions of rational agents. (TB, 27)

Dennett's expression 'not quite inexorably but with great vigour' describes the slack that intentional systems theory allows for. Rational norms do impose themselves, but do not do so perfectly. Thus the patterns revealed by the rationalizing stances are real, but they are also noisy. The point made in the quotation above applies just as much to Sphexes as it does to humans. The Sphex reliably captures crickets, reliably finds her way home, reliably builds burrows, and so forth. And she does this despite the fact that the actual conditions she faces in the world are complex and inconstant. She has, as it were, to overcome all manner of obstacles to achieve her goals, she has to absorb all manner of physical perturbations, and still arrive where she is going.

Likewise, the person having made a plan to get from home to work on time, reliably manages to do so, despite traffic jams, bus strikes, leaves on the line, and so forth (see the details of Dennett's Martian tale in TB, 26–7). To switch from the intentional stance to the design or physical stance in the case of the Sphex is to abandon the distinction between the results of her activity that relate to her goals and the results of her activity that are the result of random physical perturbations. Likewise, to switch from the personal level to the subpersonal level in the case of the person is to abandon the difference between what the person does and what merely happens to her or merely happens within her body. In either case it means giving up the distinction between activity that is, as it were, 'meant' and activity that is not. And if we give that up then we have to give up on rationalizing explanation altogether. We have to, because we do not know if any given case is like doing something or having something happen to you, such as, say, walking, as opposed to tripping over. But if we do not know if any case is like one or the other, we must take the most general approach and fall back on non-rationalizing explanation. And then we have simply abandoned looking at the real patterns in Sphex and human behaviour that are out there to be discerned (cf. the Edinburgh brogue story in chapter 2).

Dennett still insists that the rationalizing stances are primary, but happily allows that they can be supplemented by a set of empirical generalizations concerning such issues as burrow-checking behaviour or crowd-and-volunteering-help behaviour. Actual agents – that is agents that are built out of mechanistic bits and pieces – will have their foibles, their deviations from the norms of the intentional stance or the norms of the personal stance. These foibles cannot be captured by the rationalizing stances. But some of them can be readily captured by means of empirical observation. But allowing that there are *some* causal laws of psychology does not mean admitting that all the principles of psychology are causal laws. The principles of psychology are, on Dennett's view, a mixed bag of rational norms and causal laws.

Dennett's understanding of rationality

The idea of rationality plays a central role in Dennett's theory. To this point I have avoided offering any definition. Dennett, likewise, usually avoids defining or even glossing his idea of rationality. But Stich claims that empirical research as well as ordinary observation shows that human beings are often highly irrational. For the most part, Dennett does not dispute the empirical research or the ordinary observations, so it would seem that Dennett and Stich understand something rather different by rationality. Stich's critique has provoked some helpful if somewhat elusive clarification from Dennett. He first tells us what he does not mean by 'rationality'.

> [Rationality] is not deductive closure . . . Nor is rationality perfect logical consistency . . . [And] I am careful *not* to define rationality in terms of what evolution has given us . . . What then do I say rationality is? I don't say . . . (MSO, 94–6)

Deductive closure – that is working out all the implications of all the beliefs that you hold – is too demanding. It is not the kind of rationality that any agent built out of mechanistic parts could have, unless, that is, the agent operated in a very, very restricted environment. Similarly, perfect logical consistency sets the net too high. No actual agent of interest will be perfectly logically consistent. But to deny that the agent is rational is, for Dennett, an over-reaction. If either deductive closure or perfect logical consistency are what rationality really is, then there is a lot less rationality about than we thought. On the other hand, if rationality is simply 'what evolution gives us' then it sets the net too low. It tells us we cannot ever call any organism irrational. And, again, this seem like an over-reaction. (Though, of the two options, Dennett is clear that he thinks the latter is more appealing.) So are there other ways in which we can define rationality? Dennett resists a definition, but he does go on to say something more positive:

> I want to use "rational" as a general-purpose term of cognitive approval – which requires maintaining only conditional and

revisable allegiances between rationality, so considered, and proposed . . . methods of getting ahead, cognitively, in the world. I take
this usage of the terms to be quite standard, and I take appeals to
rationality by proponents of cognitive disciplines or practices to
require this understanding of the notion. (MSO, 97)

The claim here is that we can work with the idea of rationality as
cognitive approval and get all the results from his account that we
need. So long as we can reach agreement on a reasonable number
of cases about what is and what is not to be counted as rationality
– and we do, presses Dennett, otherwise we could not talk about
the arguments of various 'proponents of cognitive disciplines or
practices' – then we need not press the issue further.[3]

How does Dennett respond to the claim that humans and other
agents are often governed by psychological principles that are not
rational, the claim that Stich thinks gets him into trouble? Given my
discussion so far, we might expect the response to be simple. We
might expect Dennett to emphasize the mixed-bag approach and
point out that he can accommodate a considerable number of non-
rational principles provided a real, albeit noisy pattern of rationality is preserved. Consider that even to be a candidate for a
psychology experiment a person must by and large conform to the
canons of idealized rationality. If we did not assume a great deal of
rationality, we would not even be able to make sense of the noises
that the subjects of experiments utter (see *CE*, 72–8). The very fact
that we can ask a person questions about, say, whether some
notional person is a philosopher or a hairdresser and the person
understands the question, already shows that we are dealing with
an entity that by and large does conform to rational norms. And, of
course, we do assume, with good grounds, that they understand the
question and assume, again with good grounds, that what they say
in response is intended to be an honest and sincere reply. So while
it is true that there are important, and in the context highly salient,
failures of rationality, they take place against a background of rational success. They take place against the background of behaviour
that conforms very well with rational norms. Contrary to what Stich
suggests, there is no reason for Dennett to give up the claim that by
and large the activity of human agents conforms to the standards
of idealized rationality.

This sort of response can be discerned in Dennett's reply to Stich
(MSO), though it derives as much from comments that he makes in
other contexts. Moreover, on balance I think it is the best response

to this kind of criticism and one which Dennett should have given, and should give, more emphasis. However, in his reply to Stich another kind of response receives quite a lot of attention.

An alternate response

Dennett's alternate response is to argue that what Stich thinks of as irrational can, from a different perspective, be described as rational. Earlier I mentioned that disciplines such as psychoanalysis and sociobiology aim to expand what can be counted as rational. The psychoanalyst brings to bear beliefs and desires that lie outside of awareness to make otherwise irrational actions rational. For example, beliefs about one's parents might, in some roundabout way, make good sense of your obsession with washing your hands many times a day. The action is shown to be rational by the lights (including the unilluminated lights) of the agent. It thus falls into the scope of rationalizing explanation. Of course, in such a case, we also think something has gone wrong. Somewhere along the line, though perhaps for good reasons, the agent has acquired some distinctly odd beliefs and desires. Dennett's move is in some ways similar to that of the psychoanalyst, except that he shifts attention away from particular actions – such as explaining why, contrary to appearances, washing my hands twenty times a day is rational given my unconscious beliefs and desires – and towards general policies or rules of thumb.

First, he argues that the apparently irrational procedure may be (or may be close to) 'the best' or 'the optimum' procedure that an agent built out of mechanistic parts could achieve. Second, he argues that the apparently irrational procedure may be (or may be close to) 'the best' or 'optimum' procedure that an agent designed by Darwinian processes could achieve. In this way Dennett is shifting his 'cognitive approval' away from particular actions of the agent and on to the design of the agent. He is saying that certain procedures are the best procedures that could be installed. And this is not the same as saying that these procedures achieve the best results in any given circumstance.

The first of these arguments is straightforward. It would not be 'rational' for a finite agent to explore every implication of the action it is about to perform. Mechanisms require both time and component parts to consider and weigh options. And both time and component parts are always in limited supply. So it is not 'rational' to consider every implication. It just takes too long. Whereas it is 'rational' to consider fewer implications, and run the risk of missing something important, rather than to sit around all day trying to make the best decision (*BC*, chapter 11). We will offer more cognitive approval to an agent that gets on and makes decisions – even if she sometimes makes mistakes – than one that is so concerned to get things right that she never gets around to acting. This much said, it is worth noting that the argument does not tell us just how much 'looking before we leap' is appropriate. It simply says that rationality lies in the balance of 'looking ahead' and of 'getting on with it'.

The second argument can be more involved. Basically, the argument is that the apparently irrational procedure (or sub-optimal trait, cf. chapter 7), is the most rational there is given the constraints or limits imposed by the process of design. When the design process is evolution by natural selection a number of constraints arise. Consider, for example, three constraints: tradeoffs between the power of a solution to a problem and the costs of implementing the solution; the requirement that all new designs must build on pre-existing designs; and, third, the inability of natural selection to look ahead.

We might be able to show that, contrary to appearances, the Sphex's burrowing foible is rational, by appeal to any one or more of these factors. In the case of tradeoffs, a cheaper but less general solution to a problem may be favoured over a more expensive but more general solution. In order to avoid slipping into the trap that actual Sphexes slip into, a rival Sphex would need a bigger and better brain. But costs are involved in growing and maintaining such a brain. And these costs will not, in the actual Sphex environment, bring any benefits. So, if all other things are equal, the smarter Sphex will actually be at a disadvantage to the duller Sphex.

With these two kinds of argument Dennett can show how, from the perspectives of 'building-within-constraints' and 'designing-within-constraints' certain policies that may, at first sight, seem irrational, can be seen as rational. What he is doing, then, is offering 'cognitive approval' with respect to the design of the agent, rather than cognitive approval to individual actions of the agent. We can offer 'cognitive approval' of the Sphex wasp's design, noting that the mad experiment is highly artificial and is hardly likely to give actual Sphexes real problems in real environments. But, at the same time, we can withhold 'cognitive approval' of the Sphex's action in a particular case. We can disapprove of the Sphex's action on, say, the thirty-second trial, when once again she drags the cricket to the edge of the burrow and goes down for yet another check. I do not want to push too hard this distinction between rationality qua design and rationality qua particular actions. But I think the distinction can bear enough weight to offer an insight into why Dennett's response to Stich does not quite meet the mark.

Stich's concern seems to be this. According to Dennett's account, systems must exhibit rationality qua particular actions in order to qualify as agents. When Dennett says that sometimes what seems irrational can be reinterpreted as rational, he does not meet this criticism. For what in effect this response comes to is this: because of the ways in which they are designed and learn, natural systems are rational qua design. Systems that are irrational qua design do not survive the rigours of natural selection or of trial-and-error learning. That is why, for the most part, there aren't any. Stich could, though it is not clear that he would, agree with Dennett that natural agents are rational qua design. But, in any case, his concern that they are not rational qua particular actions is untouched. This is why I think that Dennett would do better to emphasize the mixed-bag approach. What that says is that for the most part agents are rational qua particular actions. That is it takes direct issue with Stich's pessimistic assessment of the rationality of natural agents. Agents are rational for the most part, but there will be some deviations from rationality: some will be ad hoc, as when the agent makes a mistake, and others will be systematic, as when they are allied to a bad procedure. But none of this undermines the primacy of the rationalizing stances so long as a real, albeit noisy, pattern of rational (rational qua particular actions) is maintained.

4.5   Micro-features of action

In this section I want to turn to another limit on the scope of the rationalizing stances. Dennett asks us to think about a case where we have used the intentional stance, or, using my more circumspect terminology, the personal stance, to predict that a stockbroker will order 500 shares of General Motors. The actual movements that the stockbroker undertakes will take a precise form, but if we do not recognize that:

> indefinitely many *different* patterns of finger movements and vocal cord vibrations . . . could have been substituted for the actual

particulars without perturbing the subsequent operation of the market, then [we] will have failed to see a real pattern in what [we] are observing. (TB, 26)

If we concentrate on the precise pattern, we miss the real pattern that is present at the higher level. The rationalizing stances deliberately distance us from such precise details, and so allow the real pattern of rational agency to be discerned. What this means, however, is that if we want to predict or explain precise details of an action, the rationalizing stances are often no use to us. For they often have nothing to say about whether the action will turn out this way or that way, or why an action did turn out just like this and not just like that. At the level of generality at which they are working, such differences do not feature; they are, to use an expression Dennett employs in another context, 'don't cares' (see chapter 7, p. 224). The rationalizing stances are not concerned with what we might call 'micro-features' of action. These are not part of the proper subject matter of those stances. Rather, the rationalizing stances focus on the bigger trends in an agent's activity.

So, for example, the personal stance may be used to predict that Alice will knock on my door at about 2 o'clock. The prediction is based on the fact that Alice believes she has arranged to call for me at that time. But the stance cannot be used to predict the precise moment of the knock nor the precise sequence of taps. Such micro-features are beyond the scope of the personal stance.

The time at which she knocks is determined by Alice. Knocking just then is something Alice does. And the sequence of knocks is determined by her too. Again, knocking in just that way is something Alice does. So the action, in all its precision, is, as it were, owned by Alice. But when the doing is specified in such a precise way, there simply is no personal level explanation to be had. Knocking at the door at the time arranged is simply something that Alice can do. It is, as it were, a basic unit of action, one that cannot typically be broken down further. And because it cannot, there is nothing, at the personal level, to say about why the micro-features of the action fall just where they do. If we are unsatisfied with an early end to explanation here, we must switch to the sub-personal level, to the non-rationalizing stances. For, of course, micro-features need be neither inexplicable nor unpredictable. It is just that they are inexplicable and unpredictable from the vantage point of the rationalizing stances.

Note that what counts as a micro-feature can vary from case to case. For example, a micro-feature can be promoted to a macro-feature if, first, something turns on the action having this precise feature rather than that, and, second, when the agent is actually in a position to control the relevant feature. If all I know about Alice is that she said she would knock on my door at 2 o'clock, then I can make no prediction about the precise time or precise sequence of knocks. Nor would I attach any significance to differences in the precise time or sequence of knocks. But consider a different scenario. Alice and I are spies closely watched by enemy agents. Earlier we agreed on a signal that Alice would give to indicate whether or not her cover was blown. If all is well, Alice is to knock dead on 2 o'clock with three regular taps no more than half a second apart. With this background in place, we can use the personal stance to predict precisely when the knock will happen and what its nature will be. The knock will be when Alice believes it to be 2 o'clock, which, knowing that Alice's watch is two minutes slow and that she does not know this, I predict will be at two minutes past two.

The success or failure of skilled action sometimes turns on what I am calling micro-features. A well-trained racing-car driver can reliably make minute adjustments in the way she drives. She can, further, deliberately make small changes to these adjustments on each lap, and thus self-consciously work to improve her lap times. In this way, what for the less skilled driver would be micro-features can be regarded as macro-features, that is, reliable and rational trends in the person's behaviour. But with skilled action there is often a limit to the precision that can be achieved, even by the most skilled performers. Perhaps at a critical time our driver succeeds in shaving off a few hundredths of a second on her qualifying lap. But, from her own perspective, she did nothing differently on this lap than she did on the last. Nevertheless, the good lap puts her in pole position. Achieving pole by driving the quickest lap is clearly something our driver did. It is an action of hers. And so, we might now ask, what is the personal level explanation of her gaining pole over her rival?

José Luis Bermúdez discusses a similar case, involving a tennis match. All the personal level facts about his opponent – his desire to win, what he thought about the shot, and so forth – are compatible with the winning shot being out instead of in. But the fine-grained details of the stroke meant Bermúdez lost the game.

No explanation proceeding purely in terms of personal level events will be sufficiently fine-grained to explain why that shot was played then – to explain why my opponent extended his racket precisely that distance at precisely that angle. On the other hand, this seems to be a paradigm of a personal level event. After all, he won the game and we can't explain why he won the game without explaining why he played that shot then. (Bermúdez, 2000, 79)

Bermúdez suggests that to explain why his opponent won the game we must switch to the sub-personal level. If he is right, then the same would apply to our racing driver. For the personal level is simply not fine-grained enough to explain how the precise muscle movements occurred that led to the winning shot or the fastest qualifying lap. Once all the personal level details are provided, there is still a certain amount of slack as to how the precise micro-features pan out. In the case of the skilled tennis player or skilled driver, this slack is massively reduced. What for ordinary people would be micro-features become part of the patterns that 'impose themselves . . . with great vigour'. But these patterns are 'not quite inexorably' imposed. Once we move beyond the real pattern that does impose itself with great vigour, we are, as far as personal level explanation is concerned, in the realm of noise.

And this means, for Dennett, that there is no personal level explanation of why the driver achieved pole position or why Bermúdez's opponent won the match. Of course, there is plenty to say at the personal level. Getting in the right zone, getting very close to the best qualifying time or very close to the baseline, is something that the person can take full credit for. But that she drove just that tiny bit faster on this lap or was just the right side of the baseline on this occasion, these are not events that have a personal level explanation. If the margin of error falls beyond what she can reliably achieve, falls outside the patterns that she can reliably deliver, then all we can say is that she was lucky on this occasion. On another occasion, with all the same skills and training, she might have been less lucky. Of course, it is no accident that the competitors are in the right zone. That is not luck. But where the margins of error are very fine, Dennett's view implies that there is no interesting explanation to be had of winning or losing.

But what about Bermúdez's suggestion that we switch to the sub-personal level to explain what he describes as 'a paradigm of a personal level event'. As before, the difficulty on Dennett's account is this. As we switch from the personal to the sub-personal, from the rationalizing stance to the non-rationalizing stance, we abandon the subject matter with which we began. We end up explaining not why a person achieved pole, but explaining why the person's body moved in a particular way such that pole was achieved. For Dennett, these two events have to be considered as distinct. The person vanishes from sight when we descend to the sub-personal level. We can, of course, readily relate the sub-personal level to the personal level by means of labelling various sub-personal features in the light of the contribution that they make to personal level capacities. But, as argued above – in the case of the lemonade-seller – the sub-personal level cannot repair the lack of precision that is present at the personal level. The precision runs out because the rational pattern that is vigorously imposed on behaviour only has so much detail in it. Beyond that, there is not more detail, just noise.

4.6   Where things stand

Agent explanation is diverse. When a person does something, we may ask why. We seek to make sense of the action. For Dennett the most basic way of making sense of an agent is by appeal to a rationalizing stance. We point to what the agent thinks and values and show how her action is reasonable in light of this. But sometimes this method cannot make sense of an action. The agent may have made a mistake. Or she may be locked into a bad cognitive procedure, an irrational method of thinking or deciding. Or we may have described the action in such a way that there is just no explanation to be had in terms of what, on this occasion, the agent had any control over. When appeal to a rationalizing stance fails us, we must turn to various supplementary strategies.

The first set of supplementary strategies involve empirical generalizations or causal laws that tell us how the agent operates in certain conditions. All Sphex wasps can be caught out by the experimenter who moves the cricket away from the burrow entrances. Some humans, those with dyslexia, cannot learn to spell certain words however hard they try. When we employ these sorts of generalizations or laws we are working at the same level as the relevant rationalizing stance. We are not, that is, abandoning the subject matter of the agent and her doings.

By contrast, the second set of supplementary strategies do involve a change of subject matter. These strategies involve turning

Styles of agent explanation

Rationalizing stances	• personal stance (or the personal level) • intentional stance (or the agent-other-than-a-person-al level)
Non-rational laws and generalizations	• intentional antecedents and intentional consequences • intentional antecedents and non-intentional consequences • non-intentional antecedents and intentional consequences
Non-rationalizing stances	• design stance (or the sub-personal level) • physical stance (or the sub-personal level)

away from a rationalizing stance and adopting a non-rationalizing stance, that is, either the design or physical stance. Dennett also describes this as switching to the sub-personal level, though, as noted above, the same terminology is also applied to agents that are not persons. Strictly speaking, when we turn away from the rationalizing stances we 'abandon the subject matter' of agents and their doings. But by labelling the mechanistic elements in our sub-personal explanations we can recover this subject matter. This labelling is always done with an eye to the picture of the agent revealed by the rationalizing stance. The labelling employed at the sub-personal level is, then, dependent on the successful application of a rationalizing stance. The whole agent does not get its intentionality from the intentionality of its sub-personal part. Rather, we can label the sub-personal parts in virtue of the intentionality of the whole agent. This last point, as we shall see in the following two chapters, is vital for understanding Dennett's account of consciousness.

Further reading

Fodor, Stich, and Churchland are all key players in the folk psychology debate. Despite substantial differences in their attitudes to folk psychology, they are all committed to the homogeneity of the logical status of its principles. See Fodor, 1987, chapter 1; Stich, 1983, chapters 1 and 2; and Churchland, 1989, chapters 1 and 6. Churchland's, 1988, chapter 3, contains a friendly introduction. Folk psychology is much discussed in the technical literature and there are a number of collections about or featuring sections on the topic, for example, Greenwood (1991) and Lycan (1990). Peter Strawson's paper 'Freedom and Resentment' (Strawson, 1962) presents an important look at 'the fundamentally different attitude we adopt towards the insane'. Stich's critique of Dennett is concentrated in his 'Dennett on Intentional Systems' (1981) but is further refined and developed in Stich (1983) and Stich (1990). A variation of Stich's criticism that Dennett rules empirical inquiry into the limits of human rationality is developed by Fodor and Lepore (1993 or 1992, chapter 5). See Elton (1998) for a response. Gardner (2000) explores the relationship between personal level explanation and psychoanalytic explanation.

An account of the psychological studies that appear to show people are less rational than folk psychology and philosophy typically allow can be found in Nisbett and Ross (1980). The philosophical backlash begins with Cohen (1981). Stich (1990) provides an introduction and a convenient, if partisan, entry point to the literature. Dennett discusses a popular example of a cognitive shortcoming, that revealed by the Wason Four Card Test, in *DDI*, 488–9.

For a range of responses to Dennett's distinction between the personal and the sub-personal, see McDowell (1994a), and *Philosophical Explorations* 3,1 January 2000, a special issue dedicated to the topic. An excellent example of the box-and-arrow approach in cognitive psychology, along with a discussion of its merits, can be found in Ellis and Young, 1996, in particular chapter 8 and the model presented on page 222ff. On the 'question-and-answer game of giving reasons for [our] actions' being the distinctive mark of the personal as opposed to the intentional stance, see Dennett, CP; BS, chapter 16; and ER, chapter 4. For two key historical sources of this idea, see Anscombe (1957) and Sellars (1956). A more recent articulation is McDowell's *Mind and World* (McDowell, 1994b) which, I argue (Elton, 2000), is more in tune with Dennett than McDowell himself allows. This idea is further explored in the section on the self in chapter 6 and in chapter 8.

5

Explaining Consciousness: The Basic Account

People do get awfully excited about consciousness. They say it is the last great mystery. They say it is logically impossible to solve the mystery, or that it is logically possible, but mere human beings are not up to the task. Some suggest that consciousness somehow lies outside the causal order. Others argue that vast resources must be pumped into neuroscience if we are even to take a few tentative steps forward on the path to a solution. It is against this sort of background that Dennett published his cheekily entitled book *Consciousness Explained* (1991). The book met with a lively reception, but Dennett's bold claim to have explained consciousness has not yet won widespread approval. *Kinds of Minds: Towards an Understanding of Consciousness* (1996) has a much more modest title. With that book and comments in various papers Dennett may seem to have backed off. However, in this chapter and the next I shall rally to the title of *Consciousness Explained*. I shall argue that Dennett does offer a very plausible explanation of consciousness. And, most critically, he shows that there is nothing in the phenomena of consciousness that cannot be reconciled with the mechanistic world view. Consciousness gives us no reason to think that science is somehow incomplete. Nor does it give us a reason to think that we need to turn to supernature if we are fully to account for our own self-conception. Dennett shows that consciousness is not such a difficult problem after all.

I begin by distinguishing two senses of consciousness that are the source of excitement, those concerned with experience and self-awareness respectively. I then turn to a vigorous reconstruction of

Dennett's positive account, highlighting two distinctive features of Dennett's approach that are often submerged in his writing. The first is that, in my view, Dennett's work interweaves two distinct strands: a strand concerned with the level of the agent and a strand concerned with the sub-personal level of the agent's parts. The second is that Dennett's account relies on a critical distinction between two different ways in which an agent can be aware of herself and the world around her. By keeping these two distinctive features clearly in mind, we can see how Dennett's account of consciousness dovetails with his account of agency and how it provides a satisfying explanation of an initially puzzling phenomena.

Having accentuated the positive in this chapter, in the following chapter I turn to some of the discrepancies between my reconstruction of Dennett's view and his texts. I trace some of the changes and developments that Dennett has made to his account, and comment on how his presentation of his views has often obscured the two distinctive features I champion. I then turn to some sceptical challenges. To persuade the sceptic, Dennett needs to deflate our concept of consciousness. For Dennett, if we agree that we are built only out of mechanistic bits and pieces, then certain deeply appealing ideas about consciousness must be rejected. But what we are left with can be wholly satisfying. Finally, I turn to Dennett's account of the self or the subject of consciousness.

5.1   The agent level

The very term 'consciousness' is used in a variety of ways (*CC*, 114–16; *CE*, 21–5). For our purposes, however, it will serve to distinguish just two. The first sense refers to experience: having pains, tickles, or itches; hearing music; taking in the visual scene; tasting a flavour. How is this sense problematic? Consider an electronic device that is very good at telling red apples from green ones. Unless we hear a very elaborate story about the device, we would normally assume that it has no experiences of red and green (cf. *CC*, 126). If we ask 'what it is like' for an apple-sorter to detect a red apple or a green apple, the answer is, surely, that it is not like anything at all. Our intuition tells us that what the electronic apple-sorter is missing and what the human apple-sorter has, is a feeling or an experience of the apples' redness or greenness, as well as their roundness, smoothness, odour, and so forth. What the electronic apple-sorter lacks and what we have is experiential consciousness.

The second sense of consciousness refers to an awareness of who and what we are, one that is reflective and that can be critical. This sense of consciousness is often referred to as self-consciousness or self-awareness. It is a common intuition that animals have consciousness in the experiential sense. We think, for example, that their pains hurt, that they feel, more or less, to the animal the way our pains feel to us. And it is also a common intuition that animals lack self-consciousness. As she goes about her business, we tend not to think of an animal pausing and wondering what she is doing and, perhaps more critically, why she is doing it. We speak, of course, of people who are more or less self-conscious, more or less reflective. But for the sense of self-conscious that is critical here, every healthy human being is fully self-conscious. They are because they are able to think about who they are now, who they have been, and what they will become. There is no need to have particularly deep or exciting thoughts about such issues to be self-conscious in the sense at hand. To have any thoughts at all about such issues is to be very different from, say, an ant or an apple-sorter. Ants and apple-sorters do not merely lack interesting thoughts about who and what they are, they lack any such thoughts altogether.

Dennett's account of consciousness comprises two strands, strands which he usually intertwines in his presentation. The first strand is an agent level account of consciousness, one which analyses consciousness in terms of special intentional capacities of the agent. The second strand concerns the sub-personal mechanisms which underpin those special intentional capacities. I want to separate the two strands as much as possible. I should note, however, that while I think my interpretation correctly captures Dennett's view, it does require setting aside certain remarks and generously interpreting others (see chapter 6). This caveat aired, we can now turn to the first strand.

Two kinds of awareness

The most fundamental tenet of Dennett's agent level account is that there are two ways in which an agent can perceive or be aware of a state of affairs. There is a mode of awareness that serves only to influence the control of behaviour. And there is a mode of awareness that serves not only to influence the control of behaviour, but also to influence the agent's own narrative of what she is and is not aware of. In *Content and Consciousness* Dennett calls the latter 'awareness₁' and the former 'awareness₂'. These labels were fairly soon abandoned after *Content and Consciousness*. But Dennett tells us that he never intended to abandon the distinction itself. Rather, he judged that his terminology, and also the tactic of bringing this distinction to the foreground, was not helping to persuade his critics (see *CC*, 2nd edn, xi; *BC*, 358–9; Dennett, 1994, 544–5). Here I shall reinstate the distinction. However, partly for the sake of clarity – that is, to avoid those awkward numbered subscripts – and partly because the way Dennett has understood the underlying distinction has shifted since 1969, I shall use different labels. I shall talk about 'behavioural awareness' and 'narrative awareness'. Behavioural awareness, which corresponds to Dennett's awareness₂, is the kind of awareness that involves modulating one's behaviour appropriately in response to the state of the environment. Narrative awareness, of which Dennett's awareness₁ is a formulation, is the kind of awareness that involves the capacity to consider what one is aware of and what one is doing. In *Content and Consciousness* Dennett characterizes narrative awareness by identifying it with the capacity to make an introspective report. You are narratively aware that there is a tree in front of you if you are in a position to give a report to that effect. Giving a report is, of course, a kind of behaviour, but a very special kind.

Behavioural awareness is exhibited by all agents. When we observe that a 'bee diverts from its beeline to avoid collision with a tree' (*CC*, 116) we quite naturally say that the bee is aware of the tree. But in saying that the bee is aware, we do not need to imagine that anything very exciting is going on with the bee. All the bee needs to do to qualify as being behaviourally aware is to avoid trees reliably. If you can behave appropriately in the light of some state of affairs, and do so reliably, then you are behaviourally aware of that state of affairs.

By contrast narrative awareness is exhibited by very few agents. Indeed, it is only persons that unproblematically exhibit the capacity for narrative awareness. We can gain a clearer sense of narrative awareness by considering cases where a person is and is not narratively aware of some state of affairs. 'Consider the man who reasons thus: I must have been aware that the glass had reached my lips, or I wouldn't have tipped it' (*CC*, 117). Now if the man's claim is that he was behaviourally aware that the glass had reached his lips, we should have no argument with him. But if we are supposed to think that he was narratively aware, then Dennett tells us we must resist. The man may infer that he was behaviourally aware.

But to be narratively aware is to be able to make a non-inferential report as to how you take the world to be. And this, distracted as he was by conversation and not thinking about the glass, the man cannot do. On another occasion, when he was concentrating on his sip, perhaps savouring the moment, he would be narratively aware.

Dennett emphasizes that his account of consciousness begins from the third-person perspective (*CE*, 70ff). The first-person perspective is what I have on my own consciousness and you have on yours. But because I have no tools for directly observing what goes on in your mind, it initially seems difficult for me, some other person, to study and theorize about the contents of your consciousness. If I have access to fancy equipment I can, of course, directly observe what goes on in your brain. But as we have already seen in the case of intentional states, how we understand what appears in the brain needs to be interpreted in the light of the behaviour of the whole person. Just being able to look inside the head does not, of itself, move us forward. Since 1982 Dennett has defended what he describes as a third-person method of gathering information about and describing the contents of someone's consciousness. He calls his method 'heterophenomenology' (*CE*, 72ff; see also Dennett, 1982, and *BS*, chapter 10) – it is just like phenomenology, i.e. observing and reflecting on our own experience, except that it is done by an other (hetero).

Heterophenomenology involves interpreting an agent's behaviour in order to work out what the person thinks her experience is like. But, argues Dennett, what a person *thinks* her experience is like just *is* what her experience is like. For example, he denies that 'there's a difference between thinking (judging, deciding, being of the heartfelt opinion that) something seems pink to you and something really seeming pink to you' (*CE*, 364; see also *CE*, chapter 11 *passim*). Experience, he presses, does not outstrip our capacity to be aware of it. Not everyone agrees, as we shall see later in this chapter and in the next. But, granting this for the time being, we can see how Dennett thinks that, heterophenomenology can reveal what someone else is experiencing. If a person sincerely reports, 'I see a tree before me', then the heterophenomenologist can conclude that the person has an experience as of a tree. If a person is asked to press a button when she sees a red dot on the screen, then, on observing her press the button the heterophenomenologist can conclude that the person has an experience as of a red dot. But in this latter case there may be more data to come. The person may press the button and then say, 'Oops, I'm sorry. I did not mean to press the button. I did not see a red dot.' In this case the initial conclusion would be amended. The heterophenomenologist would conclude that, after all, there was no experience of a red dot.

The method is a third-personal one because it does not matter who the heterophenomenologist is. Two or more different practitioners of the art will, by and large, agree on their conclusions. And this also makes the method objective (*CE*, 72). However, in saying that it is objective Dennett is not implying that we must not bring certain values to bear in interpreting the data. The most objective data might be, as it were, mere sounds and bodily movements. But that would be of no use to us at all. Heterophenomenology requires that its practitioners adopt a rationalizing stance (*CE*, 74–8). Moreover, I think that it requires what I have called the personal stance rather than the vanilla intentional stance. The intentional stance cannot distinguish between what the agent takes herself to experience and what, in her behaviour, she shows herself to be sensitive to. But these two can come apart, as we shall see shortly. By contrast, the personal stance only discerns that which the agent takes herself to experience. It is blind to that which she merely shows herself to be sensitive to, to that which, as we might say, she has no consciousness. (In chapter 6 I discuss further the use of the personal as opposed to the intentional stance in this context.) In drawing conclusions from a verbal report, we must assume the person means what she says and is not just making some noises. And in drawing a conclusion about experience from a button push, we have to assume that we are dealing with a rational agent capable of understanding and following our instructions.

The method of heterophenomenology is the means by which we determine the contents of an agent's narrative awareness. In *Content and Consciousness* Dennett argues that the only tool for (what he later called) heterophenomenology was the verbal report. Of course, verbal reports do not necessarily require speech. We can, as it were, say things by raising an eyebrow, so long as we have earlier agreed what the signal is supposed to mean. Or we can use sign-language or write things down. All these modes, however, are part of what Dennett was driving at when he discussed verbal reports. There are some signs that he may have backed off from this position (see chapter 6), but I shall proceed on the assumption that verbal reports (as just glossed here, i.e., to include such things as eyebrow raises and sign-language) are the only tool for heterophenomenology.

Introspection and control – I

Why does Dennett want to say the bee is not aware of the tree in the same way that we can be, that is, in the sense that there is something that it is like for the bee to be aware of the tree? It will take some time to present Dennett's argument. To begin with, however, it is worth asking how we might determine that it is like something for the bee to be aware of the tree. An important point for Dennett is that we cannot ask the bee (*CC*, 116 and 120; cf. *CE*, 446 and 447). Unlike the person, the bee is not capable of delivering an introspective report through language or through any other means. So, to credit the bee with experience like ours, we must suppose that there is something that it is like for the bee 'on the inside', but that it is simply unable to express this or indicate that it is so. This idea does have some initial appeal. But Dennett aims to show it does not hold water.

Indeed, Dennett thinks this idea gets things quite back to front. For him, it is being equipped with an ability to make reports – to others or even just to yourself – that leads to it being the case that there is something that it is like to experience the world. So, for him, it does not make sense to think that there could be something that it was like to experience the world independently of whether or not reporting could take place. It is not as though the subject matter of the reports is there whether or not the reporting skill is there. Rather, it is the very capacity to make a report that gives sense to the idea of there being an 'on the inside', of there being something that it is 'like' for a creature. This, in any case, is the interpretation of Dennett which I want to defend. Dennett himself does not present his view in quite this way. However, as I shall argue below, this interpretation is the only one that is fully compatible with Dennett's account of agency.

Discussing the two kinds of awareness, Dennett warns that the two are often 'run together' (*CC*, 121). And, indeed, this is not surprising given that 'there is a high degree of coincidence of the two in human affairs' (*CC*, 121). But they can and do come apart. Neither, he suggests, should be taken to be the correct analysis of our ordinary term 'aware' or our ordinary term 'conscious of'. Instead, we simply need to note that the ordinary term does dual service, covering the ground of both narrative and behavioural awareness.

Dennett thinks we need to break the link between narrative awareness – what we are aware of in introspection – and behavioural awareness, which only explains appropriate responses to our environment. There are many occasions when human beings respond appropriately to their environment, but have nothing to report. For example, we turn in our sleep to avoid muscle cramps. This shows all the hallmarks of a response to mild pain. And yet we have nothing to say about such pain. Whether we have a pain or not is perhaps no more than a terminological issue. But in the absence of any inclination to report, at the time or later, it seems clear that we do not *feel* the pain.

A similar example is that of the walker who has a stone in her boot. She is engrossed in conversation and not, she might say, aware of the stone. And yet her gait is subtly altered to avoid pressure on her foot. She is, then, behaviourally aware of the stone, and this explains the appropriate modulation of her behaviour. But she is not narratively aware of the stone. This explains why she has nothing to say about the stone. Again, whether she has a pain is not so important. But again, in the absence of any inclination to report, at the time or later, there seems little reason to say she *feels* the pain (cf. *CC*, 125).

Empirical psychology provides a host of further examples which are most naturally described as behavioural awareness in the absence of narrative awareness. Take the phenomena of 'priming'. A word is flashed up on a screen so quickly that the subject cannot recognize it. If awareness for introspection and awareness for control must always go together, then we would think that which word was flashed up could have no effect on subsequent behaviour. But this turns out not to be the case. If a word such as 'doctor' is flashed up too quickly to be recognized, but slowly enough for it to have a causal impact on the visual system, this will 'prime' the recognition of a word with which it is strongly associated, such as 'nurse'. That is to say, subjects will be able to recognize the word 'nurse' more quickly after, as it were, having failed to see the word 'doctor'. In some sense, then, the subject has recognized the word 'doctor' even though she cannot report any awareness of this. Indeed, she reports quite emphatically a failure to recognize any word at all.

Narrative awareness is not then required for control of action. Behavioural awareness will often suffice on its own. This is Dennett's contention. Why should we object? To the extent that these notions are just technical terms of Dennett's theory, he can stipulate whether they are logically related or not. But the issue becomes critical when we turn to Dennett's bold move, parallel in some ways to the bold move of claiming that agents just are intentional systems that we encountered in chapter 2.

The bold move is this: Dennett claims that the exciting kinds of consciousness are wholly accounted for by narrative awareness. '[There] is no important residue in the ordinary concept of awareness that is not subsumed under either awareness$_1$ [narrative awareness] or awareness$_2$ [behavioural awareness]' (CC, 121, cf. CE, 280–2, and chapter 14). Without narrative awareness, there is no self-consciousness and no experiential consciousness. But with narrative awareness comes both of the exciting kinds of consciousness. So narrative awareness is both necessary and also sufficient for the exciting kinds of consciousness.

If Dennett's claim is true, then to explain consciousness Dennett needs only to explain narrative awareness. And although there is work to do in explaining narrative awareness, the project does not appear to be intractable. Indeed, it looks very manageable.

But is Dennett's bold claim true? Is it even plausible? Although narrative awareness looks like a good candidate to account for self-consciousness, it is not clear at this stage that it has anything to contribute to an account of experiential consciousness. Key to Dennett's argument is the premise that what we think our experience is like, just is what our experience is like. Two worries arise immediately. First, simply having thoughts or entertaining beliefs does not seem to be like, say, seeing or hearing. The two seem altogether different in kind. Second, many experiences cannot readily be put into words if, indeed, they can be put into words at all. Many experiences seem ineffable or, put bluntly, unreportable. I turn to these two issues in a moment, but first, with Dennett's bold claim on the table, we need to re-examine the relationship between introspection and control.

Introspection and control – II

Consider two folk psychological claims about consciousness:

- *Whatever can be experienced can be reported upon*, for example, you cannot be in pain and yet be unable (now or on some later occasion) to report that you are in pain.
- *Only that which is perceived, where perception entails experience, can influence the control of behaviour*, for example, unless you have seen something, then your behaviour will not be rationally influenced by the visual presence of that something.

I do not want to say that either of these claims are universally held. But they are certainly not uncommon. Of course, the two claims leave the term 'experience' ambiguous between Dennett's two senses of awareness. This is as it should be if Dennett is right that common sense does not usually distinguish between his two senses. If we substitute 'narrative awareness' for 'experience' in the above two claims, the second claim comes up false. We do not need to be narratively aware of something for that something to rationally influence the control of our behaviour. On the other hand, if we substitute 'behavioural awareness', the second claim turns out true but the first turns out false: we cannot always report what we are behaviourally aware of.

Dennett's proposal, in effect, is that we revise the two folk psychological claims, taking advantage of his distinction between two modes of awareness. One understanding of experience is tied to introspection. This is the understanding of experience that is cashed out by narrative awareness. Another understanding of experience is tied only to control. And this is cashed out by behavioural awareness. The deflation of our understanding of consciousness, if it is a deflation, comes in separating out the idea of control and introspection. The two do not need to go together.

As we have just seen, there are examples both from the everyday and from empirical psychology that seem to support the dissociation between control and introspection. Can we respond to these examples in a different way from Dennett? Consider two alternative explanations.

Suppose we want to insist that the sense of 'experience' in the two folk psychological claims is just the same. There is one notion of experience. And we might add, it is just that kind of experience that is common to people, cats, and bats. On this understanding we need to explain how control occurs in the apparent absence of experience, where the apparent absence is indicated by the inability to report. Here is what we might say: there is a brief experience, a moment where the relevant factors were available for introspection, but that, with the passage of further events, the experience is then forgotten. So we might say that the walker was introspectively aware of the stone and the discomfort it was causing, but forgot, or put this thought to the back of her mind. Or we might say of the experimental subject that she did recognize the word 'doctor' in the ordinary way, that it was briefly available for introspective report, but then she forgot this experience. Her forgetting explains her denial of ever having experienced it, but the experience itself explains how it can come to have an impact on the control of behaviour.

What encourages this kind of response is the intuition that for an agent to respond rationally to an experience the experience must somehow be played before her mind. It is this that Dennett is complaining about when he talks about the Cartesian Theatre (*CE*, chapter 5, esp. 107–11; *CE*, *passim*; TO). The Cartesian Theatre is supposed to be a functional or even geographical centre in the brain where thoughts and experiences are 'made available' to consciousness. If, as Descartes suggested, we were disembodied souls operating our bodies by, say, radio control, then the Cartesian Theatre would make perfect sense; the data gathered by our senses would need to be collected together before transmission to the soul (cf. *BC*, 132).

This first alternative saves both folk psychological intuitions at the price of saying that no sooner than we have had many of our experiences we instantly forget them. Perhaps the most apt thing to say about this suggestion is that it is baroque; in any case, it is quite some bullet to bite. Let us turn to the second alternative. This alternative favours the folk psychological claim about control as opposed to the claim about introspection. It accounts for the dissociation data by dropping the insistence on a necessary link between experience and report. The claim is that you can have experiences without any inclination or disposition to report. These are, as it were, unconscious experiences.[1]

Once again, something like the Cartesian Theatre seems to feature in this approach. The move does not broaden out experience in an open-ended way. So it does not imply that when we exhibit a reflex response, such as jerking our leg in response to a hammer tap on the knee, we have an experience. And, given this, the view needs to distinguish between modes of awareness that are genuine experiences (such as 'feeling' the pain in your foot) and modes of awareness that are not (such as 'noticing' the hammer tap on the knee). What serves to distinguish the two? It is perhaps tendentious to insist that it is something like the Cartesian Theatre. But we need some criteria that are both (a) independent of our capacity to report and (b) such that they make it plausible that there is something that it is like to have the experience. In effect, Dennett's talk of the Cartesian Theatre is a metaphor for a criterion that meets these requirements.

What can be said in favour of the second alternative, the alternative that allows for unreportable experiences? One attractive feature for some is that it accommodates the widespread intuition that animals can have experiences, experiences which are just like ours, and yet be quite unable to report them or even reflect on them to themselves. Similarly, when discussing cases such as the walker with the stone in her boot, many have the intuition that it makes perfect sense to say that she has the pain, the very same pain she has when she can report it, only that in this case she is unable to make the report.

Consider how we might tell whether an anaesthetic has success-fully suppressed the presence of pain. We ask the patient to tell us whether or not she feels the pain. If she can confidently report that she does not, then we take it that she does not. For a pain scientist, say, to come along and insist that contrary to the patient's report she really is in pain (though not the sort of pain that generates suf-fering) seems almost nonsensical. Yes, the pain scientist might have identified a theoretically interesting brain condition, one that has strong correlations with pain reports. But if she insists that the subject is genuinely in pain might we not reasonably insist that she does not really understand what we mean by the term 'pain'? This is the sort of move that Dennett wants to press. If we allow the idea of experience to detach from reportability, it is not clear why we should want to adopt that idea of experience.

Dennett spends much of *Consciousness Explained* trying to make this point (especially chapters 10–12). Time and again he empha-sizes that the contents of the heterophenomenological text, that is the full account of what the subject is able to report, exhausts all there is to say about the contents of her consciousness. Anything that escapes that text simply does not deserve to count as a content of consciousness. And it does not, because it does not connect up in the right way with the agent's sayings and doings.

Dennett does not merely think that saying there could be ex-periences that we cannot report is false. He thinks it is incoherent. His thought is that the very idea of an experience – an experience in the exciting sense, in the 'what is it like to be' sense – breaks down if we allow that it could occur without reporting. For the most part Dennett does not argue the point, but rather tries to get his readers on side by developing intuitions about puzzle cases. However, there is scope for argument here. We can offer an argument on Dennett's behalf – I say this because if the argument is present in Dennett it is very far from explicit. The argument takes as a premise that any account of experience must meet two interrelated constraints: first, it must show that experience is something that we actually care about and, second, it must offer a coherent account of the subject of experience.

Consider the first constraint. In effect, Dennett needs to insist that a constraint on any account of experience is that the presence or absence of experience is something that really matters to us. This does seem like a reasonable constraint to insist upon independently of Dennett's account. And, of course, Dennett's account does meet this constraint. If experience can be present in the absence of any report – e.g., we are in pain but cannot report that we are in pain – then, for all that we are able to speak, ponder, and worry, the experience might just as well be absent. And this, for Dennett, means we just cannot be talking about experience in anything like the ordinary sense, the sense in which we care about having it or not. At best, such a notion of experience must be technical, useful perhaps for psychological theories, but not critical to our self-conception.

The second constraint concerns the role of the subject of experience. Suppose we assert the modest premise that where there is experience so there must be a subject of experience. Who is the subject of unreportable experiences, such as the pain caused by the stone in the walker's boot? Let us say that the 'essential you' experiences the pain. It is the 'essential you' that is the subject of the pain experience. But now it turns out that the 'essential you' is out of kilter with the 'authorial you', the you that is the author of your verbal reports. The 'authorial you' reports different things about what she experiences than the 'essential you'. But who do you want to identify with? Are you the 'essential you' or are you the 'authorial you'? Dennett's view implies that the 'essential you' is a dead option. (I revisit this move in chapter 6 when I discuss the 'inner witnesses' and 'authors of our reports'.)

In speaking of the Cartesian Theatre Dennett reveals his suspicion that something like this extra shadow subject is being introduced. In terms of that metaphor, the 'essential you' is the audience of the drama played out on the inner stage. But this 'essential you' is a strangely passive subject. It cannot be identified with the subject that is responsible for your actions or your reports. That subject could only be the 'authorial you'. And, in the end, this extra shadow subject looks to be more a product of confused thinking than anything else.

I would not assert that either of my arguments, or any of Dennett's, are utterly decisive against those who claim there is more to consciousness than can be captured in the heterophenomenological report. But I think the case for Dennett's view is a very strong one. Those who object to his view need to be very clear what they are offering in its place. And, in particular, they need to be very clear in their account of the subject of experience. Dennett's view makes it quite clear how the subject of experiences – experiences of pains, itches, colours, and so forth – is one and the same as the subject who is the author of our reports and the owner of our actions. I cannot see any reason, and nor can Dennett, for accepting an account that does not clearly meet such a criterion.

We shall return to this issue when we look at some sources of scepticism later in the next chapter (6.2). But now I want to return to the two issues identified a little earlier. Dennett's claim is that the contents of consciousness are exhausted by the contents of the heterophenomenological text, and that this text can be extracted by any qualified third party. But if this is so, then, first, why is it that vision has a distinct phenomenology from, say, taste or hearing? How could this difference be represented in the heterophenomenological text? And, second, why is it that we have the strong conviction that many experiences are ineffable, are incapable of being expressed or reported at all?

5.2   Seeing and believing

Is seeing believing?

Dennett touts the slogan 'seeing is believing' in a section title in *Consciousness Explained* (CE, 362). And to a crude approximation this just is Dennett's account of the experience of seeing. Seeing is believing. And so is hearing, tasting, smelling, feeling, sensing the positioning of your body, and so forth. All these are just cases of believing. For Dennett, experiential consciousness is simply a matter of coming to acquire a variety of intentional states.

But at first blush this does not seem right at all. After all, being told that there is a cat on the mat by a reliable source gives rise to the belief that there is a cat on the mat. But there is either no phenomenology to having such a belief or, if there is, it is quite unlike the experience of actually seeing a cat on the mat. So how can seeing be simply a matter of believing? What is clear about Dennett's theory is that the difference between seeing the cat and being told that the cat is there is to be accounted for solely in terms of intentional states. Dennett presents a fairly detailed case as to what intentional states are associated with seeing and what with being told (see *CC*, 132–41; *CE*, chapter 11). That said, he tends to approach the issue somewhat obliquely, for example, through the issue of mental imagery (*CE*, chapter 10; *BS*, chapter 10; *CC*, chapter 7) or 'filling in' (*CE*, chapter 11). Here I shall express Dennett's view more directly than he does himself, tackling the issue head on.

When one sees that the cat is on the mat one acquires a great deal of information that is lacking when one is simply told that the cat is on the mat. When one sees the cat one comes to know a great deal about its position, its orientation, its colours, its size, the way it looks in the prevailing lighting conditions, how like or unlike it is to other cats one has known, and so on. And, of course, when one is told that there is a cat on the mat, one acquires some information that could not be acquired by perceiving this to be so. For example, one comes to know a great deal about the sound of the voice that is doing the telling, whether it has an accent, whether it is male or female, and so forth. And we can go on to elaborate further differences. So there are plenty of differences in beliefs between the case where I see the cat and the case where I am told that the cat is on the mat. If phenomenology does depend on belief, then, there is plenty of scope for Dennett to account for the fact that seeing has one kind of distinctive phenomenology and being told has another. This is not quite the same as convincing us that just these differences can actually account for the difference in phenomenology. But it is a good start.

What Dennett's position needs is an argument to show how the ready availability of certain sorts of belief could plausibly account for the phenomenology of vision. (And, of course, the same task will need to be repeated for all the senses.) Perhaps one of the most striking features of vision is the sense we have of taking in the whole field of view before our eyes all at once. Leonardo da Vinci captures this intuition nicely, commenting on the relative merits of painting and poetry:

> The poet in describing beauty and ugliness of any figure can only show it to you consecutively, bit by bit, while the painter can display it all at once. (Sturgis, 2000, 61)

This idea has often been repeated in discussions of art and there is *something* right about it. But in fact it does take us time to take in what our eyes make available to us, whether we are looking at a picture or at the world. This is made clear by studying the way in which the eye and brain operate. The eye can only detect rich detail in a narrow region, and so to detect all the detail in a picture the eye must scan the picture, building up detail as it does so.

The same point can be revealed more simply. If shown an image only briefly, our experience is that we have taken in the whole picture and that we have seen all of the picture with the same amount of detail. But we can see this is not the case by checking how much we are actually able to recall about the picture. When we are pressed, it turns out we may be ignorant of very basic features, such as how many figures the picture contains and even what activities are portrayed.

In *Consciousness Explained* Dennett tells us of the time he took part in an eye-tracking experiment (*CE*, 361–2). Special equipment is used to work out just where the detail-sensitive part of the eye is focusing at any given time. The devious experiment in which Dennett participated generates the appearance of a stable text on a computer screen. But, in fact, the computer replaces the words the eye is not focusing on with different words of the same length. If you are not participating in the experiment you see the screen flickering, the text in constant change. But as a subject the text on the screen 'seems to you for all the world as stable as if the words were carved in marble' (*CE*, 361). Dennett writes of his own experience: 'While I waited for the experimenters to turn on the apparatus, I read the text on the screen. I waited, and waited, eager for the trials to begin. I got impatient. "Why don't you turn it on?" I asked. "It is on," they replied' (*CE*, 361).

It is important to understand this sort of data in the right way. The data does show that da Vinci is mistaken. We do not take in the visual scene instantly. But, on the other hand, we do take it in very quickly. Psychologists writing about this sometimes make remarks that leave philosophers cringing. For example:

> What we actually see is a very rough picture with a few spots in clear detail. What we feel we see is a large picture which is everywhere as clear in detail as the favoured spot on which we concentrate our attention. (From a study reported by Sturgis, 2000, 61)

This kind of talk is akin to saying that table tops are not really solid because 'actually' there are many tiny gaps in them due to the space between the atoms that make them up. It is of course very interesting that there are gaps. But this does not reveal that table tops are not solid. That would be absurd. At best it reveals that a certain way of understanding solidity is flawed. We may need to deflate our pre-atomic concept of solidity. But, in revising our concept of solidity, we are clearly not giving up on anything important. Similarly, it is quite absurd to say that we see a very rough picture with a few spots in clear detail (cf. *CE*, 354). I might see this if someone had splattered my glasses with paint. But I do not in normal conditions.

We do better, I think, to say that when we look at a scene we often believe we have, at an instant, more information actually available to us than turns out to be the case. But the drama of all this is removed by the fact that we can very readily acquire the information that we do not have. We simply look for longer. Here, writing with breathtaking boldness, is Dennett on this point:

> If seeing is rather like reading a novel at breakneck speed, it is also the case that the novel is written to order at breakneck speed ... Whenever we examine our own experience of seeing, whenever we set out to discover what we can say about what we are seeing, we find all the details we think of looking for. When we read a novel, questions can come to mind that are not answered in the book, but when we are looking at something, as soon as questions come up they are answered immediately by new information as a result of the inevitable shift in focus and fixation point of our eyes. The reports of perception are written to order; whatever detail interest us is immediately brought into focus and reported on. When this occurs one is not scanning some stable mental image ... One is scanning the outside world, quite literally. One can no more become interested in a part of one's visual experience without bringing the relevant information to the fore than one can run away from one's shadow. For this reason it is tempting to suppose that everything one *can* know about via the eyes is *always* 'present to consciousness' in some stable picture. (*CC*, 139–40)

What is highly attractive about this account is the way in which it reconciles the psychological data – the fact that, contrary to appearances, we do not take in the whole scene at an instant – with the phenomenology of seeing. Of course we think we have the whole scene available to us. We do for two reasons. First, whatever question we may raise about the scene we can typically answer without any noticeable delay. So there is no time for a sense of absence to get a hold of us. And, second, we simply do not believe that the world has any gaps in it. Only if we did have this belief, the belief that the world was somehow gappy, would the world look gappy to us. As Dennett notes, an 'absence of information is not the same as information about an absence' (*CE*, 324).

When my glasses are spattered with paint the world can, for a few moments, look a bit gappy. But so long as I can move my head freely, this sense of gappiness is very short-lived. For even with the paint interfering with my vision, it is still the case that any question I might, as it were, pose of the world can be answered without any noticeable delay. What I notice when my glasses are paint-spattered is that I see less well. It is harder, more tiring, and I miss things more often. But I do not see differently.

Dennett argues, and I have offered some further support, that the distinctively visual phenomenology can be accounted for in terms of the acquisition of beliefs. What is distinctive about visual phenomenology is not, as da Vinci suggests, that we come to know all about the visual scene in an instant. This, for Dennett, is an inflated conception of what vision is. And, if we think about the actual practicalities of the information processing required, we can see it is an inflated conception of what vision could ever be. Nor, for Dennett, does the distinctive aspect consist of some feature that lies outside of the sets of beliefs and judgements we make when we have our eyes open and our attention engaged. Rather, what is distinctive about visual phenomenology is that in seeing we acquire the well-grounded belief that all we might want to know about the visual scene is readily available, that no question we might pose about it will go unanswered. And we have the capacity to find out more about any detail in the visual scene that attracts our attention nearly instantaneously.

Does introspection show us that there is more to seeing than this? Dennett thinks not because he thinks that '[whenever] you can answer a question without a noticeable delay, it seems as though that answer were already active in your mind' (Marvin Minsky, quoted in *CE*, 380). And *seeming* to be already active in your mind is all that is needed for the phenomenology of seeing. Of course, the argument is not utterly decisive. If we oppose Dennett's view, he may reasonably ask what more we think is needed to give an account of visual phenomenology. What is it that he has left out?

Ineffability

Something we might have left out would be the ineffable quality that experience seems to have. How can Dennett explain this? Dennett agrees that it is often 'hard to say' just what it is we are experiencing, that our words often seem to fail us. But he claims that 'this should not embarrass us, because we can say why it's hard to say' (*CE*, 382). Dennett is less explicit on this than we might like. But it is not difficult to find reasons why it is 'hard to say' what our experience is like.

First, we have to take account of the sheer amount of visual information. We are often told that a picture is worth a thousand words. But, in fact, we might reckon that very many more than a thousand are needed to capture all the judgements we can make when we open our eyes and gaze out on even a fairly mundane scene. It is, then, 'hard to say' what a visual experience is like, because there is so much to say. (Dennett hints at something like this move in *CE*, 399–400.)

Second, for many discriminations that we can make – such as noticing that this shade is darker than that – we have no ready vocabulary to draw the nuances. We can report – hence we are narratively aware – that there is a difference. But to put the nature of the difference into words, words that could have some application independently of the scene's being in front of us and our being able to point to features to elucidate our words, may not be possible. So we can only make our report using terms such as 'this' or 'that' or the equivalent. That is, we can say something along the lines of 'the colour on that curtain just above that squiggly bit and to the right of that crease'. Or we can just point, either using our fingers or, if our report is not public, simply by fixing our attention. (Dennett hints at something like this move on *CE*, 383.)

Third, when I see, taste, or hear things, I do not simply make neutral judgements about what is out there. Inevitably, my judgements come tinged with associations of various kinds. We have to take account of:

> [the] subtle individual difference wrought by epigenesis and a thousand chance encounters to create a unique manifold of . . . dispositions that outruns any short catalogue of effects. These dispositions may be dramatic – ever since that yellow car crashed into her, one shade of yellow [disturbs her] – or minuscule – an ever so slight relaxation evoked by a nostalgic whiff of childhood comfort food. (Dennett, 2001, 233)

I would like to add a fourth consideration of my own, one that fits well with Dennett's general project. It seems to me that the timing and ordering of the information that we acquire must play a role both in determining phenomenology and in making certain experiences ineffable (or nearly so). The reason why someone reading transcripts about a visual scene will not suddenly come to have visual images is that she cannot take in the written down perceptual beliefs at the same rate and in the same order as she would were she seeing. Timing and ordering matter because each time a belief is taken on it has an impact on other beliefs, desires, and so forth. And the impact that the first in a series of beliefs has alters the context in which subsequent beliefs will be accommodated. This is true of linguistic as well as perceptual beliefs, but with perceptual beliefs it seems reasonable to assume that timing and context effects are much more dramatic. I cannot know what it is like for you to read *War and Peace*, not because reading it gives rise to mysterious and thoroughly ineffable experiences. The reason is much more down to earth. I simply cannot reproduce the enormously complex succession of belief states that reading the novel sets off in you. The same is true for perceptual experience. My claim here is that timing and ordering, as well as the other factors already mentioned, contribute to the appearance of ineffability, or, indeed, to making experience actually ineffable (see chapter 6 for further discussion of ineffability).

5.3   The sub-personal level

In his presentation of his account of consciousness Dennett has, over time, given more and more space to the sub-personal level account and less and less to the personal level. My presentation in this chapter aims to counteract that trend. Dennett has spent more time on the sub-personal for at least two reasons. First, and most simply, Dennett is intensely interested in sub-personal mechanisms. He likes to find out about them and to disseminate what he has found out in a clear and accessible manner. Second, he has changed his mind a number of times, as he has found out more and science has found out more about how brains do and could work. Whereas *Content and Consciousness* was largely speculative, by the time of *Consciousness Explained* Dennett draws on a great deal of empirical psychology and brain science. So, in order to keep his audience posted on his changes of mind, he has needed to give over space to his sub-personal account.

My key concern here is not with the details of the sub-personal account. Rather, my concern is with whether or not Dennett's philosophical position can make good sense. For that to be so Dennett must show that there is some sub-personal story or other that can make intelligible the successful ascription of narrative as well as behavioural awareness. That some sub-personal story is possible should not be a big deal, unless we are to admit that consciousness requires supernature. However for consciousness to be explained, as opposed to being some brute fact, the sub-personal story must be intelligible. This is a tougher demand.

Dennett's approach here is the same approach that he applied to agency. First, we apply intentionalistic labels at the sub-personal level. And then we move between the personal and the sub-personal stance, flipping regularly between the two, with the aim of understanding how the sub-personal mechanism can underpin behavioural awareness and narrative awareness. Of course, as noted in chapter 3, this appeal to 'flipping' is not an argument as such. Rather, it is an invitation. Dennett tells us various stories and takes us through the process of flipping from one perspective to another. Through this process he hopes to take us to a position where we share (what he sees as) his insight, where we say, 'Ah yes. If we constructed a device just like that, then it would give rise to activity that could be interpreted as the activity of an agent with behavioural and narrative awareness.'

The role of sub-personal theory

In 'Towards a Cognitive Theory of Consciousness' (TCTC) Dennett acknowledges that simply examining the sub-personal account in isolation gives us no reason to think it could underpin consciousness:

> At best a sub-personal theory will seem to give us *no grounds* for believing its instantiations would be subjects of experience, and at worst . . . a sub-personal theory will seem to permit instantiations that are *obviously not* subjects of experience. (TCTC, 154)

The point here is that there is no consciousness at the sub-personal level. No module or sub-system is the specific locus for consciousness. It is the agent, and not any of her parts, that is conscious. Dennett goes on:

> Intuition then, proclaims that any sub-personal theory must leave out something vital [but intuitions] can sometimes be appeased or made to go away. I propose to construct a full-fledged "I" out of sub-personal parts.

These remarks need some interpretation. The key point is that Dennett aims to show that the intuition that sub-personal accounts must leave something out is misplaced. This is of a piece with Dennett's pursuing his naturalistic agenda. He wants to show both that consciousness is possible without appeal to supernature and also that the relation between the mechanism and the phenomenon need not be deeply mysterious. The expression 'construct an "I" out of sub-personal parts' does raise eyebrows. For this expression can make it seem as though what consciousness is, is simply an aggregate of sub-personal parts. But no aggregate of sub-personal parts could be any more conscious than a single sub-personal part. The process of aggregation cannot switch us from a non-rationalizing stance to a rationalizing stance. But to get from sub-personal parts to an 'I' we need to make just such a switch. Dennett could be clearer about the need for the switch. But he is clear enough that the question of consciousness just cannot be addressed at the sub-personal level. In making his case he states: 'The first step is to sketch a sub-personal flow chart, a cognitivistic model that by being sub-personal "evades" the question of personal consciousness' (TCTC, 154).

The second step is more complicated. It supposes that the first step is complete, that we have a satisfactory sub-personal flow chart, one that can give an account of the sort of behaviour – behavioural and narrative awareness – that we conscious agents go in for. Now Dennett goes on to ask two questions:

(1) Would an entity instantiating this theory sketch *seem* . . . to have an inner conscious life?
(2) Would such an entity *in fact* have an inner conscious life? (TCTC, 172)

Dennett is bullish about the first claim. Perhaps, he tells us, his sketch is not quite right. But something broadly akin to it could surely yield a 'yes' to the first question. The second question is harder. Dennett eschews what he calls 'doctrinaire verificationism' (TCTC, 173). That is to say, he does not want to simply insist that because such an entity would seem to be conscious it is conscious. What he actually presses is not exactly an argument, but rather what I have described as the flipping strategy:

What convinces *me* that a [sub-personal theory] could capture all the dear features I discover in my inner life is not any "argument" . . .

but a detailed attempt to describe to myself exactly those features of my life *and the nature of my acquaintance with them* that I would cite as my "grounds" for claiming that I *am* – and do not merely *seem to be* – conscious. What *I* discover are facts quite congenial to [sub-personal] theorising, and my tactic here has been to try, by persuasive redescription, to elicit the same discoveries in others. (TCTC, 173)

Dennett dramatizes the very same point in *Consciousness Explained*. He has his fictional interlocutor say the following:

When I tell you, sincerely, that I am imagining a purple cow, I am not just unconsciously producing a word-string to that effect . . . I am consciously and deliberately reporting the existence of something that is *really* there! (CE, 97)

In reply Dennett insists that his interlocutor is 'unconsciously producing a word-string' (CE, 97). She has no clue as to how she does it. There are, as he put the point in *Content and Consciousness* no mental processes involved (CC, 92–3; cf. chapter 4, p. 108). So if we want to know more about the production of the word string, we cannot look to introspection, we cannot look to anything that we, qua people, do. We must turn instead to the sub-personal. Dennett's claim, then, is that once we recognize the limits of personal level explanation, we see how little we can actually tell, from introspection, about the origin of our reports. And yet once the reports are explained, then all that is genuinely within the purview of introspection is explained.

The trouble is that we often theorize about what we do. In the case of introspection Dennett says 'we find ourselves *wanting to say* all these things about what is going on in us; this gives rise to *theories* we hold about how we come to be able to do this – for instance, the notorious but homespun theory that we "perceive" these goings on with our "inner eye"' (TCTC, 166–7). Such 'theories' can, of course, have a tremendous grip on us.

The shape of Dennett's sub-personal theories

How can a sub-personal mechanism do the sort of stuff that earns the ascription of behavioural awareness and narrative awareness? We can only answer this question by rehearsing some of the specific suggestions that Dennett has made. In *Content and Consciousness* he offers a story about the way in which one part of the person, say a visual system, is connected to various other systems, say the motor system, the navigation system, and the speech centre. The presence of connections between the visual system and the motor system can help to explain behavioural awareness. For example, such connections can help to explain how it is that the agent can steer around an obstacle, such as a tree. A message, which we on the outside interpret as meaning something like 'tree', is passed from the visual system to the motor system, and appropriate action ensues. The same message, or a similar one, may also be passed on to the speech centre. If so, this would help to explain narrative awareness. The receipt of the message by the speech centre makes possible the agent's report, 'there is a tree ahead'. In the absence of such a connection there could be no such report, there could be no narrative awareness of the tree.

Of course, this is very sketchy. We will want to know how the speech centre works. And we will also want to be clear that Dennett is not begging any questions by giving the speech centre too many powers. Were we to find that the speech centre needed to have the same capacities as a person in order to do its job, then we would have made no progress at all in explaining how the powers of persons can be underpinned by the powers of their parts. But this condensation of the *Content and Consciousness* sketch makes Dennett's basic strategy clear.

The *Brainstorms* account (TCTC) adds some detail. Dennett introduces a 'memory buffer' and a 'public relations' sub-system (which incorporates the 'speech centre'). But the basic picture is the same. Sub-personal messages can influence behaviour-controlling systems without going via the memory buffer. But only those messages that make it into the memory buffer can influence the processes of report, whether internal (introspection) or external (saying how things are with you).

In *Consciousness Explained* Dennett makes a substantial revision to his sub-personal account. I shall say more about these developments in the next chapter. But, in brief, he abandons the ideas of discrete centres of control within the brain. So there is no longer one 'memory buffer' or 'public relations' system. The work of these systems is distributed about the brain. The criterion of making it into the 'speech centre' is replaced by the more diffuse criterion of succeeding in influencing speech or memory.

Despite variations, the fine-grained details of which I am ignoring here, the core principle remains the same. In every version of Dennett's sub-personal story, there is a potential for sub-personal messages to be recruited only for control of behaviour (thus under-pinning behavioural awareness) or to be recruited for control of reporting behaviour (thus underpinning narrative awareness). For Dennett, by understanding the operation of such a mechanism and thinking carefully what it can achieve, we can come to understand how narrative awareness can be underpinned by sub-personal parts.

A case study: 'filling in' at the personal and sub-personal levels

How do the personal and sub-personal stories relate to one another? We can best illustrate this by working through a case study. The phenomenon known as 'filling in' (*CE*, 344–56) is where an agent seems to be aware of parts of the world about which she has no information. As we have already seen, ordinary vision involves 'filling in'. For in vision, although the brain sometimes has not had a chance to acquire information about a region of the visual field, the person still seems to be aware of the right sorts of thing in the 'missing' region.

Consider Dennett's case of the Marilyn Monroe wallpaper (*CE*, 354). You enter a room with a 'regular array of hundreds of identical' Marilyn images on the wall. Now:

> You would see in a fraction of a second that there were "lots and lots of identical, detailed, focused portraits of Marilyn Monroe." Since your eyes only saccade four or five times a second at most, you could foveate only one or two Marilyns in the time it takes you to jump to the conclusion *and* thereupon to *see* hundreds of identical Marilyns. We know that parafoveal vision could not distinguish Marilyn from various Marilyn-shaped blobs, but nevertheless, what you see is *not* wallpaper of Marilyn-in-the-middle surrounded by various indistinct Marilyn shaped blobs. (*CE*, 354)

At the personal level what goes on here is that you reach a judgement, namely that the wall is covered by hundreds of identical Marilyns. It turns out that this judgement is sound. You can keep looking at the wall, scanning it carefully, and it will not seem any different. To understand this experience we need know nothing about what is going on inside your head. Just as the rationalizing stances can be formulated, understood, and applied without knowing anything about a system's insides so too can Dennett's account of consciousness. And yet, we still can ask and may want to ask, 'How is all this achieved given that conscious agents are made out of mechanistic bits and pieces?' To answer that question we turn to the sub-personal level.

Here is a rough gloss of what is going on: your brain is gathering information about the wall and processing it in various ways. When the parts of the brain that contribute to reporting make a 'probe' (*CE*, 113, 135–6), that is, request a tentative conclusion about what is out there in the world, then a signal meaning 'the wall is covered by hundreds of identical Marilyns' is returned. And this signal modulates what you say or think about what is out there.

It is critical to realize two things about such sub-personal stories. First, a variety of different sub-personal stories are compatible with one and the same personal level story. So the sub-personal underpinnings of seeing the Marilyn wallpaper can be quite diverse, even while the nature of the conscious agent's experience is quite uniform. Second, the talk of 'meanings' and 'conclusions' or of 'understanding' at the sub-personal level is wholly metaphorical. While such talk gives us a way of relating the sub-personal processes to what is going on with the agent, it is not meant to imply that there are any personal level capacities required or present at the sub-personal level. Let me try to illustrate these two points.

Consider a scenario in which you are doing the representing rather than your brain. Suppose that you used file cards as a means of representation. How, using the cards, could you represent a wall papered with 1,000 Marilyn Monroe images? One option would be to use 1,000 cards each bearing a Marilyn image. Another option would involve just two cards: the first would bear a Marilyn image, and the other would bear an inscription: 'The image on the other card repeated 1,000 times over.' Clearly enough these radically different representational strategies deliver the same message. Of course, if you, a person, were actually using physical file cards you would be acutely aware of the differences between these two modes of representation. You would be aware of both the medium of representation and the message that is represented. You would be aware of the different steps you would need to take to construct and manipulate these representations. Nonetheless, if you were asked to pass on the message, and *just the message*, your report would be the same in both cases.

Now if the 'user' of the representations is not a person at all, but simply part of a mechanism, as in a computer system or a biological brain, then differences in the medium of representation largely drop away. The only feature of such internal representations that will have any impact on the rest of the mechanism is the message. I say 'largely' drop away, because it is possible to investigate the nature of the medium of representation indirectly (*CE*, 354). Again, imagine that you are doing the representing and not your brain. How long would it take you to answer the question: Are there more than 500 Marilyn images on the wall? If you are using the 2-card method, it should take hardly any time at all. On the other hand, if you were using the 1,000-card method, it could take longer. You might have to manually count the cards to make sure there were at least 500. It is this sort of principle that is appealed to when psychologists attempt to work out the media of brain representations. Although the nature of the media is invisible to introspection, we can expect different media to work faster or slower faced with some visual problems, or to fail in different ways. The point is, however, that differences in style of representation do not affect what goes on at the personal level. Whether your brain uses a 2-card or a 1,000-card representational strategy, it is still the case that you see the Marilyn wallpaper at a glance. You make no inferences, undertake no mental processes. You simply see the wallpaper. And so:

> The question of whether the brain "fills in" in one way or another is not a question on which introspection by itself can bear, for . . . introspection provides us – the subject as well as the "outside experimenter" – only with the content of representation, not with the features of the representational medium itself. (*CE*, 353–4)

In a very important sense, then, it does not matter how the brain represents, only what it represents. Your experience is no different if your brain uses a 2-card or a 1,000-card strategy, or something in between, or something else again. Provided they do the same job, these sub-personal factors have no bearing on phenomenological consciousness.

At the sub-personal level we simply have a collection of interconnected parts sending signals to one another. But we, from the outside, can interpret these signals as messages meaning this or that. And we can interpret the parts as systems working to achieve this or that end with respect to the agent's overall goals. For example, we can interpret a sub-personal signal as a message meaning 'there is a wall covered with 1,000 identical Marilyn images'. And so we think of this internal signal as a representation.

But note the difference between this representation and more familiar representations such as pictures and words. There is no witness to this representation. There is nothing inside the head that looks upon this message as a representation. To look at something as a representation is to be in the position of the person with the file cards. That is, it is to be aware of both medium and message. But internal sub-systems are not aware of the medium. They simply respond to the message. Of course, they do not do so by understanding the message. Just as assigning a meaning to the signal is a matter of heuristic labelling, so is assigning the power of understanding the message to a sub-system. Inside the head it is all mechanisms. There is no understanding going on. There are no meanings being recognized. But, for all this, talking as though understanding was going on and as though meanings were being recognized is a brilliant way of understanding how the sub-personal processes underpin the personal level capacities. Indeed, in the case of complex systems it is not clear that any other approach can make that underpinning process intelligible.

The preceding paragraph demonstrates how hard it can be to keep the personal and the sub-personal levels clearly apart. Once we begin the process of heuristic labelling, it is hard to back off. But we need, at least at the level of philosophical theory, to back off from time to time and remember that all this talk is no more than heuristic talk. The parts that make up a conscious agent are not conscious, nor do they understand the meanings we assign to internal signals. Once we are clear about that, it is easy to be clear that different ways of arranging these parts, that achieve the same job, could not have any effect on the nature of an agent's conscious experience.

5.4 Where things stand

I have presented a reconstruction of Dennett's account of consciousness that aims to capture the central elements of his account and cast them into clear relief. According to Dennett the exciting kinds of consciousness can be reduced to the acquisition of intentional states. Agents that are conscious are agents that not only rationally respond to the world and their own states but can also generate a narrative about how they take the world and themselves to be. For example, seeing quite literally is a matter of believing. The beliefs that seeing generates are rich in detail and highly context specific. And, unlike the 'beliefs' of, say, a chess machine or a dog, they are beliefs that we can report. Being able to report them entails that we can rationally reflect upon them, qualify them, and so forth. And in particular we can qualify such beliefs with the expression 'or so it seems to me'. This capacity for reporting, reflecting, and qualifying is not available to agents such as chess machines and dogs. While such agents can be behaviourally aware, they cannot be narratively aware, and hence cannot be conscious in either of the exciting senses.

We have also seen that while narrative awareness initially looks ill-placed to account for experiential consciousness, Dennett has plenty of scope to argue for a strong link. Beliefs strike us as having either no distinctive phenomenology or none appropriate to the different modes of perception. But when we consider the availability or generatability of beliefs in answers to questions that might arise, when we consider the speed and ordering of belief acquisition, and so forth, we can see how beliefs alone can give us a rich account of visual phenomenology. And, in principle at least, it looks as though similar accounts could be developed for other perceptual modes. Finally, we have seen how a sub-personal account is possible and potentially illuminating. That it is possible shows we have no need for supernature. That it is potentially illuminating shows that consciousness is not nearly as mysterious as some would like to make out. And, in examining the role of the sub-personal, we have seen how sub-personal mechanisms are more or less irrelevant to fixing the nature of consciousness. What consciousness is and what consciousness is like is something established at the level of the agent. What is inside the agent, provided it does not operate by miraculous means, does not matter.

This chapter has been unrelentingly positive about the power of Dennett's account to explain consciousness. And, in addition, I have ruthlessly emphasized the features of Dennett's account that I think are most critical to its success and to its compatibility with other aspects of his philosophical work, and have largely ignored any of his remarks that are at odds with my interpretation. In the next chapter I look at some discrepancies between my reconstruction of Dennett's view and the various versions of his view that he has presented in *Content and Consciousness*, *Brainstorms*, *Consciousness Explained*, and elsewhere. I also examine some key sources of scepticism concerning Dennett's view, tracing some of Dennett's responses. Finally, I turn to Dennett's conception of the subject of experience and of self-conscious reflection. For Dennett, being able to generate a narrative effectively introduces a new kind of point of view, what Dennett has called 'the narrative self'. I relate Dennett's account of the self to the concept of the person, and argue, contrary to Dennett's own rhetoric that, in any interesting sense of the terms 'real' and 'fiction', the self is real.

Further reading

Consciousness: is a mystery (Fodor, 1992); is a problem it is logically impossible to solve (Nagel, 1974); is a problem it is logically possible to solve but mere human beings are not up to the task (McGinn, 1989); is a phenomena that lies outside the causal order (Jackson, 1982); can be tackled through neuroscience (Flanagan, 1992). That expression 'what it is like' comes from Nagel (1974), who asked, 'What is it like to be a Bat?' Nagel concluded it *is* like something, but that we cannot know what it is like. Flanagan (1992) provides a useful general survey of philosophical and psychological work on consciousness. Block et al. (1997) is an extensive collection of papers, both old and new, on the topic, and also includes a lengthy introduction.

I develop and defend the terminology 'narrative awareness' and 'behavioural awareness' in my paper 'Consciousness: Only at the Personal Level' (Elton, 2000). The case of the stone in the walker's boot is based on a case discussed in Armstrong and Malcolm's *Consciousness and Causality*. Armstrong and Malcolm each push a different interpretation of the puzzle case (see 15–16, 124ff). The phenomena of 'priming' is discussed in most textbooks on cognitive psychology. Dennett discusses pain at length in 'Why You Can't Make a Computer that Feels Pain' in *Brainstorms* (chapter 11). As in the other papers in *Brainstorms* (see my chapter 6), in that paper Dennett is pessimistic about the cogency of our ordinary concept of 'pain'. It is because the concept is confused, not because computers might lack anything critical, that Dennett concludes we cannot build a computer that feels pain. Post-*Brainstorms* Dennett is more friendly to ordinary concepts, arguing that we undertake gentle deflations rather than give up on them altogether. Were he to rewrite the pain paper today, it might be called, 'Why You Can Make a Computer That Feels Pain, So Long as You Are Prepared to Undertake a Modest Deflation of the Concept of Pain'. Armstrong (for example, Armstrong and Malcolm, 1984; 173) is one notable supporter to the view that 'seeing is believing', although in other respects his views are quite unlike Dennett's. Churchland and Ramachandran (1993) aim to criticize Dennett's account of filling in.

Against them I argue (Elton, 1998) that they simply illustrate how various psychological investigations can tell us about the medium of representation in the brain, without upsetting Dennett's central claim that introspection, and hence consciousness, is blind to the medium.

6

Explaining Consciousness: Developments, Doubts, and the Self

I begin this chapter by looking at some discrepancies between my reconstruction of Dennett's view as outlined in the last chapter and some of Dennett's own remarks. At best Dennett sometimes pays too little attention to critical distinctions, and in particular his own personal/sub-personal distinction. At worst, Dennett exhibits some serious confusion. I then turn to sources of scepticism concerning Dennett's account, sources that claim he does not take seriously enough the special nature of experiential consciousness. Finally, I sketch out Dennett's account of the self, criticizing Dennett's own characterization of the self as a fiction, but defending Dennett's underlying doctrine.

6.1 Developments and discrepancies

Dennett's account of consciousness was first formulated in *Content and Consciousness*. It is developed, not always for the better, in the papers in *Brainstorms*, and then further in a set of less well-known papers. The material in these papers was reworked and combined with new material, not least his collaboration with Marcel Kinsbourne, 'Time and the Observer' (TO), to yield the expansive *Consciousness Explained*. Despite many changes in the style of presentation and in the fine-grained details, one strand of the account has remained remarkably stable. But it is difficult to see this unless the two strands of his account are clearly distinguished, as I am doing here. It is the first strand, the agent level account, that remains stable. And this is what we might expect from what is a philosophically driven analysis. The second strand, Dennett's story of how the sub-personal mechanisms that underpin consciousness are or could be arranged, has changed as he has learned more about, and science and engineering has learned more about, how brains do work and how they could work. And, again, this is what we might expect from an empirically driven analysis.

The distinction between what I have called narrative and behavioural awareness, and a fairly strict adherence to the distinction between the personal and the sub-personal level are easy to find in *Content and Consciousness* (though see below for a caveat). However, these distinctions are harder to recover from *Consciousness Explained* and *Brainstorms*. In this section I show how these distinctions arise in those texts and also examine some of the developments in Dennett's account.

Two kinds of awareness: Consciousness Explained

In *Consciousness Explained* Dennett talks repeatedly about discriminations made in the brain, which he labels 'context-fixations' (*CE*, 365) or just 'contents' (*CE*, 135). He uses the term 'draft' to describe a set of such 'contents' linked together by a common theme:

> While some of the contents in these drafts will make their brief contributions and fade without further effect – and some will make no contribution at all – others will persist to play a variety of roles in the further modulation of internal state and behaviour and a few will even persist to the point of making their presence known through press releases issued in the form of verbal behaviour. (*CE*, 135)

Here Dennett makes it clear that it is only a selection of the available 'contents' or 'drafts' that modulate reporting. At any given time, there are many sets of available drafts or competing interpretations of the world and competing plans for action. The succession of such drafts yields 'something *rather like* a narrative stream' . . . but it is 'only rather like a narrative because of its multiplicity' (*CE*, 135). He goes on: 'Probing this stream at various intervals produces different effects, precipitating different narratives – and these *are* narratives: single versions of a portion of "the stream of consciousness"' (*CE*, 135). A 'probe' is simply a demand for a report, a demand that may be either internal or external. In either case, the results are '*judgements* about how it seems to the subject, judgements the subject himself can then go on to interpret, act upon, remember' (*CE*, 169). The sub-personal process of probing is what underpins narrative awareness. Drafts that do not yield such judgements are drafts that underpin behavioural awareness.

Note that Dennett seems to allow that some drafts will not even contribute to behavioural awareness ('some will make no contribution at all'). This looks like a departure from his strict adherence to only ascribing intentional states (i.e. states with content) on behavioural grounds. In fact, since, as I shall argue below, the 'content' of Dennett's drafts is sub-personal, i.e. no more than a case of intentionalistic labelling, this need not be of concern. States that do not contribute to behaviour on a particular occasion can still be given intentionalistic labels that help us understand their role in the operation of the brain.

Dennett also reveals his ongoing commitment to a distinction between narrative and behavioural awareness in his discussion of heterophenomenology. The heterophenomenological text yields a description of an inner world that is: 'populated with all the images, events, sounds, smells, hunches, presentiments, and feelings that the subject (apparently) *sincerely believes* to exist in his or her (or its) stream of consciousness' (*CE*, 98, *my italics*). And of the text itself Dennett is clear that: '[We] must move beyond the text: we must interpret it as a record of *speech acts*; not mere pronunciations or recitations but assertions, questions, answers, promises, comments, requests for clarification, out-loud musings, self-admonitions' (*CE*, 76).

These comments make clear, I think, that heterophenomenology is concerned with narrative and not behavioural awareness. The text is based on the agent's reports about how she thinks things are with her. It is not derived simply by noticing what discriminations she shows herself able to make in her behaviour. The 'pains' of the sleeper lead her to turn over. This demonstrates that she is behaviourally aware of these 'pains'. But these 'pains' will not feature in her heterophenomenology. Only what she can report features in her heterophenomenology. And this is why, in the last chapter, I insisted that to gather heterophenomenology we had to adopt the personal stance and not merely the intentional stance. The intentional stance does not distinguish between unreported 'pains' during sleep and wholly reportable pains that occur when the subject is awake.

However, while I think this interpretation makes best sense of Dennett's theory, it is at odds with his remarks about non-human animals. Discussing bats he notes that although they cannot talk: 'They can, however, behave in many non-verbal ways that can provide a clear basis for describing their heterophenomenological world. . . . Heterophenomenology without a text is not impossible, just difficult' (*CE*, 446). This is quite at odds with his attitude in *Content and Consciousness* (126–7; 130–1) where he is quite clear that animals lack narrative awareness and hence lack the sort of con- sciousness that generates excitement. Of course, he is also clear there that, on his account, an animal's lack of consciousness does not mean we cannot appeal to intentional states in explaining its actions. That he can appeal to intentional states to explain animal behaviour without having to ascribe the exciting kind of con- sciousness to them is, for Dennett, a key advantage of his theory. In *Consciousness Explained* Dennett fudges the issue. He thinks, in keeping with his general approach, that suffering – and, after all any notion of 'pain' that is not linked to suffering is, surely, not a notion worth caring about – involves a great deal of cognitive sophistication:

> Suffering is not a matter of being visited by some ineffable but intrin- sically awful state, but of having one's life hopes, life plans, life pro- jects blighted by circumstances imposed on one's desires, thwarting one's intentions. . . . [The] capacity to suffer is a function of the cap- acity to have articulated, wide-ranging, highly discriminative de- sires, expectations, and other sophisticated mental states. (*CE*, 449)

And yet he is also able to write: 'Many, but not all, animals are capable of significant degrees of suffering' (*CE*, 451). If we combine this remark with the relevant part of the earlier passage we have Dennett saying:

> Many, but not all, animals [enjoy the] capacity to have articulated, wide-ranging, highly discriminative desires, expectations, and other sophisticated mental states.

If 'sophisticated mental states' are supposed to be self-conscious states, or states of narrative awareness, and it is not clear what else they might be, then Dennett has got himself into trouble. For he pre- sents us with no reason to think that the language-less are gener- ally capable of such sophistication. But, without language, it is not obvious how an agent can think about past and future, can think about her projects and plans, can tell a story of her own life to herself. This is not to say it is impossible; the issue is controversial. But Dennett's own view seems to be that very few non-human animals have any great sophistication here. They do not because, according to Dennett, that kind of sophistication comes only with culture (see chapter 7, and also *CE*, chapter 7; *DDI*, chapter 12).

And so we would expect Dennett's views would lead him to say that animals do not suffer, and hence do not feel pain in any interesting sense of the term pain. And yet he persistently shies away from any such conclusion. I suspect he does so because he thinks the conclusion might licence, or might lead some to think that it does licence, arbitrary treatment of animals. But, as Dennett himself points out, there are many other ways of arguing for kindly treatment to animals (*CE*, 452–3). We do not need to think that animals suffer, or, more carefully, are aware of the thwarting of their interests, to think that harming them in various ways is morally suspect.

Two kinds of awareness: Brainstorms

Does something like the distinction between narrative and behavioural awareness occur in *Brainstorms*? In 'Towards a Cognitive Theory of Consciousness', for a long time Dennett's flagship consciousness paper, Dennett draws this distinction by reference to whether or not we have 'personal access' to processes that 'happen in me and to me' (TCTC, 150). 'Personal access' corresponds to narrative awareness. And, though it receives relatively little emphasis, he is careful to note that, as well as the information that we do have personal access to, 'perceptual analysis provides information about the world that is utilised in the control of behaviour but is not accessible to introspection or consciousness, on any familiar understanding of these terms' (TCTC, 169), i.e., he is careful to acknowledge what I have been calling behavioural awareness.

It is worth noting that in 'Towards a Cognitive Theory of Consciousness', and the other papers in *Brainstorms*, Dennett makes no attempt to fix on particular senses of terms such as experience, consciousness, pain, and so forth. He tells us that:

> A plausible theory of experience will be one that does justice to three distinguishable families of intuitions we have about experience and consciousness: those dealing with the role of experience in guiding current behaviour [my behavioural awareness – ME], those dealing with our *current* proclivities and capacities to *say* what we are

experiencing [my narrative awareness – ME], and those dealing with
the *retrospective* or *recollective* capacity to say [again my narrative
awareness – ME] . . . A theory that does justice to these distinct and
often inharmonious demands must also do justice to a fourth: the
functional saliencies that emerge from empirical investigation. ('Are
Dreams Experiences?' *BS*, 147–8)

Dennett notes that nothing may meet all four conditions. That
might lead us to abandon the concept of experience altogether. This
is an occasion where something like an eliminativist streak shows
through in Dennett's work. But on other occasions, and it is from
those that I have taken my cue in describing Dennett's position, he
wants to hang on to reformed versions of ordinary concepts – ones
that have had all infection by bad philosophical theory removed. In
the case of experience, this requires us to distinguish between narrative and behavioural awareness, and then to recognize that
nothing of what we care about is left out. However, I have been
aggressively clear that these notions do not have to do justice to
Dennett's fourth condition in the quote just given, namely, that they
tally well with the 'functional saliencies that emerge from empirical investigation'. In contrast to both earlier and later work, when
discussing experience in *Brainstorms*, Dennett tries to meet both
common-sense constraints and to respect functional saliencies. But
if his account of intentionality is right, and Dennett if anyone will
think that it is, then it should be no surprise to him that both constraints cannot be met.

Time and the observer

Perhaps the most striking development in Dennett's account of consciousness is his claim about locating conscious experiences in time.
He first introduces this theme in 'Are Dreams Experiences?' (*BS*
chapter 8). When we report a dream, we subjectively locate the time
of experience in the past, during the time while we were asleep. In
fact, as Dennett is aware, describing it this way may sound like an
insult. For we want to say that it is not just that I report having had
my dream during the time I was asleep, I actually experienced it
while I was asleep. This is the 'received view' of dreaming: dreaming is a matter of having experiences during the time you are asleep,
some of which you can recall on waking.

Norman Malcolm has provocatively challenged this claim, arguing that dreams, far from being experiences, are simply dispositions to tell a story when awake. Dennett shows a great deal of sympathy for Malcolm, but in 'Are Dreams Experiences?' he does not take quite such a hard line. He does not because, during this period, he is tempted by the idea that we can have a concept of experience that does meet the four constraints of guiding behaviour, generating reports, laying down memory, *and* respecting the 'functional saliencies that emerge from empirical investigation' (*BS*, 148). So, in this paper, he thinks that when we claim to have experiences while asleep we are supposing – tacitly, of course – that 'having an experience' is a concept that has some sub-personal criterion, and, as such, empirical investigation could confirm or refute the hypothesis that we have the experiences when we seem to have them. Moreover he is open to the idea, though not irrevocably committed to it, that this could be the right way to understand our ordinary concept of experience. If it is, then whether dreams are experiences or not would be an empirical issue. As we have just noted, Dennett normally steers away from such a view in favour of a concept of experience rooted in the first three constraints but not in the fourth.

He does so because on the whole – though less so in *Brainstorms* than elsewhere – he wants to allow that introspection is the ultimate arbiter of what is in consciousness. Of course, sometimes our introspective reports come with excess baggage: that is, our reports are conditioned by 'theories' (TCTC, 166) we have about what experience could be. We 'mistake theorising for observing' (*CE*, 94) and hence are inclined to insist that dreams must actually have been experienced while we were asleep or that we really manipulate mental images in our minds or that we really have complete information about the Marilyn Monroe wallpapered wall at an instant. In the dream case, it is not a datum that dreams are experiences we have while asleep. The datum is that dreams seem to have been experienced while we were asleep. His method of heterophenomenology makes this clear: what we need to explain is not the nature of the items in our heterophenomenological realm, but the production of a text which is about the items. Or, put another way, what we have to explain is not the supposed fact that there are things within our minds – or even in our brains – that correspond to experiences, but the uncontroversial fact that things seem to us like that.

Introspection or heterophenomenology cannot tell us when the sub-personal processes take place that account for our capacity to 'recall' our 'dream experiences' when we wake. Dennett advances this point by asking us to imagine what, according to the 'received view', technologically advanced dream scientists should be able to achieve:

> We can even imagine that they will be able to obliterate the "veridical" dream memory and substitute for it an undreamed narrative. This eventuality would produce a strange result indeed. Our dreamer would wake up and report her dream, only to be assured by the researcher that she never dreamed *that* dream, but rather another, which they proceed to relate to her. (*BS*, 134)

The point is that for all the confidence we have in our judgements about how things seem to us, these judgements may have, as a causal basis, either a 'veridical dream memory' or an artificial insertion. According to the received view the former was something genuinely experienced by the subject, but now forgotten, and the latter is something that was never experienced. But we cannot, by introspection, tell one from the other. If Dennett persuades us of this, he has paved the way for his more radical point, namely, that there is never any need for an 'inner presentation' of the dream prior to our waking recall. We cannot distinguish between cases where, on the received view, there has been an 'inner presentation' and cases where there has not. So what is the presentation process supposed to add? Indeed, what reason have we to believe that there is any such presentation process? Dennett thinks he has shown us that the fact that it seems to us that the dream has been presented is not a reason to think that some presentation process has occurred. The causal basis for experience – that is what underpins experience at the sub-personal level – needs only to establish a memory trace that is later used to produce a report. There is no need for the addition of any kind of presentation process, for any kind of playing out in the Cartesian Theatre.

In *Consciousness Explained* (and TO) Dennett develops the point made in the dreaming paper in a different context. Looking at short intervals of time, he examines the connection between the experiences that we report – which are items described by our heterophenomenological text – and the causal processes that underpin our successful perception and action. It seems to us that our experiences are inner states that are the causal intermediaries between perception and action. But, as Dennett is at pains to emphasize, how things seem to us give us no insight into our sub-personal workings. The attempt to identify episodes described by our heterophenomenological text with distinct sub-personal episodes runs into a whole host of problems (*CE*, 459; *CC*, chapter 1).

Let me try to make this issue clearer. Suppose a red light is flashed up on a display. We see the light. There is an episode that we can report; there is a feature that is described in our heterophenomenological text, the experience of a red light, or, more cautiously, seeming to see a red light. There is an episode that is a projection of the text, in just the same way that Sherlock Holmes is a projection of Conan Doyle's texts (*CE*, 79–81). Call this the 'projected episode'. Dennett typically describes such items as fictions not projections (though see *CE*, 127–32), but, as with his other uses of the term 'fiction', I find this distracting and misleading. There is also a sub-personal process that causes the production of a text which features the description of the projected episode. (Dennett does not use the term 'sub-personal' in *CE* or TO. I am imposing that terminology.) Call this the 'sub-personal episode'. The issue at hand, then, is the relationship between the projected episode and the sub-personal episode. Dennett's contention, as I am glossing it, is that serious problems arise if we attempt to identify the projected episode with the sub-personal episode.

The first problem is that where short intervals are concerned the sub-personal episode may not occur at the same time as the time at which the projected episode seems to occur. It may seem to you that you saw the red light at *t*1. But the sub-personal episode that underpins the production of heterophenomenological text from which we learn about the projected episode may have occurred at *t*0 (earlier) or *t*2 (later).

The second problem is that there may be a whole host of content-fixations taking place during a given interval. Which content-fixations influence reporting is settled only as a result of a probe. So until and unless a probe is made, there may be no clear fact of the matter as to what the projected episode actually is. Moreover, probing at different times may yield quite different projected episodes.

We can illustrate these two problems by looking at one of the many cases Dennett presents (in both *CE* and TO), the 'cutaneous rabbit':

The subject's arm rests cushioned on a table, and mechanical tappers are placed at two or three locations along the arm, up to a foot apart. A series of taps in rhythm are delivered by the tappers, e.g. five at the wrist followed by two near the elbow and then three more on the upper arm. . . . The astonishing effect is that the taps seem to the subjects to travel in regular sequence over equidistant points up the arm – as if a little animal were hopping along the arm. Now at first, one feels like asking *how did the brain know* that after five taps on the wrist, there were going to be some taps near the elbow? The subjects experience the "departure" of the taps from the wrist beginning with the second tap, yet in catch trials in which the later elbow taps were never delivered, subjects feel five wrist taps at the wrist in the expected manner. (CE, 143)

Dennett shows how we could preserve the identity of the projected episode and the sub-personal episode in two different ways (CE, 115–26; TO). The Orwellian theory allows that we really did experience 'five taps at the wrist' but our memory of this was wiped as information about the later taps came to the fore. Now when we think back to our experience, we have a false memory, a memory of having experienced a sequence of taps moving regularly up our arm. This is akin to the rewriting of history that Winston Smith undertakes in Orwell's *1984*. The Stalinesque theory requires no slurring of our capacity to remember, but does involve 'show trials'. Here the sub-personal episode is just there to generate a 'real experience', a show trial, a short time after the actual events. This is what we report and what we remember. Of course, this does mean that consciousness lags behind action somewhat, but since we can unconsciously respond to events before the 'show trial' takes place, this is not noticeable (CE, 122). But Dennett thinks that the distinction between the Orwellian and Stalinesque theories is bogus and he applies his method of de-differencing (see chapter 2). Both theories appeal to the idea of an inner fact, a fact about what is really experienced, that somehow gets to the truth where introspection or heterophenomenology cannot. But according to Dennett no sub-personal fact could play this role, could make the difference between something being conscious or not. That difference is a difference at the personal and not at the sub-personal level.

The Orwellian theory assumes that, say, after five taps on the wrist there must be an experience of five taps on the wrist. Indeed, it assumes more. It assumes that after every tap we must have an experience of that tap. But these assumptions are false. And they are false because they make claims about very small time intervals, time intervals about which our introspective judgement has no authority. And, more fundamentally, about which there are no introspective judgements made at all. The Stalinesque theory rejects the possibility of systematic mis-remembering and so insists that there cannot have been consciousness of the five taps while they were still in progress, or indeed of all ten taps. Rather, once the brain has gathered all its information, an inner experience is generated. This is an experience that makes good sense of all the information, and it is one that is reliably remembered.

For Dennett, there simply need be no fact about what is and what is not conscious until a probe occurs. If the probe occurs after five taps and before any other taps, then the heterophenomenology will yield a projected episode of five taps on the wrist. If the probe occurs after all ten taps, then the projected episode will be of taps hopping along the arm. Dennett argues for this point by showing that there are no means, introspective or otherwise, of distinguishing the Orwellian from the Stalinesque strategy, just as there are no means of telling whether dreams are presented to us while asleep or only seem to have been presented to us while asleep.

In fact, although Dennett does not make it himself, there is another powerful argument available to him. As Dennett does elsewhere, we can press the point that we are made of mechanistic bits and pieces, and, because they take time to do their work, it just must be the case that there are points in time when there is no fact of the matter as to what we are conscious of.

Consider the following analogy. We enter a sum into a pocket calculator, such as '12 × 9'. At $t0$ we press the '=' key. At $t2$, a fraction of a second later, the answer '108' flashes up on the screen. But we know that between $t0$ and $t2$ the calculator has undertaken hundreds if not thousands of internal steps. Now suppose we pressed the question of what the calculator 'thought' the answer to the sum was at $t1$, some time after $t0$ but before $t2$. Clearly, there is just no answer to this question. Nor is it mysterious that there is no answer to the question. For practical purposes, there is always a determinate answer to what the calculator thinks the answer to a sum is. But that is because we only 'probe' the calculator for an answer when it is good and ready.

In the same way, Dennett thinks that until a heterophenomenological text is generated, there is no fact of the matter as to what is conscious. What is interesting about us, and one of the factors that makes us different from the calculator, is that we can be probed earlier or later. When a probe takes place a particular narrative is 'precipitated' (*CE*, 135 and 169). That is, some determinate answer to how the subject takes things to be is given. There is a good evolutionary reason for this; sometimes we have to act quickly and act on the best information we have gathered to date. This means that initially puzzling cases, such as the cutaneous rabbit, can occur. These cases are not particularly important in themselves, although it is clearly a virtue of Dennett's theory that he can accommodate them. What is important about them is that they can be used to show that there is no scope for an identity between projected episodes and sub-personal episodes, any more than, in Dennett's view, there is scope for an identity between intentional states and sub-personal states.

Dennett's overall message is that:

> Certain sorts of questions one might think it is appropriate to ask about [conscious experiences] have no answers, because these questions presuppose inappropriate – unmotivatable – temporal and spatial boundaries that are more fine-grained than the phenomena admit. (*BC*, 135)

Just as we cannot keep refining our account of what someone believes and desires beyond a certain point, so we cannot keep refining our account of what someone experiences. And the level of temporal and spatial refinement that is appropriate to sub-personal processes is inevitably finer-grained than the level of refinement for personal level processes. Sub-personal processes can be located within specific regions of the brain, and very many processes can take place in a fraction of second. Personal processes cannot be located more precisely than the rough region of the head, if that, and typically take whole fractions of a second to complete.

The personal/sub-personal distinction

My reading of Dennett's position has been constrained by a strict adherence to Dennett's distinction between the personal and the sub-personal levels. Unfortunately, Dennett himself is rarely as sensitive to his own distinction as I might like. Nonetheless, despite many explicit remarks that are at odds with strict adherence to his distinction, Dennett's key arguments invariably respect it, and often turn on respecting it. And it is for this reason that I place it at the heart of my interpretation.

In defining the two kinds of awareness in *Content and Consciousness* he writes:

> (1) A is aware$_1$ [narratively aware] that p at time t if and only if p is the content of the input state of A's 'speech centre' at time t
>
> (2) A is aware$_2$ [behaviourally aware] that p at time t if and only if p is the content of an internal event in A at time t that is effective in directing current behaviour. (118–19)

These two definitions mix the personal and the sub-personal levels. And indeed, Dennett explicitly acknowledges this, saying that he is providing sub-personal criteria for a personal level concept. He remarks that this 'may seem like an admission of madness, but there is no alternative method of analysis in this case' (CC, 119). As we have seen, I think Dennett is quite wrong about this. The whole thrust of Dennett's account of agency is that we do not need and could not reasonably require a sub-personal criteria for the application of any personal or agent level term. So it is odd to see a mixing up of levels here. And, indeed, such a mixing up of levels threatens to undermine Dennett's whole approach. But by keeping the two strands apart, we can avoid this problem and, at the same time, not give up on anything that is important to Dennett. We simply recast the definitions wholly within agent level vocabulary and then add a separate sub-personal commentary. The two definitions, recast at the agent level, will read something like this:

(1) A is narratively aware that p around about time t if and only if the belief that p is effective in directing her current (or, with caveats, future) reporting of how things are with her at around about time t^1

(2) A is behaviourally aware that p around about time t if and only if the belief that p at time t is effective in directing current (or future) behaviour.

These new definitions, I contend, capture what Dennett needs, but without introducing any explicit sub-personal criteria. Moreover, these two definitions are independent of any of the sub-personal variants that Dennett has offered. They fit just as well with the 'speech centre' of *Content and Consciousness*, with the 'memory buffer' of 'Towards a Cognitive Theory of Consciousness', and with the competing collections of content-fixations that make up the multiple-drafts model of *Consciousness Explained*. Consider, for example, two different sub-personal commentaries on narrative awareness:

> *Content and Consciousness:* Instances of narrative awareness are underpinned by a flow of sub-personal signals (which, in the light of the agent's capacity as a whole are assigned various meanings) into the sub-personal module called the speech centre (so called in light of its critical role in underpinning the agent's capacity for speech).

> *Consciousness Explained:* The capacity for narrative awareness is underpinned by a collection of sub-personal signals (which, in the light of the agent's capacity as a whole are assigned various meanings), also referred to as content-fixations, actually having an influence on the control of the sub-personal mechanisms that underpin reporting and/or underpin the construction of an auto-biographical narrative.

Fame and multiple drafts

The later Dennett gives us a picture of lots of sub-personal contents washing about in the brain. This image occurs, for example, when he is talking about the multiple-drafts model of consciousness. The key idea in that model is that there are always many different 'drafts' or provisional 'takings that' that the brain keeps active at any one time. Only a selection of these multiple drafts gets to influence our reporting behaviour and hence gets to count as conscious or, more carefully, gets to contribute to narrative awareness. Some drafts never get to influence anything very much, and do not even contribute to behavioural awareness. And, finally, some drafts contribute to behavioural awareness but not to narrative awareness. One of the important ideas behind the multiple-drafts model is that it allows us to make sense of the subtle ways in which control and report can come apart. On any given occasion, the draft that contributes to control may be a different draft from that which contributes to consciousness.

In work after *Consciousness Explained* he suggests that what makes some content-fixations contribute to consciousness and others not, is closely akin to the phenomenon of fame (*BC*, chapter 7; Dennett, 2001): 'Consciousness is cerebral celebrity – nothing more and nothing less. Those contents are conscious that persevere, that monopolise resources for long enough to achieve certain typical and "symptomatic" effects – on memory, on the control of behaviour, and so forth' (*BC*, 137).

Dennett asks us to consider Andy Warhol's imagined future where everyone is famous for fifteen minutes. This future, he argues, makes no sense. Someone might be on TV for fifteen minutes, and seen by millions, but that in itself would not make them famous. To be famous requires that you stick in people's minds for a while. Similarly, for Dennett, 'being an item of consciousness is *not at all* like being on television'. Whereas a TV appearance is an episode that has a precise beginning and an end, and one that can take place whether or not it is remembered by anyone, whether or not it leaves any lasting impact, fame is not like this at all. 'Instantaneous fame is a disguised contradiction in terms, and it follows from my proposed conception of what consciousness is that an instantaneous flicker of consciousness is also an incoherent notion' (*BC*, 138).

Dennett's fame analogy is helpful for explaining the claims he develops in *Consciousness Explained* (and TO). That is, it helps explain his insistence that for all that it feels as though conscious experience occurs at a precise time and place, its actual occurrence is spread out in time and spread out across the brain. However, in promoting the fame analogy Dennett sometimes seems to suggest that what matters for consciousness is simply the degree of influence content-fixations have. (This occurs in *BC*, chapter 7, in his reply to Block (Block, 1995, 252–3), and also in *KM*, 155.) On my interpretation this will not do. A content-fixation might have a great deal of influence on behaviour, for example, it might influence us to turn over in our sleep. As such it might be regarded as famous. But it will not contribute to consciousness unless it modulates the behaviour that is the source of the heterophenomenological text. It is not just fame, then, understood as degree of influence. Content-fixations must be famous in the right way to be conscious. Their influence must extend to those parts of the brain that causally underpin reporting as well as control of behaviour.

6.2   The sceptic's case

A number of Dennett's critics argue that although he may have accounted for what we say or think about consciousness, consciousness itself has been sidelined or ignored. For the sceptic there are further facts concerning consciousness that remain unfixed by all the considerations that Dennett has offered. The idea that there might be such further facts is typically supported by a range of thought experiments. I shall briefly review some of the sources of scepticism and comment on Dennett's responses. Then I turn to what I think is the deepest response that can be made to this kind of scepticism, a response that cuts across a wide range of differences in sceptical views.

Sceptical sources

Let us begin, however, with the sources. Consider first the scenario known as spectrum inversion. We are asked to suppose that when Ruth looks at the grass the experience she has of its colour is the same experience Jane has when she looks at a clear summer sky. The way green looks to Ruth, then, is the way blue looks to Jane. And, we may suppose, vice versa. But of course that is how things have always been for Ruth and Jane. Ruth calls the grass green all right, it is just that her experience of it is different from Jane's. And Jane also calls the grass green, but her experience of it is different from Ruth's. Surely, Dennett's critics urge, this is possible? And yet the possibility is ruled out by Dennett's account. After all, if our experience is no more than what we say or think about how the world appears to us, then since Ruth and Jane say the same things, they must, on Dennett's story, have the same experience. But the fact that we can readily imagine the spectrum inversion case shows, the critics press, that Dennett has missed something out of his account.

A similar scenario involves what have come to be known as 'philosophical zombies'. Imagine two agents – or what appear to be agents – that are behaviourally indistinguishable. Call them Gilbert and George. Both negotiate their environments smoothly and can make fluent and detailed comments about colours, sounds, tastes, and touches. But Gilbert, we are asked to believe, lacks experiential consciousness. Of course, we will want some reason to believe this. There must be some difference between Gilbert and George that leads to Gilbert's lack. The range of differences offered to us is wide ranging. Sometimes we are told that Gilbert's brain is made out of silicon chips instead of biological neurons. Sometimes Gilbert's brain is just organized in a slightly different way: he has, as it were, a different program inside, albeit one that achieves the same end result on the outside. More radically, Gilbert sometimes lives in a different sort of universe from George, one in which the very same physical set of facts give rise to different non-physical facts. Again,

Dennett's critics urge, this is surely possible. And again the possibility is ruled out by Dennett's account. If we apply the method of heterophenomenology to Gilbert we shall turn up just the same sort of result as we would with George. And on Dennett's account that means that Gilbert's conscious experience is as rich and interesting as George's. But the fact that we can readily imagine that Gilbert is a philosophical zombie shows, the critics press, that Dennett has missed something out of his account.

Of course, both of these scenarios appeal directly to our intuitions about what is possible. Frank Jackson, in a much cited series of papers, attempts to provide some reasoned support for these sorts of intuitions. Jackson asks us to imagine a scientist, Mary, who has never seen any colours. She is confined to a black-and-white room, there are no mirrors, she is made to wear black-and-white gloves, and so forth. But Mary is an expert on the brain and in particular the mechanisms of colour vision. Indeed, we are asked to suppose that she knows all the physical facts there are to know about colour and the brain. But for all that she knows these facts, Jackson argues, she still does not know what it is like to see red. If she leaves the black-and-white room and encounters red objects she will learn something new. She will learn what it is like to see the colour red. Jackson's point is that all the physical facts there were failed to give Mary insight into what it was like to see red. And so he concludes that what it is like to see red is not a physical fact.

Curiously, in *Consciousness Explained* Dennett suggests that perhaps Mary really could know what it was like to see red before she was released from the room. He suggests that when we think through what it would be to know all the physical facts, this outcome does not seem so unlikely (*CE*, 398–400). This strikes me as implausible. I do not see how, even if given all the facts, Mary can guarantee getting herself into the position that she would need to be in to find out what it is like to see red. Knowing everything that is said in *War and Peace* does not mean that I am in a position to know what it is like to read the book for the first time at the age of twenty-one, having never before encountered Russian fiction. And a similar problem may beset Mary. If so, Dennett is just wrong to think that we underestimate what Mary could know from within the room. But, in any case, Dennett does not need to make this move in order to fend off Jackson's argument, as we shall see in a moment.

Ned Block also tries to argue a case rather than simply presenting raw intuitions, but he adopts a different strategy from Jackson. He invites us to endorse a distinction between two kinds of consciousness. The first he calls phenomenal consciousness. Phenomenal consciousness is what I have been calling here experiential consciousness: it is concerned with what the experience is like, with what Mary the brain-and-colour expert lacks knowledge of before she leaves the room, what the zombie Gilbert lacks, and the respect in which Ruth and Jane differ. The second kind of consciousness he calls access consciousness. Access consciousness is concerned with the capacity for intentional states to exert rational control of speech or action. This notion of access consciousness covers the ground jointly covered by Dennett's narrative and behavioural awareness. But the difference that Dennett wants to make much of, between what is reportable and what merely exerts control, is not especially marked by Block.

Using Block's terminology, we can readily express Dennett's view. Dennett thinks that phenomenal consciousness is simply a sub-species of access consciousness. Phenomenal consciousness is narrative awareness as applied to perception. But Block wants to argue that access consciousness and phenomenal consciousness must be logically distinct. To this end he attempts to show that there are cases where there is access consciousness but not phenomenal consciousness and phenomenal consciousness without access consciousness. He tries to show that we can have phenomenal consciousness without access consciousness by appealing to a species of example we have already discussed. When people turn in their sleep, or while the conversing walker fails to notice the pain caused by the stone in her boot, Block thinks we have phenomenal consciousness without access consciousness. His own example involves 'hearing' without being aware of hearing a pneumatic drill that has been working for some time (Block, 1995, 386–7; cf. Dennett's clock-ticking example, *CE*, 137–8). If this is right then phenomenal consciousness cannot be a sub-species of access consciousness, because we can have phenomenal consciousness with respect to something in the absence of any access consciousness with respect to the same thing.

Showing access consciousness in the absence of phenomenal consciousness is a little more complex. Block begins with a genuine and puzzling brain pathology: blindsight (*CE*, 321–33). This is a condition where a person's visual system is damaged. The result is that she cannot recognize objects that appear in a certain region of her visual field. What is puzzling about blindsight is that if encouraged to guess what they themselves say they cannot see, blindsight subjects do much better than chance. Somehow the information is getting through, and can have an influence on guesses. But, the subjects report, they have no experience of objects in the damaged region. Dennett's take on this must be that there is some behavioural awareness, but a lack of narrative awareness. The behavioural awareness is what influences the guesses.

It is a striking and important feature of blindsight that subjects do not make spontaneous judgements about the blind region of their visual field. They have to be forced to guess. Block asks us to imagine what he calls 'superblindsight':

> [Suppose] – contrary to fact apparently – that a blindsight patient could be trained to prompt himself at will, guessing what is in the blind field without being told to guess. The superblindsighter spontaneously says, "Now I know there is a horizontal line in my visual field even though I don't actually see it." Visual information simply pops into his thoughts in the way that solutions to problems we've been worrying about pop into our thoughts, or in the way some people just know the time or which way is North without having any perceptual experience of it. (Block, 1995, 233; cf. *CE*, 328–33)

Whether or not superblindsight is a condition that could actually occur in our brains, Block urges us to agree that it is a logically coherent scenario. If it is, then there can be an absence of phenomenal consciousness even though access consciousness is unimpaired. And so it would seem that phenomenal consciousness just cannot be a sub-species of access consciousness. For we have a case where the access consciousness appears to be fully present, and yet there is no accompanying phenomenal consciousness.

Dennett's responses

Dennett has to take a tough line with these various sources of scepticism (*BC*, chapter 10). For him they depend on assumptions about consciousness that do not stand up to scrutiny. His first response, then, to spectrum inversion and philosophical zombies is simply to deny that they are coherent possibilities. That we can imagine them carries little weight with Dennett. He urges us to work our imaginations harder and hence come to see that these scenarios do not really make sense.

In the case of Jackson's argument we have seen that he actually challenges one of the claims, namely that Mary will learn something new when she leaves the room. But we can accept that claim and still find the argument wanting. If successful, what the argument shows is that knowing all the physical facts does not entail knowing what it is like to have certain experiences. But this could be true without it being the case that experience is somehow independent of the physical facts or facts about intentional states. First of all, it could be true simply because finding out what it is like to have certain experiences can be very difficult or even impossible. How would I set about finding out what it is like to read *War and Peace* for the first time at twenty-one, never having read Russian fiction before? Having read Dostoyevsky at nineteen and being over thirty make this task impossible for me. But this does not generate some great mystery. Dennett makes the same point by asking us to imagine what it would be like to be a 'Leipzig Lutheran churchgoer in, say 1720, hearing one of J. S. Bach's chorale cantatas in its premier performance' (*CE*, 387). He notes that:

> If we want to imagine what it was like to be a Leipzig Bach-hearer, it is not enough for us to hear the same tones on the same instruments in the same order; we must also prepare ourselves somehow to respond to those tones with the same heartaches, thrills, and waves of nostalgia. (*CE*, 387)

Second, fixing all the physical facts does fix (more or less – Dennett will allow for some indeterminacy) the results that the heterophenomenological method will yield. We can, then, work out everything that the person will think and say about her experience, even if we are not in a position to have it ourselves. And, on Dennett's account, knowing what a person thinks and says about her experience is knowing all there is to know about that experience. Again, talking about the Bach case, he notes that:

> we can carefully list the difference between our dispositions and knowledge and theirs, and by comparing the lists, come to appreciate in whatever detail we want, the differences between what it was like to be them listening to Bach, and what it is like to be us. . . . There would be no mystery left over; just an experience that could be described quite accurately, but not directly enjoyed. (*CE*, 388)

And yet, on Jackson's account it is supposed to be possible for the nature of experience to somehow be free to vary even once all the physical facts are fixed, even once all the facts about intentional states are fixed. And this, of course, is just the contention that the spectrum inversion and philosophical zombie cases represent. In both those cases something is kept constant, usually the behavioural profile of the agent rather than the physical composition, while it is insisted that something else, the nature of experiential consciousness, can vary. But this contention is deeply problematic. It requires us to make sense of a difference in experience in the absence of a difference in behavioural profile. And, according to Dennett, this just does not make any sense. With only one caveat, I think Dennett is completely right about this.

A deeper response

Dennett, in effect, applies his de-differencing strategy to attack the sceptic (see chapter 2). The sceptic is convinced that the nature of conscious experience can vary independently of the agent's behavioural profile. So she needs to point to some difference or some factor that fixes the nature of conscious experience while the behavioural profile remains fixed. But any candidate difference that is offered can, Dennett thinks, be found wanting. Either the difference cannot do the job or the difference can only do the job by appealing to supernature. So, if Dennett is convincing, we end up agreeing that the supposed difference was spurious all along and, hence, that the sceptic's position does not make sense.

We can see the de-differencing strategy at work in an extended discussion of a case with the same structure as the spectrum inversion. In a 1988 paper (QQ) Dennett tells the story of Mr Chase and Mr Sanborn. Both men work as coffee-tasters and both say that while they used to enjoy their jobs, they are now dissatisfied. They no longer enjoy the flavour of the coffee they taste. It is agreed that the coffee has not changed: the changes lies with Mr Chase and Mr Sanborn. Chase's explanation is that although the coffee tastes just the same to him as it always did, he no longer likes that very flavour. Sanborn's explanation is that although his aesthetic preferences are just the same, his perceptual equipment, his 'flavour analysis unit', has altered. When Sanborn drinks coffee, he says, the experience he has is a different one from the experience he used to have.

Mr Chase and Mr Sanborn are sincere and the story invites us to take what they say at face value. What Chase and Sanborn claim is that by introspection they can tell what has happened to them, they can tell, that is, the difference between having the same attitudes but different experiences as opposed to different attitudes but the same experiences. Dennett denies that introspection can tell the difference between these two stories. The apparent difference in their experiences that Chase and Sanborn draw attention to is, Dennett suggests, no difference at all. And so to the extent that the thought experiment suggests there are genuinely two options here, it is bogus. Why?

The answer is that nothing that counts in favour of Chase's theory could count against Sanborn's, and nothing that counts in favour of Sanborn's could count against Chase's.[2] Of course, Chase and Sanborn want to insist that there is a fact here, regardless of the evidence that can be gathered from the third-person point of view. They want to insist that there is an experiential difference between one story and the other. But, what could explain such an experiential difference? A dualist would allow some supernatural difference between the two cases. But, setting that aside, the experiential difference must be backed by some sort of material difference. Does this present a problem? Surely Chase and Sanborn can argue that their difference in experience follows from differences in the way in which their brains, their sub-personal machinery, have changed. Over time, for example, Chase's preference unit has altered whereas for Sanborn it is his flavour analysis unit that has changed.

This is the critical step. *The intelligibility of the thought experiment appeals to the intelligibility of there being a sub-personal difference that underpins the experiential difference.* Now, if one does not look closely at how sub-personal theory can be constructed, then the thought experiment will receive no resistance. But if, as Dennett does, we think very hard about how sub-personal mechanisms could and could not operate, we quickly see that something has gone badly wrong.

To diagnose what has gone wrong we need to look at the role of the intentionalistic labels we apply to sub-personal components, labels such as 'preference unit' or 'flavour analysis unit'. There is no agent that takes up the output of the 'flavour analysis unit' and compares it with stored memories in the 'preference unit' (cf. my discussion of representation in chapter 5, pp. 163–5). Were there such an agent, the difference that Chase and Sanborn try to establish would make sense. It would, because such an agent could, for example, remember how the outputs of the 'flavour analysis unit' used to look and notice the difference. Imagine the output, when Sanborn was tasting coffee, takes the form of a coded number, say, the number 617. But Sanborn's 'flavour analysis unit' is wearing out and now, for the same input, it outputs the number 412. If, inside

Sanborn's head, there were an agent connected to the output of the 'flavour analysis unit' she could reflect on this difference. But there is no such agent. The whole point of the sub-personal story is to tell a story about the components that make up an agent, and not to reintroduce the agent, reintroduce the entity that has the experiences, on the inside. I suppose that in principle there *could* be something like an inner agent in the brain. But this does not affect the basic thrust of Dennett's position. For we simply rerun the same argument again, this time targeting the inner agent. Something must stop the regress. Dennett urges we might as well stop it at the first step (cf. TO, 185).

Of course, if just one sub-personal component changes its output, from 617 to 412, it will make a difference to the agent of which the component is a part. But if, 'further down stream', the sub-personal components that make use of that output are also changed so that they now respond to 412 in the way they used to respond to 617, then the change cannot make any difference. If we imagine that the 'preference unit' is the only one that responds to the output of the 'flavour analysis unit', and if the preference unit now responds to 412 as it used to respond to 617, then the change has no scope to have any effect on experience. All that has happened here is that one realization of a functional system has been replaced by another realization of the very same functional system. No one and no thing inside is sensitive to the change in the coding of the signal that 'means' coffee-of-this-sort.

Neuroscientists or cognitive psychologists may prefer one way of carving up the sub-personal processes to another (cf. QQ, 630). And one way might yield something that plays the role of a central system, the reporting unit, the biographer-maker, or whatever. But although that way of carving things up might be based on sound theoretical motivations, it can provide no basis for reforming our understanding of the idea of experiential consciousness. The only reason any sub-system earns the right to have a label such as 'visual system', a 'flavour analysis unit', or a 'central executive' is because it is a component part of an agent that can see or can taste or integrate a variety of perceptual and cognitive information. It is not, then, as though sub-systems do some seeing, some tasting, or some thinking, and then pass the results on to the person. Change the surrounding context in which the 'visual system', 'the taste analyser', or the 'central executive' works, and it will no longer warrant the label. For after all it is the person and not her assembled parts that sees or tastes and thinks.

We are now in a much better position to see why Dennett must take a hard line on zombies and spectrum inversion cases. Indeed, although he sometimes compares his denial of the existence of zombies and spectrum inversion cases to a denial of the existence of gremlins (*CE*, 406; *BC*, 177), we can discern within his work a stronger denial. Given Dennett's view, it at least makes sense that gremlins exist – it is just that we have no evidence at all that they do. But it does not even make sense that zombies and spectrum inversion cases exist. For these scenarios can only make sense if we allow that the link between having experience and being in a position to report experience is severed. And Dennett resists any severing of this link. He does, I suggest, because he thinks that what it is to be a subject of experience – the kind of experience for which the question 'what is it like' is appropriate – is to be a narrator or a reporter. This point cuts two ways.

First, in the absence of something to report or to narrate, to oneself or others, Dennett thinks the very idea of experiential consciousness breaks down. And, of course, what we say conforms with Dennett's view. When we cannot report, we say that we have had no experience, we say we noticed or perceived nothing at all. In the grip of a certain kind of theory, we might infer that we must have had an experience. But why should we think this 'experience' is part of what we normally think of as experiential consciousness? After all, as far as we are concerned, there was not anything it was like to undergo the experience.

Second, in the presence of reports and narratives, made to oneself and others, Dennett thinks that we have all we need for experiential consciousness. And, again, what we say conforms with Dennett's view. When we report sincerely that we have had a certain experience, we do not expect to be challenged. The sceptics insist that there must be something more to having the experience than generating a report. Dennett contests this by asking the sceptic to say exactly what this more might amount to. The 'something more' seems to be independent of our reports. But if the 'something more' has no power to influence our reporting and narrating, then what has its presence or absence to do with us? Are we supposed to think that there is some inner subject inside, an 'inner witness', that enjoys this unreportable experience? For there to be experiences there must be some subject. But even if we allow such inner subjects, what have they to do with us? They are not authors of our reports. They do not enthuse about positive experiences or complain about negative ones. They are, after all, mute. What are these inner subjects? Not anything we can identify with for sure. And, for Dennett, they are simply artefacts of a misbegotten theory (cf. the discussion of the 'essential you' and 'authorial you' in 5.1).

Block and superblindsight

I have already presented the case against Block's contention that there can be phenomenal consciousness in the absence of access consciousness. But what about the claim that there can be access consciousness in the absence of phenomenal consciousness, the case that superblindsight is supposed to illustrate? The very first point to note here is that the access consciousness of the superblindsight subject and the ordinary subject are not the same. What is leading to the rational control of speech in the ordinary subject cannot be the same as what is leading to the rational control of speech in the superblindsight subject. If they were, then both subjects would offer up the same reports. But the superblindsight subject says she cannot see. So we do not have a case where there is the very same access consciousness and only a difference in phenomenal consciousness.

But there is more to say to undermine Block's case. Following Dennett's method of de-differencing, we can examine the case more carefully and try to figure out what difference is supposed to make the difference between the superblindsight case and the ordinary case. When we do this, we realize that there are two distinct scenarios that Block may have in mind. Neither can help Block establish his point.

In the first scenario the superblindsight subject exhibits the same capacities as the ordinary subject. Suppose she were looking at the Mona Lisa, with half the painting in her 'blind' region and half in the normal region. On this scenario her aesthetic appreciation would be undiminished. She could, we might suppose, deliver a fluid monologue on the merits of the painting, including seamless comments on features, such as the smile, that might span across the seen and 'unseen' region. The only difference between her looking at it in this way, and her looking at it such that the whole picture fell into the normal field, would be that she would add the comment 'but I can't see half of the picture'. But now do we not start to think that what is wrong with her is not a lack in her consciousness but a peculiarity in her commentary about her consciousness?

If we apply the method of heterophenomenology to the subject, we find that she has a full and rich visual phenomenology. She talks about the smile, the way it is painted, the way it curves, and so forth. And so, as heterophenomenologists, we infer that the smile appears a certain way to her. Of course, as heterophenomenologists we also have to take into account her claim not to see. But this one factor is massively outweighed by many other factors. As such, the most natural interpretation is to suggest that something has gone wrong with the subject's understanding of what seeing is, rather than that something has gone wrong with her sight. This, I think, is as far as we need to go to undermine this scenario. Dennett goes further (*CE*, 331–3). He argues that the subject's inclination to say that she can see flows from her ability to offer a fluid monologue on the merits of the picture and the features of the smile. It is because she can do this, it is because this information is so readily available to her, that the subject knows that she is seeing. So, for Dennett, the very idea of this kind of superblindsight makes no sense. Restoring the capacity to comment fluidly on the whole of her visual field is, for Dennett, just restoring her sight.

However, perhaps we should understand Block's case in a different way. A second scenario would insist that the superblindsight subject could identify all the features of objects in the 'blind' region, but insist that she can do so only by laboriously setting herself guesses and waiting to hear her own answers. We could concede to Block that she might, in this way, gain all the information about the object in the 'blind' region that she could have were it in the normal region. But the information has arrived in a slow and piecemeal fashion. And this, surely, is more than enough to account for the difference in phenomenology. As discussed already, what is characteristic about vision is the way a vast array of information is made available not in an instant, but very quickly and without awkward delays. Moreover, the phenomenology of vision excludes the need to engage in discrete mental processes, acts of guesses, acts of inference, and so forth. If we need to go in for these activities in order to find out what something looks like, then although we may reach the correct conclusions, it will not feel like seeing. And so when the subject says she does not see, we can happily concur. But again Block's attempt to show that phenomenal consciousness is logically independent from access consciousness is scuppered, as we concur on the basis of a difference that we understand in terms of access consciousness.

This, in any case, is the response to superblindsight that I think Dennett ought to give. In fact, when he replies to Block (Block, 1995, 252–3) he focuses on the idea that as richness of content is restored to the blindsight patient so too will be the phenomenology. But richness of content is not the only issue. After all, without my glasses, the richness of the content of my visual perception is seriously impaired, but the visual character of the phenomenology is undiminished. What matters is not the richness itself – though richness will be required for normal visual phenomenology – but the kinds of influence that the content has. What is lacking in blindsight is influence on the capacity to spontaneously generate reports about what is before one's eyes. To the extent that the superblindsight scenario can be understood as restoring this capacity, so it should be understood as restoring visual phenomenology.

Two minor concessions

Although Dennett has to be hostile to spectrum inversion and zombie cases in order to protect the integrity of his view, he can make some minor concessions. In the case of spectrum inversion Dennett need not rule out the idea that different individuals may see colours or taste flavours in rather different ways. Suppose that Ruth and Jane describe a colour as fire-engine red. They always agree on their judgements about which samples are and are not fire-engine red. This does not mean that their experiences are identical. The 1720 Leipzig churchgoers might use the same words to describe certain aspects of a cantata performance as we would, and yet we can fully understand that their experience would be different from ours. In the same way Ruth and Jane may also differ. Perhaps Jane associates fire-engine red with certain events. These need not consciously come to mind when she sees that colour, but nonetheless they may have a range of subtle and hard to detect impacts. If some of these impacts affect her reporting then they will affect her experience (cf. Dennett, 2001, 233; and chapter 5, p. 156).

To make the point clear consider a crude case. Suppose Jane sees fire-engine red and it makes her feel good. She says this to herself or to Ruth. Ruth sees the colour, and agrees with Jane that it is fire-engine red, that it is just the same colour as the boots Jane lost on holiday, say. And yet, seeing the colour does not make Ruth feel good. Indeed, it makes her feel mildly anxious. She says this to herself or to Jane. Now it might be argued that both Jane and Ruth have a pure fire-engine red experience, and in the wake of this experience there are particular associations. But according to Dennett's theory it is not always possible to separate out the associations from the experiences. To the extent that the associations do not come apart from the experience then, for Dennett, they just are part of the experience. And if this applies in the crude case just given – that is, if Jane just cannot shake off feeling good in the face of fire-engine red and Ruth just cannot shake off feeling mildly anxious – then their experiences of fire-engine red just are different from one another. This sort of story makes good sense of the expression 'the way red looks to Jane is not the same as the way red looks to Ruth'. But in making sense of that expression it does not challenge Dennett's account of experiential consciousness.

Dennett could also make a concession concerning philosophical zombies, although he chooses not to (Dennett, 1993, 923–5). A distinctive feature of Dennett's view is that an agent's innards do not determine what its intentional states are. Intentional states are fixed by sustained patterns of behaviour and not by facts about the agent's innards. And the same applies to the agent's conscious states. Indeed, given that Dennett's view just is that – that conscious states depend wholly on intentional states – this is no surprise. Against this view Ned Block (1981), amongst others, has pressed an interesting species of counterexample: the giant look-up table.

Here is my version of the giant look-up table example. Suppose we look inside (what we think is) an agent and find instead of a complex and powerful computing device there is a giant look-up table filled with reasonable responses to external stimuli. The idea here is that whenever a stimulus arrives from the outside, the internal machinery simply looks up in the table what the appropriate response should be and then generates it. The look-up table must be absolutely vast. To see this, consider a much simpler case, one where there are only five possible stimuli. A five-entry look-up table will suffice for the first test we give the device. But if we are to observe the device over time then the table size must be much, much larger. For appropriate responses in the wake of stimulus A may not be the same as after stimulus B, C, D, or E. If you poke me in the eye twice, then I will respond differently the first time than I did the second. So for the second stimulus I need five extra look-up tables each with five entries in them. But the same problem will arise on the third stimulus. Only now I need an extra twenty-five look-up tables with five entries each. Already I have collected 31 look-up tables, and I am only on to the third stimulus. Add another step and it is up to 156 tables (125 + 31), and then 781 (625 + 156), and then 3,906 (3,125 + 781), and then 19,531 (15,625 + 3,906), and so on. The number keeps on getting bigger, and getting bigger faster. But to cope with hundreds of stimuli, and stimuli that could arrive simultaneously, we will need very, very many more tables. The numbers here will be even bigger and, for the device to cope with even a modest number of stimuli, the numbers will make the mind boggle.

So of course the idea of a look-up table that could speak and act like a human being is daftly implausible. Dennett sometimes just dismisses this sort of case when it is used as a counterexample on the grounds that it is practically impossible (Dennett, 1993, 923; *BC*, 12–13). But on at least one occasion he has suggested that were such a device to be built it would in fact be as conscious as you or I (Dennett, 1993, 924). This seems quite crazy. If the theory really insists that systems with only look-up tables inside are conscious, then surely something has gone wrong. But does he really need to bite this particular bullet? It is not clear to me that he does. Two things are important to Dennett. The first is that behavioural criteria for consciousness are the most basic criteria. The second is that what goes on inside an agent's head cannot be miraculous. And so his view is that, barring miracles, if it behaves as if it is conscious, then it is conscious. To the extent that the look-up table is miraculous, Dennett simply does not think it is his concern to worry about the case. In fact, this point needs a bit more finesse. Dennett could concede, I think, that there are some broad constraints about innards. It must be that the very same innards would, in similar but different situations, produce appropriate behaviour. And it must be that the innards are of a 'reasonable' size. Taken together, these two conditions should rule out look-up tables. But these conditions are very general. And they are proscriptive (ruling things out) rather than prescriptive (saying what must be there). As such they do not in any way threaten the primary role for behavioural criteria.

Another condition is required to rule out a different kind of case that is sometimes raised. Something that looks like a person may be nothing more than a remote-controlled robot, controlled by a committee of scientists (see Peacocke, 1983, chapter 8). To rule out this sort of case, Dennett could insist that the innards themselves do not achieve their functionality by an essential use of parts that themselves have the kinds of capacities the innards are supposed to underpin. I say 'essentially', because Dennett need not rule out the idea that a person be a part of some other person. This is, in effect, what happens in Searle's famous Chinese Room thought experiment (Searle, 1980; 1992, chapter 3). A person replaces a chunk of neural machinery. But the fact that a person does so is not essential.

A dumb bit of machinery would do the job of the person in the room just as well. Having person A as part of another person B's innards in the way Searle imagines is not, for Dennett, any reason to think that person B is not a fully-fledged conscious agent. But in Peacocke's thought experiment, the persons could not be replaced by dumb bits of machinery. And for this reason, Dennett, were he to adopt my proposal, could exclude that set of innards.

6.3   Soul pearls and persons

In writing about consciousness Dennett battles against the idea that somewhere inside a person there is a 'witness' (*CE*, chapter 11), something that takes in experiences. And similarly he rails against the idea that there is a 'central meaner' (*CE*, chapter 8), something whose ideas and intentions are subsequently translated into action. The problem with the idea of an inner 'witness' or a 'central meaner' is that to do their job they must have the very capacities that we are setting out to explain. That is, they must be capable of understanding, thought, experience, and free choice. But inside the person there are only mechanistic bits and pieces. And none of these bits and pieces themselves do the person's thinking or have the person's experiences. They are simply parts of the person.

Most naturalists would sign up to what has just been said. But many are more cautious about some of the implications. For there is a great reluctance to give up on the idea that our essence, what we call the self, is indivisible and determinate. That is to say the self cannot divide or fracture and it is always clear whether or not a self is present at a particular time and place. When we think of ourselves in this way, Dennett says we think of ourselves as 'soul pearls' (*CE*, 423). While Dennett's label may be tendentious, the intuitions to which it alerts us are both common and attractive. But these intuitions form part of an inflated conception of the self, a conception that is incompatible with our being made from mechanistic bits and pieces. But what are we if we are not soul pearls? What account can Dennett offer that deflates our concept but keeps in touch with what we hold dear? He comes close to an explicit definition in the following remark: 'A self . . . is an abstraction defined by the myriad of attributions and interpretations (including self-attributions and self-interpretations) that have composed the biography of the living body whose Centre of Narrative Gravity it is' (*CE*, 426–7).

The self, Dennett is clear, is not the same as the human being. Rather, he thinks of the self as a product of the human being. Just as spiders produce webs, beavers make dams, and bowerbirds build their bowers (elaborate displays to attract a mate), so:

> the strangest and most wonderful constructions in the whole animal world are the amazing, intricate constructions made by the primate *Homo Sapiens*. Each normal individual of this species makes a *self*. Out of its brain it spins a web of words and deeds, and, like the other creatures, it doesn't have to know what it is doing; it just does it. (*CE*, 416)

He contrasts the biological self and the narrative self. The biological self just is the agent or intentional system by another name. But the narrative self is a product or artefact of that agent.

> These . . . streams of narrative issue forth *as if* from a single source. . . . [Their] effect on any audience is to encourage them to (try to) posit a unified agent whose words they are, about whom they are: in short, to posit a *centre of narrative gravity*. . . . We heterophenomenologists appreciate the enormous simplification you get when you posit a centre of narrative gravity for a narrative-spinning human body. Like the biological self, this psychological or narrative self is yet another abstraction, not a thing in the brain, but still a remarkably robust and almost tangible attractor of properties . . . (*CE*, 418)

In describing the self in this way, Dennett is working to break down what he sees as a pernicious, inflated, and generally unhelpful understanding of the self, namely the vision of selves as soul pearls. However, in working to break down this conception, I think he over-eggs the pudding. For example, he is quite prepared to countenance the idea that the self is no more than a 'theorists' fiction' (*CE*, 429). Indeed, he seems to revel in this idea. But, as with the discussion of intentional states (chapter 3), I think that this way of speaking is ultimately misleading.

The positive point Dennett is trying to make is that when, and only when, we adopt the personal stance towards healthy human beings, we come to discern a real pattern, albeit a noisy pattern, of self-conscious rational activity. We do not, as with the vanilla intentional stance, simply discern an agent pursuing its goals in an unreflective way. Rather, we come to see a self that not only acts on purpose, but has a grasp of its own purposes, that can weigh and consider different plans, and that can rehearse alternative options.

Most important of all, we come to see a self that can offer reasons to itself and others, and a self that can act because it recognizes a reason as a reason.

By talking of selves as artefacts of the human agent, Dennett makes them seem somehow separate from that agent. Indeed, all this talk of the self chimes very well with a Cartesian way of looking at things, where there really is a clear distinction between the human animal and the human soul, and where the person is a composite of the two. In adopting talk of the self, then, it is almost as though Dennett is trying to naturalize the soul. A better move for him to make, and one that is more in keeping with his general approach, is to refuse to separate out the self and the person. This way of putting things must have some appeal to him. Consider the tension in the following remark:

> "Call me Dan," you hear from my lips, and you oblige, not by calling my lips Dan, or my body Dan, but by calling me Dan, the theorist's fictions created by . . . well, not by me but my brain, acting in concert over the years with my parents and siblings and friends. (*CE*, 429)

Who is 'me' here? Surely it is a person, a fully embodied thinker, something that acts and perceives, that fully occupies the space of her body? It seems odd, for Dennett of all philosophers, to say that the 'me' here is fundamentally a self. For the most part, I think Dennett's view is much better expressed using the vocabulary of persons. I am not, most fundamentally, a narrative self. I am not that much of an abstraction. Rather, I am, most fundamentally, a person. And a person is a narrative agent. As such, she is a different kind of agent than most, certainly than most if not all animals. But like other agents, a narrative agent is a material entity. She is made out of mechanistic bits and pieces. She has mass and extension, and so she is hardly an abstraction or a mere theorist's fiction.

A narrative agent is not like a star, a mountain, or an atom. And it is tremendously important to be clear about that. And if to be real you must, in the relevant ways, be like a star, a mountain, or an atom, then she is not real. But Dennett has already done plenty of work to diffuse that sense of real (see chapter 3). He would do better, then, to insist that persons are narrative agents, rather than composites of human beings and selves, and such agents are as real as anything needs to be. This much said, I do not want to fuss too much about talk of selves. For in some contexts it is more useful to talk about the self than the person. So long as this talk does not run away with itself, no harm need be done.

Dennett does not draw an explicit connection between his discussion of selves and his talk of real patterns, but we have just seen how the real pattern idea can be applied straightforwardly to selves. Let me put the point in terms of persons, or narrative agents, rather than selves. A person is a real pattern sustained by the activity of a biological agent. It is not the pattern revealed by the intentional stance. Rather, it is the pattern revealed by what I have called the personal stance. With the intentional stance, we can only discern an agent so long as we can interpret a system's activity as the more or less rational pursuit of its overarching goals. With the personal stance further demands enter the picture. For it is not enough that from moment to moment the agent is rational. In addition, the agent must be able to present itself to itself and others as a rational agent. This is the point of Dennett's talk about narrative.

The key claim here, tacit in Dennett but required to make sense of his view, is that in the absence of a story linking what I am doing now with what I have done and what I am going to do, the idea of a self cannot be sustained (see chapter 8). In the absence of such a story, although my actions may be understood as rational, they will not be understood as the actions of a person. My turning in my sleep is rational. But it is not typically part of the story I tell of what I do, and what I do for reasons that I can recognize. And as such, it is not something that is done by the person, though it may be something done by the human being.

I shall return to the idea of narrative and the distinctive contribution it makes to the nature of persons in chapter 8. But enough has been said here to return to the issue of how Dennett's view is at odds with the conception of our essential selves as soul pearls. How does Dennett's account of persons stand up to the intuitive requirements that a self be indivisible and determinate?

A different kind of person

When we see ourselves as essentially soul pearls then a whole host of worries about who we are, about what philosophers call 'personal identity', simply cannot arise. If we are soul pearls, then it could never be the case that a person could somehow split into two parts. And it could never be the case that it was not clear – as a matter of fact and not just as a matter of finding out – whether a person was present or not. For if the soul pearl is present, then the person is there. There is no room for indeterminacy. But, for Dennett, the soul pearl view simply does not hold up. He thinks that once you start to think about persons as entities made from mechanistic parts you have to give up on the idea of indivisibility and determinacy.

I want to address determinacy first, and to do so I shall return to talk of the self rather than talk of the person. For Dennett the selves of human beings do not have clear boundaries. It is not clear when a self arrives on the scene. Is there a self at the moment a human being is born? Dennett thinks not. For the self only comes into being with the onset of narrative capacity. But such a capacity is acquired through culture and primarily through language. No doubt there are some features of the self that will finally emerge that can be detected very early on. But the self, for Dennett, is something that is constructed and not something that is present all the time, but simply deaf and mute.³ So, strictly speaking, at the moment of birth Dennett thinks we have a potential person, but not an actual person. The infant grows into personhood, she is not born into it.

Similarly, it is not always clear when the self leaves the scene. Dementia, Alzheimer's disease, and various psychiatric disorders are all pathologies of the self. They affect the extent to which you can remember what you have done and what you plan to do. When memory and intention begin to fail, so the self begins to break down. But the point at which the pathology becomes so bad that we say the self has been destroyed may be quite unclear. And, again, the lack of clarity here is not a problem of our not knowing or not being sure when the self breaks down. Rather, it is that there is no fact of the matter as to when the self has or has not collapsed. In Dennett's view, there is no reason why there should be a determinate fact of the matter. Both in arriving and departing, the self is a delicate construction, a complex behavioural profile which is sustained both by well-functioning brain processes and an appropriate environment. But if brain processes or environment are disrupted in various ways, then the self may suffer, may falter in complicated ways, ways that are hard to describe. They are hard to describe, of course, because our ordinary concepts more or less presuppose that our selves are soul pearls. And this is fine for the most part. But when selves do not behave in the usual way, when they do not behave as if they were soul pearls, our ordinary concepts can run into trouble.

Let me now turn to indivisibility. In one sense we have to think of the self as something indivisible. This is an interpretative constraint on the self, just as being rational is an interpretative constraint on being an agent. But just as actual agents approach purity from impurity in the domain of rationality, so actual selves approach purity from impurity in the domain of narrative coherence.

In the case of the actual selves of human beings it is possible, though uncommon, for there to be genuine doubt as to when and where a self is located. A whole genre of thought experiments, initiated by the British philosopher John Locke (1632–1704), generate puzzles. For example, suppose Cicely's memories and personality traits are somehow wiped from her brain, and they are replaced with Emily's memories and personality traits. This process is achieved by scanning Emily's brain and using the information so gathered to reorder the connections of Cicely's brain. As a first case, imagine that Emily was on her deathbed just as the memories and personality traits were gathered. Now there is some pressure, I do not say how much, to say that Cicely has not survived the operation but Emily has. Emily's self, some are tempted to say, has been moved from her dying body to Cicely's healthy body. Cicely's self, however, has been destroyed. Now it is interesting to consider a second case. Suppose that Emily is not on her deathbed and survives the scanning process unharmed. For many this leads to a revised judgement about Cicely. They may say that Cicely has survived, but her memory has been altered. Or they may say that she has not survived. But in this case people rarely say that Emily's self has transferred across to Cicely. For Emily still seems to have her own self with her.

There are many variants on these kinds of puzzles and many interesting solutions. The point I want to make here is that the pressure these puzzles generate arises directly from the tension between a concept of the self as soul pearl and a concept of the self as a construction. Were the self a soul pearl then there would always be a fact as to who was Emily and who was Cicely. Check who is who by checking which body has which soul pearl. And there would always be a fact as to whether a person had come into being or if not. Just check for the presence or absence of the soul pearl. For soul pearls are either there or they are not there. There are no in-between states. Perhaps you cannot always check, perhaps your knowledge will be limited. But on the soul pearl view, the facts are always fixed one way or the other.

But selves are not soul pearls. Sometimes it is hard to say whether a self is there or not. And once we think hard about the fact that persons, or human beings with selves, are made out of mechanistic bits and pieces all this starts to make sense. What underpins a person can be slowly split into two, in the manner of an amoeba. Or it can be duplicated, like a piece of paper in a photocopier. After such a transformation, we will be able to apply the personal stance towards two different systems, to discern two different persons. And so the question will arise which person is the original person, if either. It is not clear how we answer this question. The deflation of our concept of the self that Dennett is promoting explains why it is not clear, but goes further, and insists that we are mistaken to try to make it clear by looking for deeper or more fundamental facts. Because selves are not soul pearls, or anything like them, there are no deeper facts.

Once we think of persons or selves as discerned by the personal stance, we cannot rule out as metaphysically incoherent such cases as two persons in one body (*CE*, 419–20), or one person across two bodies (*CE*, 422). Dennett reports empirical evidence that invites us to describe certain human beings and their selves in just this way. But, turning to much more everyday phenomena, the fact that we are underpinned by mechanisms means that by stages the applicability of the personal stance can become more and more marginal, thus making it unclear whether we are dealing with a self or not. This is what happens in dementia. And, in the case of infants for whom the personal stance is not clearly applicable, by stages it becomes more and more applicable, until it is obvious that we are missing out on something if we fail to apply it. Both cases show that we are left with times where it is just not clear whether or not we are dealing with a self. These two cases again work to undermine the soul pearl view.

Further reading

Between *Brainstorms* and *Consciousness Explained* Dennett developed his account of consciousness in a series of papers, most notably 'Quining Qualia' (QQ) and 'How to Study Human Consciousness Empirically' (Dennett, 1982). (See *IS*, x.) For two rather different interpretations of Dennett's account of consciousness, see Symons (2001) and Akins (1996). For doubts about my application of the distinction between the personal and the sub-personal to Dennett's later work, see Hornsby (2000). Much has been written on the differences between human and animal thought and consciousness. Norman Malcolm's 'Thoughtless Brutes' (Malcolm,

1973) is a classic and an important discussion. Jonathan Bennett (1964; 1976) has thought more carefully about this issue than most. MacIntyre (1999) briefly surveys these and other contributions in a very interesting discussion of animals. Dennett's discussions of animal thought and experience, which to my mind become increasingly evasive and equivocal, can be found in *BS*, chapter 16; *ISCE*; *CE*, chapter 14; *KM*, 161–8; *BC*, Section III. The possibility of extracting a heterophenomenological text from animal behaviour has excited some psychologists. See, for example, Cowey and Stoerig (1991).

Malcolm's views on dreaming are set out in his classic 'Dreaming and Scepticism' (Malcolm, 1956) and then in his monograph *Dreaming* (Malcolm, 1959). Dunlop (1977) is an excellent collection of essays on dreaming, including Malcolm's and Dennett's. Two places where Dennett talks about 'fame' as a metaphor for consciousness are 'Real Consciousness' (*BC*, chapter 7) and 'Are we Explaining Consciousness Yet?' (Dennett, 2001).

The possibility of spectrum inversion and of philosophical zombies are issues discussed at inordinate length. The papers in Block et al. (1997) are as good an entry point into this literature as any. The story about Mary appears in Jackson (1982) and is further elaborated in Jackson (1986). Critical discussion can, again, be found in Block et al. (1997). On Gilbert's lack of consciousness: as due to silicon chips inside (Searle, 1992); as a different program inside (Dretske, 1995); as due to different laws of nature (Chalmers, 1996). Block's distinction between phenomenal and access consciousness is presented in Block (1995), along with a series of commentaries, including one from Dennett. Block's distinction is also briefly presented and criticized in Flanagan (1992). The key reference for the giant look-up table thought experiment is Block's excellent paper 'Psychologism and Behaviorism' (Block, 1981). There is a good discussion of Block's case in Kirk (1994). Dennett discusses the case in his article 'The Message is there is no *Medium*'(1993).

Readers familiar with the literature on consciousness may have noted that I have not made any use of the term 'qualia'. Dennett has twice argued (*QQ*; and *CE*, chapter 12) that the term, which refers to items of, or properties of items of, phenomenal consciousness, has too many unhelpful and potentially question-begging connotations to be worthwhile. We can say all we want to say about consciousness without use of the term, as I have here.

For Locke on puzzles of personal identity, see *An Essay Concerning Human Understanding* (II.27). See *BC*, chapter 17, for Dennett's contribution to the genre instigated by Locke. The examples of Emily and Cicely are based on Williams (1970). Derek Parfit's *Reasons and Persons* (Parfit, 1984) presents a view of personal identity that is in many ways in tune with Dennett's, although Parfit does not share Dennett's concern with narrative. There are many papers and books on the topic of personal identity, with no sign of the trend slowing down. A demanding but important book, which explores some ideas that Dennett no more than touches on, is Carol Rovane's *The Bounds of Agency* (Rovane, 1998).

7

Dennett's Darwin

Dennett has explicitly discussed Darwinism at great length in *Darwin's Dangerous Idea*, but the theory of evolution by natural selection is also a constant background theme in the rest of his work. In this chapter I outline Dennett's particular take on Darwinism and show how it is a counterpart to his account of intentional systems. I also discuss some of the more controversial aspects of Dennett's take, in particular his defence of adaptationism and his critique of contingency.

7.1   Darwinism

Dennett's Darwinian agendas

In *Darwin's Dangerous Idea*, his extended monograph on Darwinism, Dennett has a number of different agendas. The dominant agenda is a defence of naturalism against a certain sort of sceptic. Here the sceptic is someone who thinks that natural forces alone cannot account for the origin of so many diverse biological organisms and cannot account for their highly subtle designs. Many such sceptics are creationists. That is, they are upfront about their appeal to supernature; God, they say, had a hand in producing the biological realm. Dennett does want to address the creationist. However, he also addresses those who would like to disavow supernature, but are still puzzled by how mere mechanism could be responsible for all that apparent design. Finally, he also wants to address those who see themselves as agreeing with Darwinism while suspecting it has few if any implications for fields of endeavour beyond the purely biological.

For Dennett, Darwinism is not simply about explaining how the biological realm could have come to be in the absence of a supernatural designer. He also wants to appeal to Darwinism in order to introduce useful constraints on empirical inquiry into the way in which humans and other organisms operate. A failure to take Darwinian thinking seriously gives, he suggests, credence to possible ways in which the brain might be designed that have little or no plausibility. Not to take evolutionary constraints seriously when thinking about and investigating mechanisms, such as the mechanism whereby humans acquire language, is, for Dennett, simply to countenance the possibility of supernature being exercised in our evolutionary history. This is something he suggests Chomsky and Fodor's work does (*DDI*, chapter 13). By denying that highly useful native endowments are best explained by appeal to natural selection, Chomsky and Fodor provoke sceptical doubts from many quarters, and not just from Dennett.[1]

Dennett also *seems* to want to appeal to Darwinism in order to better our understanding of human nature, of consciousness, of free will, and of ethics. And, more generally, he wants to put forward Darwinism as a powerful unifying theory: 'In a single stroke, the idea of evolution by natural selection unifies the realm of life, meaning, and purpose with the realm of space and time, cause and effect, mechanism and physical law' (*DDI*, 21). The term 'unifies' needs some comment. A naive reading of this passage might take it to imply some sort of reduction of intentional concepts to non-intentional concepts. And in *Darwin's Dangerous Idea* Dennett does use the term 'reduction' with enthusiasm. But he also distinguishes between what he calls 'greedy reductionism' and 'good reductionism' (*DDI*, 80–3). The former, Dennett tells us, is hostile to distinct levels of explanation; rather, it represents the drive to explain phenomena in terms of the lowest possible level. In caricature, then, it might aim to explain human action, something done for reasons, by reference to the activity of neurons. By contrast the only requirement Dennett places on 'good reductionism' is that no supernatural forces are invoked.

In the terminology I have been using throughout the book, 'good reductionism' just is naturalism, i.e. the ruling out of supernatural forces. Because Dennett is not merely tolerant of but insistent on distinct self-standing levels of explanation, levels of explanation that cannot be 'reduced to' (or 'derived from') lower levels, I shall continue to describe him, contrary to his terminology in *Darwin's Dangerous Idea*, as an anti-reductionist. He is, at any rate, an anti-greedy-reductionist.

Darwin's big idea

Darwin's theory of natural selection explains the presence of traits with highly subtle designs that 'fit' organisms to their particular niche. And it also explains why there is a wide diversity of species. Consider the following premises:

- *Variation*: when organisms reproduce, offspring tend to vary in small ways from parents.
- *Heritability*: when organisms reproduce, offspring tend to inherit the features of parents (including features that are the result of earlier variation).
- *Struggle for existence*: very many organisms do not survive long enough to reproduce.

These are the basic premises, though not the only premises, for an argument for evolution by natural selection. Because there is a struggle for existence, many organisms in a population will not survive long enough to reproduce. But which do and which do not survive is not purely a matter of chance. For if, through variation, an organism has a minor advantage, she has a greater chance of surviving long enough to reproduce. If she does so survive, then her offspring will tend to inherit the feature that gave her that advantage. And, while conditions remain stable, these offspring will similarly have a greater chance of surviving long enough to reproduce. In this way, more and more of the population will come to have the advantageous feature. Variations that confer an advantage will tend to be preserved in a population, and variations that do not, and hence, relatively speaking, carry a disadvantage, will tend to be removed.

This simple argument can explain why, say, the neck of the giraffe may grow taller and taller across successive generations. Natural selection favours those giraffes who have a longer reach. The argument also explains why the neck does not grow beyond a certain length. There are, after all, costs to the animal in having a long neck. When these costs start to outweigh the advantage of a long neck, then natural selection acts. The result is that, while the environment remains stable and while other variations which might upset the balance of costs and benefits do not appear, the giraffe neck is maintained at a certain length – a length that is, given the available opportunities, optimal.

The case of the giraffe is easy to understand and immediately appealing. But the very same argument can be employed to explain the evolution of very complex traits, such as the eye and the brain. The eye is a standard 'difficult case'. How, the sceptics cry, could an organ as subtle and complex as the eye develop through this trial-and-error method?

The scepticism can readily be met. First, the Darwinist emphasizes scale. There is a great deal of time available for natural selection to do its work. That there is this time is a further premise in the Darwinian argument and, indeed, a premise that was famously disputed in Darwin's day. We are now much more confident of the earth's age and the premise is uncontroversial. Second, there are very many examples of eyes of different degrees of complexity to be found in the biological realm. That is, we can observe, as it were, the various intermediate stages between, say, the human eye, and the most primitive light-sensitive cells, such as the cells that run along the body of a worm. There is a path, on which each step is an ever so slightly better eye, that takes us from primitive light-sensitive cells to simple lenses, to focusing and moveable eyes. And the steps on this path are small enough to arise by chance. Hence, given enough time, there is no need for miracles, or even exceptional amounts of luck, in order for complex eyes to evolve.

Darwin's simple argument can also explain diversity. What begins as a relatively uniform population can diverge into two or more groups, with each group being characterized by the increasing dominance of a particular kind of variation. Although it is not absolutely necessary, we can best grasp how natural selection explains divergence by thinking about a uniform population that divides into separate groups, say, either side of a mountain range. This is because geographical separation is one way of preventing interbreeding. In one group a camouflage strategy might develop, i.e., variations that increase survival on account of being better camouflaged are favoured. In the other a running strategy might develop, i.e., variations that increase survival on account of running faster are favoured. Over time, the two populations will diverge. And having begun, more divergence may follow. As the environment changes, variations that are good for camouflaged creatures may not be good for fast-running creatures. So an initially small divergence can become large. Although there are plenty of further caveats and complications, this is basically how Darwinism explains diversity as well as design.

Darwin's big idea, then, is that there is a special class of natural processes that can generate both subtle designs and also immense diversity. There is no need for God, or any intelligent agent, to intervene in the process of generating the biological world.

The Darwinian stance

The way Dennett reads Darwin's big idea has very close parallels with his account of agency. The key assertion here is that the patterns of change that unfold over evolutionary time are rational patterns. Organisms, just as human-designed artefacts, are 'a product of a process of *reasoned* design development, a series of *choices* among alternatives, in which the *decisions* were those *deemed best*' (*DDI*, 230).

On occasion Dennett puts the rationale into the mind of a fictional agent, Mother Nature. We should set aside Dennett's 'Mother Nature' option. Even by his standards of what can count as real, there is no case for treating Mother Nature as a real agent as opposed to a fiction. We do better to endorse his alternative suggestion, which is to 'personify a species [or lineage] . . . and treat it as an agent or practical reasoner' (*DDI*, 133). Support for the coherence, and indeed attraction, of the proposal comes from an influential lobby in the philosophy of biology. David Hull and others have forcefully argued that species are historical individuals: they have a beginning, a middle, and an end; they are not kinds or classes in the manner of gold or water. And as against the Mother Nature suggestion, if we do 'personify' or make an agent of a lineage, what we are personifying is something which is made of matter. And, further, something which has mechanisms 'inside it', as it were, that enable the lineage to tune and retune the design of its member organisms towards better designs and away from worse designs.

Because Dennett thinks that the unfolding of the lineage over evolutionary time is best understood from the intentional stance, he thinks of lineages as intentional systems. Lineages are systems whose behaviour – where behaviour is understood as the change to the design of the individuals that make up the lineage – is best predicted and explained by assuming that the lineage is rationally pursuing the interests of persisting and prospering. I earlier distinguished the personal and the intentional stance (chapter 4) –

something Dennett does not generally do. Here I shall again deviate from Dennett's own terminology and speak not of the intentional stance but of the Darwinian stance. On my terminology, then, the Darwinian stance is an additional member of the family of rationalizing stances. The point of distinguishing different stances within the broad family of the rationalizing stance is to draw attention to different standards of rationality. To be rational, a person must be able to justify her actions. This is more demanding than the standard of rationality for agents other than persons. In the Darwinian case the standard of rationality is, or certainly appears to be, lower still. Lineages have no foresight at all. Indeed, it is not clear that they have anything that is even equivalent to sight. They cannot look before they leap. They just leap – but leap in a variety of directions at once – and find out what happens afterwards.

If we adopt the Darwinian stance to lineages we will, Dennett claims, come to see real patterns of evolutionary change, patterns that we could not discern from any other stance. From the Darwinian stance lineages can act. The typical (the only?) action of a lineage is to alter the standard template of the organisms which make it up from one design to another. For example, over many successive generations the lineage might turn the coats of its members from brown to white. The way a lineage performs an action is, however, rather different from the way an ordinary agent does. The lineage constantly produces variations on the standard template of the organisms that make it up. Natural selection then does its work. And over successive generations, if there is selection pressure, the standard template will shift from one design to another.

Some readers may find talk of lineages doing things a bit difficult to take. Is this not a metaphor too far? Dennett does not push the parallel with agency quite as bluntly as I just have. But this is what his view amounts to. And, moreover, he is not offering a metaphor. He thinks that, in the sense I have just described, the actions that lineages take are just as legitimate members of the general class 'actions' as my reaching out for a bagel. To the extent that this may seem weird, then Dennett's view will appear very radical and, indeed, implausible.

Design

Dennett argues that when we do encounter organisms we more or less cannot help but assume that their traits and features are designed, are, as he puts it, ordered for a purpose (*DDI*, 64–5 and see 7.2 below). This assumption is revealed, for example, in the way in which we so readily think of particular organisms as healthy or unhealthy, normal or deviant. The healthy or normal organism is one that is structured as and behaving as it is supposed to. Our very appreciation of organisms brings in such normative claims. Dennett's way of making good sense of all this is to accept that, quite literally, the organism has been designed. If the Darwinian stance can be successfully applied to lineages, we can justify this assumption. If the traits and features of an individual organism are, quite literally, the result of a sequence of rational choices made by the lineage, then they are, quite literally, designed.

So, unlike many Darwinians, Dennett does not seek either to reduce design to something else, e.g. complex historical properties, or to eliminate it (and thus leave only the task of explaining the appearance of design). He insists that evolutionary design is real and not really anything else (*DDI*, chapter 9, and 80–3, 100–3). In fact, he takes exactly the same approach to design as he does to intentionality (see chapters 2 and 3). Design is real and is so because it is part of a real pattern.

More specifically, design is the process where a rationale – such as persistence or reproductive success – shapes and structures an entity. And so, as Dennett writes, '[design] work is discernible . . . only if we start imposing *reasons* on it' (*DDI*, 133), that is only if we presuppose some sort of rationale. A failure to impose a rationale on lineages would mean that we would have no means for claiming that selected variations were better – better in terms of the persistence of the members of the lineage and hence of the lineage itself – than non-selected variations. All we could say is that the variations were different. If we eschew the idea of a lineage having an interest in persisting, then although we can still track changes in lineages, we cannot interpret these changes as developing the design of the species. But, maintains Dennett, there is a real but noisy pattern of rational changes to design in the face of environmental shifts. This pattern can only be discerned from the Darwinian stance. To eschew the stance is, then, to miss out on something that is really there and, indeed, something that is very significant.

To say that evolutionary trajectories are best predicted and explained from the Darwinian stance is not to say they will be perfectly predicted in this way. Bearing in mind the parallels with the account of agency, we can see that, for Dennett, rival methods of prediction and explanation, such as appeal to the design or physical stance, while they may help fill in some gaps, cannot displace the Darwinian stance. At best these stances can predict the ordering of an organism's structure. To recover design, to recover order for a purpose, requires interpretation, interpretation that cannot be achieved without the resources of the Darwinian stance. And, like the other rationalizing stances, Dennett's thought is that the Darwinian stance will pull out real patterns, rational patterns that will reassert themselves in a wide range of different particular circumstances.

Explaining degrees of design

Dennett draws a distinction between 'order' and 'design' (*DDI*, 64–5). Order involves regularity. It is what, as the universe expands and cools, there is less and less of (see *DDI*, 68–9). Nonetheless, order does arise quite spontaneously as a result of natural processes: stars, crystals, and solar systems all exhibit order. Design, on the other hand, is not just order, it is order for a purpose. The solar system exhibits *order*, but the eye is *designed*: it is a highly complex arrangement – highly ordered – but ordered towards some end, namely, enabling vision.

Darwinism offers a naturalistic explanation of how organisms are redesigned so that they are better adapted to their prevailing environment. Dennett's claim, and, indeed, any naturalist's claim, is that Darwinian explanation is sufficient to account for all the design we encounter in the world, from the design of viruses through to the design of the human brain and, indirectly, on to the design of human artefacts from computers to paper clips. But, for Dennett, some things, such as the eye, are more highly designed than others. By saying it is 'highly designed' he seems to mean that very many design 'decisions' must have been taken in order to produce the eye, where 'decision' here is understood as the outcome of the selection of a fitness-conferring variation. So for Dennett design comes in degrees. And the degree to which something is designed, he claims, is a measure of the amount of design work that has led to the final product.

Dennett also talks about the idea of a design space – a multi-dimensional space of all the possible designed entities, including all possible and actual organisms, all possible and actual artefacts. Although Dennett remarks that there 'is no single summit in Design Space' and that 'we cannot expect to find a scale for comparing amounts of design work across distant developing branches' (*DDI*, 134), he nonetheless seems to endorse the idea that design space has a vertical ordering. For design work is glossed as a move upwards in design space. In the lower reaches of design space there is simply a lack of order. In the higher reaches are persons, agents with the capacity for thought, free action, and consciousness. Bacteria appear below multi-cellular organisms, and eagles appear above, say, frogs, but still below dolphins, chimpanzees, and humans.

Now, of course, this ordering scheme makes a great deal of sense to us. As Dennett himself points out, it is supposed to be a naturalized version of the 'Great Chain of Being' (see *DDI*, 64), the scheme in which God is the highest kind of being, with angels below, then humans, and then all of God's other creatures from the highest to the lowest, all occupying their slots in strict order. The 'Great Chain of Being' is an intellectual idea that has deeply influenced Western thinking, arguably as far back as Plato, and continues to do so. So we find it easy to share Dennett's intuitions about 'height' in design space. Moreover, there may be some way to make these intuitions objective, for example by adverting to, say, computational power or to number of heterogeneous component parts. However, if there is a non-anthropocentric way of cashing out his metaphor of height, Dennett does not make it clear to us.

Degree of design, as measured by the amount of intellectual work undertaken, and 'height' in design space are, for Dennett, supposed to be one and the same thing. This is surely a mistake. Bacteria are constantly being redesigned by natural selection, but in so doing it is far from clear that they move 'upwards' in design space. Moreover it seems quite plausible that as much 'intellectual work' has been invested in modern bacteria, if not more, than in the design of human beings. Or then again, consider the case of a species that evolves some very complex traits and then, under new selection pressures, simplifies its design, losing body parts and behavioural sophistication. Such an organism may be the product of very much more design work than that of a very distant cousin who never evolved the complex traits in the first place, and so never had to lose them. Nonetheless, we would not expect to place the organism with the more complex history higher in design space. It is not all that clear what turns on the failure of 'height in design space' and 'degree of design' to coincide. Certainly it matters little as far as Dennett's response to the basic sceptic about the power of Darwinism. It may matter more when we come to consider large-scale trend in evolution (7.3).

In Dennett's metaphors, the question of whether Darwinism can explain the design we find in the world is expressed in terms of 'lifting'. He writes:

> imagine all the 'lifting' that has to get done in Design Space to create the magnificent organisms and (other) artefacts we encounter in our world. Vast distances must have been traversed since the dawn of life with the earliest, simplest self-replicating entities, spreading outward (diversity) and upward (excellence). (*DDI*, 75)

What Dennett has in mind here is not just the way that natural selection favours organisms that are 'better' than their conspecifics. For 'better' here does not equate with 'higher' in design space. It simply means 'better' in the given context, and does not guarantee a move 'upwards'. Rather, what Dennett has in mind are design innovations that somehow open up new possibilities, that boost, in some sense or other, the sophistication of organisms.

Dennett is thinking about moves such as the step from prokaryotes (cells lacking a nucleus) to eukaryotes (cells with a nucleus), the step from single-celled organisms to multi-cellular organisms, the invention of the lens, of sex, of language, and so forth. These substantial steps up in design complexity have clearly taken place. But, the sceptic asks, does natural selection really have the power to account for the lifting that is required to take these steps? One Darwinian response is simply to insist that, yes, it has. Evolution has had plenty of time, so even very unlikely innovations have had an opportunity to arise and become established. Dennett has a different response. If, for the sake of argument, the vanilla form of natural selection cannot explain such innovations, then we can agree that other forces are needed. Dennett then suggests that such forces can come in only two varieties: skyhooks and cranes. A skyhook is a supernatural lifting force, such as an act of God. By contrast a crane is: 'a sub-process or special feature of a design process that can be demonstrated to permit the local speeding up of the basic process of natural selection, *and* that can be demonstrated itself to be the predictable (or retrospectively explicable) product of the basic process' (*DDI*, 76).

As a naturalist Dennett wants to show that no skyhooks are needed. Cranes can do all the work. Sexual reproduction is a crane. It allows evolution to proceed more rapidly, as distinct beneficial variations which occur in different individuals can come to be combined. Another crane much admired by Dennett is the Baldwin

Effect (see *DDI*, 77–80; *CE*, 182–7). Think of a behavioural trait, such as an enthusiasm for red-spotted leaves. Having this trait may be a real boost to fitness. Normally, 'nearly having' a given trait is of no benefit to an organism. However for organisms that can engage in lifetime learning the story is different. Such creatures can turn a near miss into a hit, for example by learning to be enthusiastic about the red-spotted leaves. This is good for the individual organism. But, more importantly, it creates a new selection pressure. It is not only variations that already have the red-spotted leaf behaviour that tend to be preserved. Now those variations that are fairly near, and the nearer the better, will also tend to be preserved. A lot more variations are available for selection to work on, and this increases the speed with which the red-spotted leaf behaviour can become dominant. Finally, closer to human beings, culture – or, more basically, the ability to trade behavioural strategies between individuals – is another powerful crane.

Dennett wants to emphasize cranes in order to persuade the sceptic that the basic process of natural selection can be boosted in various ways. But these ways are wholly naturalistic, and wholly in keeping with the spirit of Darwinism. Cranes help us appreciate the capacity of purely mechanistic processes to account for all the lifting that has been achieved throughout evolutionary history.

We see here an instance of one of Dennett's general strategies. He is talking up the power of science. When we look more closely at what mechanisms can do, we see that they can exhibit more flexibility and more subtlety than the image of simple clockwork suggests to us. The other side of the coin, deflating the problematic phenomena, was one of Darwin's critical contributions. By showing that the design of organisms is often gerrymandered Darwin talked down the phenomenon of biological design. Dennett's contention is that once you begin to appreciate just how powerful cranes really are, and once you recognize that biological design is good, but not at all how we would expect from a divine artificer, you will no longer need to hanker after skyhooks.

The Darwinian origin of persons

Plants and animals pursue the goals of survival and reproduction. Darwinism explains how they can continue to do this. They can because in the struggle for existence those that are better at pursuing these goals last long enough to reproduce, and hence pass their traits onto the next generation. But there is a problem when we try to apply this picture to persons. As we have seen in chapters 4, 5, and 6 – and the point will be further elaborated in chapter 8 – persons pursue additional goals. Amongst other things, persons value the truth and they value a coherent biographical narrative. But there is little reason to suppose that caring about the truth or a coherent biography gives an agent a selective advantage. Indeed, we might suspect the opposite, that caring about such things is detrimental. If this is so, how can Darwinism explain our origin, the origin of agents that really care about these things?

Dennett here appeals to the idea of cultural evolution (*DDI*, chapter 12; *CE*, chapter 7). For an animal, its modes of behaviour are either inherited or learned during its lifetime. And, for the most part, the animal can only learn directly from its own experience. But in the case of humans, and to a minor extent some other animals, the situation is different. Through the use of imitation we can acquire new modes of behaviour. For example, a technique for making pots, that may have been refined over many generations, can be learned in a single lifetime. In this way, cultural evolution acts as a crane, accelerating the ordinary process of evolution. Culture is a powerful crane, but more is needed. Dennett needs a story about how values other than survival and reproduction can drive the design process.

Here Dennett appeals to Richard Dawkins's idea of the meme (Dawkins, 1976). A meme is unit of cultural knowledge, a unit that can be transmitted from human to human. The pot-making technique can be regarded as a meme, as can the idea of the wheel, of wearing clothes, of an alphabet, of calculus, and so forth. Dawkins's theory is that there is a competition between memes for influence in the human population. Those memes that are better at spreading themselves from human to human, whether or not they aid survival and reproduction, will come to dominate. A Darwinian process kicks in where meme variants that are better at spreading themselves than others will be spread more often, and hence come to be dominant.

According to the meme theory, there is no reason why a meme for celibacy or for suicide should not arise and spread throughout the population, even though celibacy and suicide are at odds with the goals of survival and reproduction. For example, the idea that celibacy or suicide guarantee a place in heaven might, in the right circumstances, make for a successful meme. Similarly, there is no reason why memes for valuing truth or valuing a coherent biography might not gain a firm grip on humans, thus leading to the creation of persons, i.e. agents whose nature it is to value these things. Even if such memes make humans less likely to survive and reproduce, this need not curb their influence. A human can fail to reproduce, and perhaps not survive for a normal lifespan, but still succeed in passing on memes. In this way, then, memes gain a degree of autonomy from biological imperatives and can shape human behaviour in a way that is at odds with those imperatives.

For Dennett, cultural evolution and the meme theory in particular explain how distinctively human capacities could have developed in a relatively short amount of evolutionary time. He tells an exciting story about how the primitive ability to imitate one another might have led, through a series of Good Tricks (handy design innovations) and forced moves (design changes that are more or less bound to occur once a given situation has arisen), to the capacity for language and consciousness. Exactly how and why the value of truth and biographical coherence enter the scene is not altogether clear (though see chapter 8). Perhaps the development of language, which would primarily have arisen because it promoted survival and reproduction, made humans particularly receptive to these values. Once primitive language is in place, a series of forced moves might generate the traits that we associate with modern humans and lead to the creation of persons. By 'the creation of persons' I mean here the onset of a situation where we can successfully apply the personal stance, a situation where there are real patterns of self-conscious rational behaviour in the world.

Some enthusiasts for the theory (notably Blackmore, 1999) argue that meme theory provides the best and most general explanation of human behaviour. Although Dennett is highly enthusiastic about the explanatory power of memes, he does not make this move. Just as there are all manner of physical processes going on between our brains and the environment, so there are memetic processes of reception and transmission. But, as far as persons are concerned, both the physical and the memetic should be regarded as subpersonal.

The idea of a meme, as Dennett readily concedes, is beset with difficulties. But, even if many of the details are contestable, what Dennett's approach does illustrate is that the Darwinian has a rich set of resources for explaining how humans can come to have behavioural traits that do not serve their biological imperatives. There is no need to appeal to supernature to explain the origin of persons.

7.2   Adaptationism

One of the striking things about *Darwin's Dangerous Idea* is the fierce attacks that Dennett brings against thinkers who, at first sight, would appear to be friends of Darwinism. In particular, he singles out Stephen Jay Gould's work, arguing that Gould, perhaps unwittingly, is deeply unsatisfied with Darwinism. Gould does indeed argue that a range of biological phenomena are not best explained by natural selection. Other mechanisms, and indeed, sheer chance, play an important role for Gould. Dennett's response to this is to suggest that Gould is sceptical about the power of natural selection, even boosted by cranes, to do the necessary lifting work. And because for Dennett the only other explanation for lifting involves skyhooks, it might seem that Gould must indirectly endorse such supernatural devices.

While there is an important intellectual dispute between Gould and Dennett, Dennett seriously misdiagnoses the nature of their difference. Contrary to Dennett's analysis, Gould is just as committed a naturalist as Dennett. Their fundamental difference, or so I shall argue here, is rooted in the fact that Dennett believes there is much more design in the world than Gould does. To caricature: both in the results of evolution and in the historical pattern of evolution, Dennett sees design everywhere. Whereas, although Gould sees much design, he sees much that is not ordered at all, but the mere outcome of chance events, and sees much that is ordered, but not ordered to any particular purpose.

Adaptationism

Where a feature's existence and structure is best explained as the product of natural selection ordering it to serve a particular purpose, that feature is referred to as an adaptation. The giraffe's neck is an adaptation, as is the eye, as are opposable thumbs. Dennett defends the doctrine of adaptationism, which claims the features of organisms are, for the most part, adaptations. Further, the adaptationist takes it that adaptations are, given background constraints, optimal. They are, that is, the best solution to the problems the lineage has faced. And they are the best such solution, because natural selection is almost always sufficiently effective to optimize them.

By assuming features are the optimal solutions, given various *known* constraints, to a problem faced by the organism, biologists are able to make predictions about various *unknown* constraints, such as features of the environment or features of reproduction. For example, if we suppose that the light of the pony fish, which shines downwards from its belly, is there to hide the shadow the fish would otherwise cast, then we can predict that the light may vary in intensity according to how much light is shining from above. When investigated, this was found to be the case. Of course sometimes these predictions fail, leading the biologist to rethink her account. But they succeed often enough to provide good support for the adaptationist approach. The general thought, then, is that variation and natural selection generate and retain just those features that, given constraints, are optimal solutions to problems faced by the organism.

Dennett goes further and emphasizes that we only come to regard systems – or their fossil traces – as organisms because we can conjure up functions for their structure and behaviour. Were we unable to see structures as aiming to maintain bodily coherence and to pursue various goals, then we would not be inclined to identify them as organisms at all (*DDI*, 240–1). For Dennett, then, there simply is no perspective on organisms, as opposed to systems discerned from the physical or design stances, that does not imply that very many of the features of the organism are there for some purpose.

In 1978 Gould, with his co-author Richard Lewontin, ruffled many feathers with a paper called 'The Spandrels of San Marco and the Panglossian Paradigm: A Critique of the Adaptationist Programme'. Gould and Lewontin begin their paper with an example from architecture rather than biology. 'Spandrels' are tapering triangular spaces between arches set at right angles. The spandrels in St Mark's in Venice seem tailor-made to carry the images that complete the religious iconography of the cathedral. That is, it seems as if these triangular spaces were designed, ordered for the purpose, of carrying their images. However, Gould and Lewontin argue, it would be a mistake to think of the spandrels as adaptations. Rather, they are simply a by-product of constructing the arches. That the spandrels are fit for serving a certain purpose, then, plays no part in explaining the origin of the spandrels. In fact, to adopt a term also introduced by Gould (with co-author Vrba) the St Mark's spandrels are 'exaptations' (Gould and Vrba, 1982). They are 'apt' for, that is they effectively serve the purpose of, displaying the religious iconography. But, Gould and Lewontin insist, their aptness does not explain their origin. The architects did not design the spandrels in order to carry the religious iconography. Rather, they were a side-effect of the method of construction. But once on the scene, they were exapted to serve the decorative purpose. Similarly, there may be features of organisms that, while they might initially look as though they are designed to serve a purpose they currently fulfil, have their origin as a by-product of some other process. They are exaptations and not adaptations.

Further, Gould and Lewontin argue that some complex features are neither adaptations nor exaptations. The chin, for example, may seem like a feature whose origin requires some explanation. And, further, we may find ourselves eager to think of a function it serves in order to tell a story about how natural selection developed and refined the feature to optimally serve that function (given the relevant constraints). But this, Gould and Lewontin urge, would be a mistake. The chin is a feature, but it has no function. It is simply a side-effect of other evolutionary processes, in particular 'the interaction between two growth fields' (Gould and Lewontin, 1978, 77).

To my mind, the best example they give of a non-adaptive feature is the short forelimbs of Tyrannosaurus Rex. The question may be asked, and indeed has been asked: why are Tyrannosaurus Rex's forelimbs so short? What purpose does their shortness serve? Or, then again, the question can be asked in this form: to what problem are such short limbs the optimal solution? Gould and Lewontin argue that these are the wrong questions. There is no reason for the short limbs, because they are not a product of natural selection adjusting and improving the T. Rex's design. But there is a causal explanation.

Gould and Lewontin suggest that the cause of the short limbs is to do with the biological basis of increasing body size. Genetic changes that cause an organism to increase in body size do not necessarily lead to uniform increases. So, in this case, factors to do with T. Rex genetics, and not factors to do with natural selection, explain the length of the forelimbs. Think of it like this. It is as if T. Rexes get to be big animals because natural selection favours a gene that pumps them with a growth hormone. The action of the growth hormone is not uniform; it promotes more rapid growth of some body parts than of others. The forelimbs grow more slowly relatively to the rest of the body. And if it turns out that the length of the forelimb does not make any significant difference to T. Rex survival and reproduction, and Gould and Lewontin suppose that it does not, then the limb will, other things being equal, remain the length that it is.

So the origin of exaptations cannot be read off from their current function. And nor can the origin of non-adaptive features, such as chins and the length of T. Rex's forelimbs. While some exaptations may have the form and structure that they do because natural selection has designed them for some prior purpose, this purpose may no longer be apparent. And, for some exaptations and for many non-adaptive features, natural selection has not designed the structure apparent in the feature at all. Rather, the structure of the feature is an effect of other processes, which may, but need not, include side-effects of natural selection working on other features of the organism. This, in brief, is the reasoning that Gould and Lewontin present. And they present it as an attack on what they call the 'adaptationist programme'.

The 'adaptationist programme' is, they claim, a methodology within evolutionary biology that has a very strong tendency to focus exclusively on the (perceived) current function of a feature and to explain its origin by claiming that natural selection designed that feature to best serve that function (given constraints). The adaptationist, they claim, is too eager to explain the origin of features by appeal to a 'problem' that natural selection has recently 'solved' for the organism. Their concern is that, applied ruthlessly, this approach will simply ignore alternative explanations of origin. In particular it ignores the following options:

(1) The feature, though designed by natural selection, was designed for some other purpose and then exapted, for example, the turtle's flippers when used for digging.
(2) The feature was not designed by natural selection at all, for example, the chin, the length of T. Rex's forelimbs.

Dennett has no argument with the first option, but nor does he see this as any challenge to adaptationism. In making this point, Gould and Lewontin are simply urging higher standards in constructing and evaluating adaptationist explanations. They are quite correct to say that looking at the (perceived) present function is not always the best way to account for the origin of a feature. Indeed, given the opportunistic way that natural selection works – the only way it can work – exaptation is to be expected. That said, to the extent that a feature's present function is contributing to fitness, natural selection will preserve that feature and, further, differentially favour any variations on that feature that increase the organism's fitness. In one sense it is correct to say that the wing is an exaptation from a temperature regulation device. Part of its structure is best explained by reference to that problem and the way in which natural selection solved it. But part of its structure is clearly best explained by the way in which, from a particular starting point, the feature has been refined by natural selection to serve the function of enabling flight. Because of this, there is a sense in which it is perverse to say that the wing is merely an exaptation and not an adaptation in its own right.

But Dennett does have a serious concern with the second option, the option that seems to suggest that there need be no appeal to design in explaining the origin of a feature. Disregarding 'trivial features' such as 'elephants having more legs than eyes' (*DDI*, 276), Dennett seems to think that most biological features are the outcome of design decisions. Of course, as he concedes, it does depend on how you count features.[2] Does the chin get to count as a feature? Does the length of T. Rex's forelimbs? If so, then Gould presents a good case for doubting whether these features are the outcome of design decisions. For Dennett to make a case, it must be that there is some logical link between our counting something as a feature at all, and its being the product of design. But, at the same time, this link had better not be too tight, or else Dennett will seem to win the argument by mere stipulation. Clearly, with features such as limbs and wings, there is such a connection. The identifying of these features appeals to a job that they do. But in other cases it is less clear that there is such a connection. For Gould, there are plenty of features that can be picked out independently of design considerations. And, given that they are picked out in such a way, it is an open question as to how they originated.

Dennett does acknowledge that some engineering factors are what he calls 'don't cares' (*DDI*, 275–6; see chapter 4, p. 132), cases where there is no reason to prefer one way of configuring a structure rather than another. Biological 'don't cares' do not have an adaptationist explanation. In Dennett's terminology, then, Gould and Lewontin argue that such 'don't cares', which would include the length of the T. Rex forelimbs, are common in biology and are deserving of explanation. By contrast, Dennett, as an adaptationist, thinks that such 'don't cares', while possible, must be relatively uncommon and not especially deserving of explanatory attention.

In the wake of Gould and Lewontin's paper, there has been much vociferous debate about adaptationism. I shall not attempt to trace that debate here. But I do want to defend Gould against some of the charges Dennett lays at his door.

> [May] I state for the record that I . . . do not deny either the existence and central importance of adaptation, or the production of adaptation by natural selection. Yes, eyes are for seeing and feet are for moving. And, yes again, I know of no scientific mechanism other than natural selection with the proven power to build structures of such eminently workable design. . . . But selection cannot suffice as a full explanation for many aspects of evolution; for other types and styles of causes become relevant, or even prevalent, in domains far above and below the traditional Darwinian locus of the organism. These other causes are not, as [Dennett and others] often claim, the product of thinly veiled attempts to smuggle purpose back into biology. The additional principles are as directionless, nonteleological, and materialistic as natural selection itself – but they operate differently from Darwin's central mechanism. (Gould, 1997, 'Darwinian Fundamentalism')

What we see here is that Gould does agree with Dennett's principle that where there is lifting, so there must be the work of natural selection and its cranes. But Gould points to 'aspects of evolution' for which 'other types and styles and causes become relevant'. These are aspects that, as Gould sees it, do not involve design. So Gould is not looking for 'skyhooks', as Dennett suggests. He is not because, by his lights at least, the 'aspects of evolution' which he is addressing do not involve any 'lifting', they do not involve design work. Dennett's key complaint against Gould, namely that Gould doubts the power of natural selection and its cranes to do the necessary lifting, is seriously misplaced. Where Gould's view is importantly different from Dennett's concerns the extent to which design permeates through the biological realm. And it is on this issue that Dennett needs to direct his energy.

Varieties of adaptationism

The debate generated by Gould and Lewontin has revealed, if nothing else, that there are importantly different ways to understand adaptationism. We can discern at least three distinct doctrines that have fallen under the label 'adaptationism'.[3]

Call the first 'empirical adaptationism'. This is the view that, as a matter of fact, the most common causal story about the origin of a feature will be an adaptationist story, i.e., a story in which the fact that the feature served or helped to serve a particular function explains its origin. There may be other forces, but the effect of these forces is, by and large, swamped by the power of natural selection. So other forces can be safely ignored.

The second we might call 'methodological adaptationism'. This simply states that a useful, indeed the best, starting point into an inquiry about the causal origin of a trait is to look for an adaptationist story. Though strictly speaking they are independent, empirical and methodological adaptationism go readily together. If a certain type of cause is the most common, then, by and large, it makes good methodological sense to pursue causes of that type. But empirical adaptationism suggests a contingent rather than necessary connection between a certain form of explanation and the most common form of explanation. That is, it suggests that it is a matter of discovery that the most common explanation is an adaptationist one. It is not something that we could have logically deduced from already incontrovertible premises.

A third doctrine that can fall under the heading adaptationism is what I shall call 'logical adaptationism'. The key idea here is that there is a logical connection between features and adaptationist origins. Given the basic premises accepted by all Darwinians, the empirical adaptationist still thinks it is an open question as to whether the most common causal story about feature origins involves natural selection. By contrast the logical adaptationist thinks that, given those basic premises, it follows necessarily that most traits are the result of adaptation.

Dennett is certainly a methodological adaptationist (*DDI*, 257–9), and also shows a strong attraction towards empirical adaptationism. But most fundamentally Dennett is a logical adaptationist. He shares this position with Richard Dawkins (see Dawkins, 1982 and 1986), whose work is given a great deal of attention in *Darwin's Dangerous Idea*. Both think that signing up to adaptationism is a non-negotiable requirement for doing serious biology. Both think it is not an open question, and to think that it might be is a sign of deep confusion.

Consider a parallel with adaptationism: the doctrine of 'murderism'. Whenever a 'murderist' encounters a dead person she assumes that she has been murdered and sets about looking for a murderer. She asks who might have had a motive. If one person is eliminated as a possible murderer, she looks for another, but is disinclined to look at a different sort of explanation such as death by natural causes.

What could justify someone being a murderist? If one had examined very many cases, perhaps in a violent inner city, then you might have evidence for a murderist generalization. You might, that is, have evidence for the doctrine of empirical murderism. In the light of such evidence, then, you might be readily attracted to the doctrine of methodological murderism. That is, since you believe that most deaths, as it happens, are caused by murder, you may decide that the first line of inquiry should be to look for a murderer.

But murderism might be supported in another way. A logical murderist might be unimpressed by a statistical survey, and, indeed, insist that she does not base her doctrine on such evidence. Suppose she believes that death by natural causes is a highly unlikely type of event. To die of natural causes or from an accident would, on her view, involve some quite extraordinary coincidences. Perhaps our murderist has good reasons to think that people are very robust and it takes real ingenuity to kill them off. If she did believe this, then she would have a reason to think (a) that most deaths are a result of murder and (b) a good starting point for the investigation of a death is to start by looking for a murderer.

Clearly murderism is an absurd doctrine. And it is because, as it happens, people die for all sorts of reasons aside from being murdered. There are plenty of other causes of death, and none of them involve extraordinary coincidences. But can the same be said about complex biological features?

Consider the following line of reasoning. Most changes that can occur to an organism's structure will be detrimental to its interests. Natural selection is the process whereby those chance changes that are not detrimental, and indeed may even be positively beneficial, are preserved. Complex features take many evolutionary steps to develop. Given all this, natural selection is the only plausible explanation of the origin of a complex feature. Other accounts of their origins are almost always going to be unacceptable: chance is wildly implausible. And, given that supernature is ruled out by Dennett's project, it would be incredible if another kind of cause could be the fundamental explanation of the origin of a complex feature. Without natural selection it would be a miracle that the changes brought about by that other kind of cause were not seriously at odds with the organism's interest of making a living for itself.

If we agree to her premises, then the logical adaptationist seems to have a strong case. However, it is not clear that her premises are simply those truths accepted by all Darwinians nor that they follow from those truths. There is no doubt that on some occasions selection pressures are very intense. In such circumstances, there may be nothing that counts as a 'don't care' as far as the organism's phenotype is concerned. But it is not clear that Dennett or Dawkins show that there is any reason why for long periods of time selection pressures might not be very weak. If the pressure could be less intense, then there would be more 'don't cares' and so more features that are best explained in other ways. If there is no argument that takes us from premises agreed by all to a constant regime of intense selection pressures, then Dennett's and Dawkins's view looks as though it must collapse into empirical adaptationism. That there may be such an argument is not ruled out. But what it might be is not clear from either Dennett's or Dawkins's writings.

Of course, it may simply be that what authors such as Gould are prepared to treat as a feature, is just much more liberal than what Dennett is prepared to accept. If the idea of a feature is understood in a certain kind of way, as something showing all the hallmarks of design, then the logical adaptationist is vindicated. Such features can, of course, only be explained by appeal to adaptation. But victory here would seem to be won by stipulation. Gould and Lewontin's concern is that what are often regarded as features by working biologists turn out not to be adaptations at all. Dennett and Dawkins seem to genuinely disagree with this claim as presented. Were they using the idea of a feature in a different and more narrow sense, then they would simply not be engaging with the point that Gould and Lewontin are making.

Something else fuels the misunderstanding between Dennett and Gould. They clearly agree on setting high standards for adaptationists, explanations and for thinking about past function as well as present function (see, especially *DDI*, 212–20). And they agree where there is genuine design then there must have been natural selection. Where they differ is in how much design they see in nature. When Dennett looks at nature's creatures, he sees design everywhere. When Gould looks, he sees design, but he also sees the absence of design. He finds much order that is for no purpose at all, and yet that order is not random. And he wants to explain that order as well as explaining the design. For him, that order is properly part of the study of evolution, and, because Darwinism cannot explain that order, the study of evolution cannot be purely Darwinian. For Dennett, the interest of evolution is more or less exclusively an interest in design work. The other details, the details that often excite Gould, are of somewhat peripheral interest to Dennett.

7.3 Contingency and punctuated equilibria

Dennett thinks that the evolutionary trajectory of a lineage is best predicted and explained from the Darwinian stance. The Darwinian stance will pull out patterns that will reassert themselves even in the face of unknown 'physical perturbations and variations' (TB, 27) that they may face. By contrast, someone like Gould thinks that evolutionary trajectories cannot be predicted by any shortcut route. Rather, for him, we must operate at the level of the design or physical stance. As such, it is important to attend to the 'physical perturbations and variations'. Some may well be considered random, others may be law-like, but they are not reliably absorbed. Rather, they have a deep impact on the trajectory.

To help us think about evolutionary trajectories, Gould introduces an image of rewinding the tape of life and playing it again (Gould, 1989, chapter 1). What should we expect on different runs of the tape? For Dennett, on any given run of the tape we should expect certain features reliably to reoccur. If we reran the life of any given organism, we would expect that organism to do many of the same things: search for food, search for shelter, find a mate, and so forth. And, for Dennett, lineages parallel individual organisms. They will do many of the same things: develop into multi-cellular form, develop eyes, develop wings, develop varying degrees of intelligence, and so forth. By contrast, Gould is much more sceptical about there being great similarities between different runs of the tape. His scepticism is expressed both in his theory of punctuated equilibria and, more directly, in his doctrine of contingency.

Punctuated equilibria

The theory of punctuated equilibria claims that, over long periods of time, the pattern of change that we see in populations is not continuous and gradual, but rather takes the form of long periods of stability punctuated by periods of rapid change. The time periods here are relative. What is rapid, effectively instantaneous as far as the fossil record is concerned, leaves plenty of time for natural selection to render radical changes to a population. The developers of the theory, Gould, along with colleague Niles Eldredge, do not deny this. But they point out that during these periods of stability it is far from clear that the environment is stable and unchanging. If the environment is changing, and organisms are not changing in response to it, then it appears that natural selection is not acting or is not powerful enough for its action to be noticed. And so, to tell the complete story of evolution, some other forces, non-Darwinian forces of conservatism, are required. For, at least as Gould and Eldredge gloss it, if natural selection is the dominant force, then change in species should be continuous and gradual, even on the very large timescale of the fossil record. But, although some of the data is still disputed, the fossil record seems to show the pattern of long periods of stability punctuated by short periods of change.

One Darwinian response to punctuated equilibria, which Dennett rehearses (*DDI*, 293–4), is to argue that this pattern is itself generated by the force of natural selection. Although responding to an environmental change by preserving and promoting a favourable variation is something which is endorsed by reason, so too is keeping to a tried-and-tested design. Natural selection can favour the latter strategy, just as much as the first. After all, most deviations from the norm will be detrimental. And even those that are of benefit run the risk of being diluted in a large population. So it may require very strong and very focused selection pressures to bring about the sort of change that leaves a trace in the fossil record.

But a more fundamental response to punctuated equilibria, and one which is thoroughly naturalistic, is simply to deny that the large-scale patterns of macro-evolution exhibit design. If one denies this, then there is no need for a Darwinian explanation. Where there is no design, a pattern or ordering can be explained by chance, accident, or natural law. Dennett acknowledges this point in passing.

> [Perhaps] you would be foolish to try to explain some of the visible patterns of diversity in the biosphere by concentrating on the slow transformation of the various lineages, but that does not mean that they did not undergo slow transformations at various punctuation marks in their history (*DDI*, 298).

This passing remark from Dennett, I think, gets at the heart of Gould's complaint against orthodox Darwinism. For Gould really does think it is foolish, worse, bad science, to try to explain the 'visible patterns of diversity', and also the tempo of those patterns, by concentrating on the effects of natural selection. Other factors serve to explain those patterns. For example, it may be the case that evolution advances at pace only when an extant ecological system suffers serious disruption, for example, by invasion, a meteor fall, an ice age, and so forth. But such explanations really ought not to provoke any anxiety on Dennett's part. And they should not, because the patterns that Gould is explaining by appeal to non-Darwinian causal regularities are not designed patterns. There is no order for a purpose in the pattern of punctuated equilibria. Rather, if Gould and Eldredge are right, that is just how, given some combination of very general factors and perhaps some very specific factors, the evolutionary story has unfolded.

Contingency

Let us return to Gould's image of the 'tape of life'. If we rewound the tape of life and ran it again, what sort of patterns would we expect to encounter? If the biological world were constructed by God's hand, and if God acts only for the best, then we would expect the same result on every run of the tape. Every time the tape ran life would crawl out of the sea and onto the land, plants would evolve, dinosaurs would give way to mammals, and humans would eventually arrive on the scene. This would not be a contingent flow of events. Rather, it could only go that way. But we are setting aside the possibility that God constructed the biological world, and assuming natural forces alone did the work. What difference does this make?

For Gould it makes all the difference. Even if we grant, for the sake of argument, a reasonably advanced starting point, say a population of simple single-celled organisms, Gould expects different runs of the tape of life to produce very different results. This is because he thinks the rise and fall of mountain ranges, the arrival of meteors, the onset of ice ages, and so forth, can all have a dramatic effect on the way in which the tape unfolds. And, indeed, so can rather more mundane events. Moreover, he thinks that some events which are absolutely critical in our particular history, such as the invention of multi-cellular organisms or the invention of sex, may, in themselves, be rather unlikely. While there is no reason why such inventions should not occur, and while it may be true that, if they do occur, they have a good chance of persisting, this does not mean that we have a right to expect their occurrences on different runs of the tape.

Dennett's idea is that natural selection will tend to ensure that evolutionary trajectories overcome chance, and that they will guarantee upward movement in design space. So were we to wind the

tape of life back to the beginning and run it again, we would expect
certain kinds of design to be rediscovered. For example, we might
expect that creatures would evolve that had eyes or wings, we
might expect that it would evolve air-breathing organisms. This, he
claims, is supported by compelling evidence that traits such as eyes
and wings have developed independently in different parts of
the evolutionary tree (see *DDI*, 128–35, 306–8). How, he asks us,
could this be so if the occurrence of these inventions were purely
contingent?

Dennett does not go as far as to say that natural selection is
aiming at a particular final goal. Rather, he suggests that the Darwinian stance reveals the presence of an intelligent process that will
seek out good solutions to the problems it faces. Given this, Dennett
expects it to discover good solutions, to swiftly respond to what he
calls 'forced moves', and to reliably encounter what he calls 'Good
Tricks'.

The idea of the forced move is a move in design space that is
'obviously right' (*DDI*, 129, 136, 222) and one that is not a 'big deal'
to discover (222). The moves of building organisms that have an
autonomous metabolism and that have definite boundaries are,
says Dennett, clear forced moves (128). More or less any 'run' of the
'tape of life' would quickly make this move, or, of course, grind to
a halt. Given this account of forced moves, we should not be sur-
prised to see them being made again and again as the Darwinian
processes unfold.

A Good Trick is a more general notion than the forced move. It
is any move in design space that offers a significant advantage to
the organism. It is not so much a move 'dictated by reason' as one
that is 'strongly endorsed by reasons' (456). The Baldwin Effect (see
p. 216) is described by Dennett as a Good Trick rather than as a
forced move. He reserves the term 'Good Trick' for traits that need
not be specific to a particular organism. We might, then, understand
flight as a Good Trick, rather than as a forced move. It is not a forced
move, because organisms could find ways other than flight to
improve their design, but it is a Good Trick, because quite distinct
lineages could independently discover it and the way in which it
brings benefits to different lineages is roughly the same. That is to
say, flight represents a more general pattern.

It can often seem, when reading *Darwin's Dangerous Idea*, that
Dennett is aiming to show how natural selection can play the role
that was once preserved for God's intelligence. When it comes to
explaining how organisms come to be adapted to their environ-

ment, this is all well and good. But whereas God may have wanted to fill all the slots in the great chain of being, from the worm to the human, from the human to the angels, with God, itself, at the apex, 'Mother Nature' has no such agenda. All she cares about, as it were, is ensuring that evolution unfolds in an intelligent manner. Gould can agree with this, but can also insist that there is a wide variety of such unfoldings that conform to this constraint. In particular, he makes two points to support his case.

The first point is Gould's emphasis of the fact that the most common form of life in the world is the bacterial (Gould, 1992). If there is a trend in evolution at all, it is a trend towards bacterial life as the most fundamental product. By contrast, the kinds of organisms that we are typically interested in, such as mammals, represent a tiny and statistically aberrant part of the evolutionary tree. In effect, Gould sees 'lifting' as a rather uncommon process. It goes on, all right, but moves upward in design space as often as not end in failure. Every so often there will be examples of substantial upward movement – even if movement up and down in design space is random, given time, certain heights will be reached. But that such heights are sometimes reached is no evidence of a trend pushing lineages towards such heights.

The second point draws on a particular period of evolutionary history known as the Cambrian explosion. Gould argues that at this time there was a massive diversity of different body-plans, including body-plans of a form quite distinct from any that persist today. But most of these body-plans have been lost to history. What determines which body-plans survived and which did not? Just by looking at them, it is far from clear that those that did survive were obviously better. Of course, as Dennett notes, there is only so much one can tell from looking at such fossils. But Gould argues that we should at least consider the hypothesis that the designs that survived were simply lucky rather than having a definite competitive edge over their rivals. Against this suggestion Dennett writes:

> As Darwin insisted from the beginning, however, all it takes is "some groups" with an "edge" to put the wedge of competition into action. So is Gould just saying that *most* of the competition (or the competition with the largest, most important effects) was a true lottery? (*DDI*, 304)

Gould is not saying '*most* of the competition' throughout evolutionary history was a lottery. That would make miraculous the wealth of design that we observe. But he is saying first that *some* competitions that had *large* and very *important* effects could have been a lottery. Nothing in Darwinism counts against this. And second he is saying that during the Cambrian explosion there actually was just such a lottery: the body-plans that become the basis for much of modern multi-cellular life were selected by chance factors. Had the body-plans that had been selected by chance been different, then this would have had a dramatic effect on further evolutionary development.

Dennett does not accept this and presses that even if it is not obvious from the fossil record what the basis of competitive edge might be, it is still possible that we might yet be able to discern it and tell a 'convincing story about why the winners won and the loser lost' (*DDI*, 304–5). He adds, 'Who knows?' A telling remark, because Gould's complaint is precisely that what he regards as the orthodoxy *does* claim that there is, whether we know it or not, a *reason*, one to do with differential fitness, why some body-plans won out and others lost. Here is what Gould says about his lottery suggestion:

> Perhaps the grim reaper works during brief episodes of mass extinction, provoked by unpredictable environmental catastrophes (often triggered by impacts of extra terrestrial bodies). Groups may prevail or die for reasons that bear no relationship to the Darwinian basis of success in normal times. Even if fishes hone their adaptations to peaks of aquatic perfection, they will all die if the ponds dry up. But grubby old Buster the Lungfish, former laughing stock of the piscine priesthood, may pull through – and not because a bunion on his great-grandfather's fin warned his ancestors about an impending comet. Buster and his kin may prevail because a feature evolved long ago for a different use has fortuitously permitted survival during a sudden and unpredictable change in rules. (Gould, 1989, 48)

Of course, it is open for Dennett to say that Buster did have an edge. And, in the circumstances that Gould describes, he did. But this is not the sort of edge that is normally admissible in Darwinian explanation. It does not do to say that what is fitter is just that which happens to survive. In order to avoid vacuity, fitness has to be something that gives a creature a statistically better chance of surviving to reproduce (see Mills and Beatty, 1979). But the 'edge' that Buster has could well have been something that brought benefit only in the specific context of the catastrophe. If it had, then the right answer to Gould's question, 'Why did Buster and his body-plan survive the catastrophe?', would be, 'No reason. Just good luck.'

Of course, it must be conceded that between any organism now there is a continual path back to its ancestors. And at each stage the ancestors will often have exhibited some edge over rivals. But, for all that, when there is, as Gould says, a radical change in conditions, there can be a shake-out which does not operate according to the ordinary rules of natural selection. Of course, the outcome of such a shake-out process is not one which exhibits design. But it is a pattern that has an impact on evolutionary history.

7.4 Where things stand

Dennett's two central aims in *Darwin's Dangerous Idea* are, first, to show how Darwinism is the key to reconciling the different out-looks: the mechanistic and the intentional; and, second, to show just how deep Darwinism cuts into the fabric of our most fundamental beliefs (*DDI*, 18). To what extent does he succeed?

On the reconciliation issue, Darwinism clearly shows that there is no need to appeal to supernature to explain the origin of natural agents and, in particular, of persons. But if we are not concerned with origins, but only the here-and-now nature of natural agents in general and of persons in particular, do we need to appeal to Darwinism? If God had made us, using only mechanistic bits and pieces, surely we could understand ourselves by means of Dennett's intentional systems theory, and do so without any refer-ence to Darwinism? If this is right, then Dennett overstates the case for Darwinism.

On the other hand, where Darwinism clearly can help is in taking up the slack where the predictive and explanatory power of the intentional and personal stances fall short (see chapter 4). In par-ticular, where the behaviour of an agent deviates from the rational in systematic ways, looking at the forces that designed the agent's cognitive mechanism is a good way of exploring the nature of that deviation. Moreover, central to the idea of real patterns (chapter 3) is the idea of systems that can constantly tune and retune them-selves in the face of pressures from their environment. And the canonical version of this idea is, arguably, Darwinian natural selec-tion. In these two ways, at least, we can say that Darwinism is relevant to understanding the here-and-now nature of ourselves and other natural agents.

On the issue of cutting deeply into the fabric of our most fundamental beliefs, Dennett's case is much less clear. Clearly, understanding our origins is very important. And Dennett does offer an
excellent defence of his bold claim that: '[Adaptationism] plays a
crucial role in the analysis of every biological event at every scale
from the creation of the first self-replicating macromolecule on up
. . . Adaptationist reasoning is not optional: it is the heart and soul
of evolutionary biology' (*DDI*, 238).

Even if there is something right about Gould and Lewontin's
critique of the worst excesses of adaptationism, the approach is
central. We must always begin by assuming adaptationism, for
unless we do we cannot exclude the infinite variety of alternative
possibilities. Only following this starting point can we make room
for the alternative approaches. To put the point in caricature: while
we can genuinely wonder whether the length of T. Rex's forelimb
is an adaptation or not, without adaptationism we would be unable
to exclude the thought that T. Rex was a badly designed vegetarian
water-dweller.

But outside of biology, how significant is Darwinism? Dennett's
all-encompassing notion of design space shows how we can see not
only living things, but all human artefacts, as products of a Darwinian process. But if we want to understand the origin of, say, a
work of art, how helpful is it to harp on about Darwinian processes?
Of course, it is sometimes helpful: it reminds us that there are no
supernatural forces involved in the creative process. In the very
same way, it is sometimes helpful to point out that no more than
the motion of atoms and molecules were involved in the production of an art work. But, surely, much of the time we do not need
reminding of these things? When we are comparing this artist's
approach with that, we would no more expect to end up talking
about atoms and molecules than we would about Darwinian
processes. It is true, of course, that Darwinian processes can exist
and operate at many levels. Darwinism provides a much richer
range of explanatory tools than physics, something that Dennett
powerfully illustrates. But just because we can apply Darwinian
explanations to many phenomena does not mean that we should.

The mystery of our being here

Dennett is officially sceptical about the idea that Darwinism implies
progress: 'Global, long-term progress, amounting to the view that

things in the biosphere are, in general, getting better and better and better, was denied by Darwin, and although it is often imagined by onlookers to be an implication of evolution, it is simply a mistake' (*DDI*, 299). Given this, we might expect *Darwin's Dangerous Idea* to promote no more than an account of how it is possible that all the 'lifting' that is required to design persons could take place without any help from supernature. But in fact Dennett seems to go rather further. He does not aim merely to show that it is possible for natural selection and its cranes to design persons, he also aims to show that it is more or less inevitable that natural selection and its cranes will do so. Consider the following remark:

> [Gould's] main conclusion . . . is that if we were to "wind the tape of life back" and play it again and again, the likelihood is infinitesimal of *Us* being the product on any other run through the evolutionary mill. This is undoubtedly true (if by "Us" we mean the particular variety of *Homo sapiens* we are: hairless and upright, with five fingers on each of two hands, speaking English and French and playing tennis and chess). (*DDI*, 56)

The contents of qualifying brackets are critical here. Dennett seems to be saying that actually persons, if not human beings as such, are a likely outcome of different runs of the tape. This reading is further supported by later remarks. He claims that Gould offers no evidence against the hypothesis that it is inevitable and pre-dictable that 'intelligent, language-using, technology-inventing, culture-creating beings' will arise (307). Dennett concedes that we could not predict what kinds of organisms these beings might be, whether they be water-dwellers, whether they bear live young, and so forth. But since all lineages 'grope towards the Good Tricks in Design Space' (307) he does expect some lineages to find this particular region of design space, the region of which, as far as we know, we are the only current occupiers.

If this is the right reading of Dennett, then his claim is very radical. It implies that Darwinian processes guarantee some sort of progress, implies that they guarantee systemic upward lifting in design space. It implies that Darwinism guarantees the evolution of creatures that *are* just like us in a very significant sense. Although these creatures would not be like us in many ways – they might be reptilian, have six limbs instead of four, seven fingers instead of five, and so forth – they would be like us in that they were reflective, self-conscious creatures able to make use of a fully blown language and to take advantage of the repository of knowledge that is culture. They would be persons, even if they were not human beings.

Initially the claim that evolution converges on the design of persons seems very strong indeed. Against such a strong claim, Gould's contingency can look quite modest. For, although there is evidence of convergency, there is also a wealth of diversity. And, so far as we know, we are the only persons, the only 'intelligent, language-using, technology-inventing, culture-creating beings'. Despite a good press, there is no compelling evidence that dolphins, whales, or chimps are persons. If Dennett is right, we might ask, 'Why not?' Surely, on his view we would expect to find, as we do with the eye and the wing, that there would be many cases of persons in different parts of the biosphere. Of course, that we do not find other instances of persons does not of itself defeat Dennett. But it does illustrate the need for him to marshal good reasons to think that the path towards persons is an area of design space that we should expect to be revisited regularly on different runs of the tape of life.

I think Dennett is attracted to the radical claim because he thinks that, without it, there really would be some deep mystery about how we, human beings, came to be here. Darwinian evolution, of course, explains how it is *possible* for us to have evolved, but Dennett wants more. He wants it to be likely that we evolved. For, on his view, unless Darwinism makes it likely that we would have evolved, it would be mysterious that we did.

If I am right about this, it goes some way to explaining part of the very deep ideological differences between Dennett and Gould. The thought here is that Dennett thinks that there is something that needs explaining, our presence in the world, that Gould does not. How can there be two such different views? Consider rolling a dice 100 times. The chance of getting one specific distribution of rolls (one that begins 41225326 . . . and ends . . . 6632412) is tiny. But if we do throw the dice 100 times we will most definitely get one distribution or another. So when we are faced with a specific distribution we would be mad to be deeply puzzled as to why we got just this distribution and not some other one. We would be mad, say, to dwell on the tiny, tiny chance that this was the distribution that would result from 100 throws.

There would be something amazing, something to explain, if, before we had begun to roll the dice, we had written down a prediction and that prediction now turned out 100 percent accurate. Similarly certain distributions might have peculiar features. The distribution that begins with 10 ones, followed by 10 twos, 10 threes, and so forth, would be very surprising. So would the distribution that consisted of 100 sixes in a row. Unlike most distributions, that have no particular order, these distributions stand out. And so in either of these cases we would suspect something other than chance was affecting the outcome of our dice throws. And this 'something' would require explanation.

Dennett, I think, sees some kind of ordering in the biological world that Gould does not see. This is striking as part of Dennett's overall strategy is to deflate problematic phenomena as well as talking up the power of mechanisms. Here Dennett goes in for much less deflation of the phenomena, the appearance of a purposeful design in the structure of the biological realm, than he might. For him, the biological world is akin to rolling 90 sixes out of a 100 throws, whereas for Gould it is just one distribution amongst many. For Gould, the presence of persons is simply an unlikely event. It might, say, be the equivalent to a run of 10 sixes in a 100 rolls. There is nothing mysterious about such a run. No miracle has occurred. Although it is pretty unlikely, no special explanation is called for. Contrast this with Dennett's vision. The fact that we have the equivalent of 90 sixes demands, in the absence of a miracle, some other explanation. And this explanation – the power of natural selection to seek out Good Tricks and follow forced moves – is such that on subsequent turns at rolling the dice, the same sort of effects would follow.

What is not clear is how this sort of dispute between Gould and Dennett might be settled. Is our world like the 90 sixes sequence or is it like the 10 sixes sequence? Dennett and Gould both take a stand here. But what facts can support one view rather than the other? Perhaps, in the future, evolutionary simulations will tell us more. But in the absence of such data, it is not clear what factors make one view more plausible than the other. And yet, if Dennett is wrong, then much, if not all, of the force of his argument that Darwinian processes have a tendency to yield up persons, is blunted.

Further reading

Darwin's *Origin of Species* was written for a general audience. It remains an accessible and persuasive read, although occasionally the reader can feel overburdened by details. Richard Dawkins's books, especially *The Blind Watchmaker* (Dawkins, 1986), form an excellent and highly accessible introduction to the modern face of

Darwinism. Be wary of some of the more exuberant rhetorical flourishes in his *The Selfish Gene* (Dawkins, 1976). Dennett's own *Darwin's Dangerous Idea* is more philosophical, but, as I argue here, his portrayal of Gould and others who see more scope for non-Darwinian explanation in biology is sometimes less than even-handed. Kim Sterelny and Paul Griffith's *Sex and Death* (Sterelny and Griffiths, 1999) provides excellent philosophical discussion of Darwinism and of biological issues in general. On the evolution of the eye, see Dawkins, 1995, 76–83, and Dawkins, 1996, chapter 5. The idea that species are individuals is discussed by Sterelny and Griffiths (1999, chapter 9). On the idea of substantial steps forward in design, such as the invention of eukaryotes or sex, see Maynard Smith and Szathmáry (1999).

Williams (1996) is a friendly primer on adaptationist thinking and the source from which I draw my example of the pony fish. Gould and Lewontin's (1978) paper is essential reading. Dennett's initial response is in *IS*, chapter 7. A more sustained critique comes in *DDI*, chapters 9 and 10. See Dawkins (1982) for evidence that Dawkins is, in my terminology, a logical adaptationist. Sterelny and Griffiths (1999), chapters 10–11, give a good overview of the debate. See also Peter Godfrey-Smith's (2000). Punctuated equilibria theory is described and discussed by Sterelny and Griffiths (1999, chapter 12). More partisan discussion can be found in Dawkins (1986) and *DDI*, chapter 10. Gould develops his account of contingency in *Wonderful Life* (Gould, 1989). This is a long book but the central points are fully dealt with in chapters 1 and 5. His excellent, and short, *Life's Grandeur* (Gould, 1992) also deals with contingency, but concentrates mostly on opposing the idea that there are evolutionary trends towards bigger and smarter organisms as opposed to small and stupid ones.

8

A Variety of Free Will Worth Wanting

Dennett's working method involves placing empirical constraints on our analyses of concepts. The empirical constraints are made clear when we consider a range of possible scenarios in which we think a concept should or should not apply. If it turns out that no system made out of mechanistic parts could answer to the concept, and yet the concept seems to be an ineliminable part of our self-conception, then we have a prima facie case for deflating that concept, while preserving what really matters to us. An account of consciousness that requires a plain mysterious, or even supernatural, method of knowing whether or not we are philosophical zombies, fails to pass this test. And so Dennett offers us a modestly deflated account of consciousness in its place. This modestly deflated concept makes sense of persons being conscious and also of their knowing so. Similarly, an account of sensitivity to reasons that requires perfect sensitivity to reason, or perfect immunity to Sphexishness, cannot apply to any system built from mechanistic parts. But if our account allows for a few bad habits and a tendency to error, then people, animals, and chess machines, that is, agents built out of mechanisms, can count as being genuinely sensitive to reasons. We trade a modest deflation in an ordinary concept, be it reason or consciousness, in exchange for a concept that can apply to natural entities, to entities built out of mechanistic parts. But in doing so, we do not talk either reason or consciousness down so much that what we are left with is not worth having. Indeed, everything that it makes sense to care about in these concepts is preserved by Dennett's modest deflations.

In this chapter we look at how Dennett applies his method to the issue of free will as explored in *Brainstorms* (part IV) and *Elbow Room*. How can we understand concepts such as 'rational agent', 'accountable', 'responsible', 'freely chosen action', and so forth, in such a way that they can apply to entities and properties of entities that are constructed out of mechanistic parts? Of course, the sceptic may always insist that the proper understanding of these concepts is such that they cannot apply to entities (and the properties of entities) that are so constructed. Such a sceptic leaves us with two paths: abandon naturalism in favour of supernaturalism or embrace eliminativism and deny that the concepts have any useful role to play. As elsewhere, Dennett seeks to show that we can retain the richness of our concepts, the richness that is required to sustain what matters to us about our self-conception, while reconciling them with naturalism. And, as elsewhere, he eschews reconciliation by reduction. To reduce the concepts associated with free will to the concepts associated with mechanism would, for Dennett, distort these concepts beyond the point of their being worth having.

It is worth mentioning a general background thought to Dennett's approach. For him, our concepts are, for the most part, all right as they are (*ER*, 19). So what is left after any revision in the light of empirical constraints should be recognizable as a tidied-up version of what we began with. For the issues of sensitivity to reasons and of consciousness, I have argued that this strategy works well. But can Dennett make as strong a case for the issue of free will? I shall begin with a brief review of one formulation of the free will problem. I then turn to the set of concepts that Dennett aims to examine and strip of supernatural baggage. His stripped-down concepts certainly avoid any tension with naturalism. But what is less clear is whether they provide a rich enough account of agency to temper the discomfort which the problem of free will generates.

8.1 Dennett's version of the free will problem

The problem of free will is often linked to determinism, the doctrine that given the initial state of the universe and the laws of physics there is only one way in which the future can unfold. But for Dennett the real threat is not so much determinism, which modern physics suggests is false, but mechanism (*BS*, 233ff). If we suppose determinism to be false, it is still the case that our internal mechanism operates in a largely deterministic fashion. The parts from which we are built are generally reliable. Perhaps quantum effects, effects that elude the grip of determinism, play a significant factor at the level of the atom, but they will almost entirely be eliminated at the level of the neuron. Natural selection typically designs our component parts to be reliable and to compensate for or filter out any indeterministic fluctuations there may be. It typically does this because, in most circumstances, any other strategy would make an organism less fit. So, even if determinism is false, the mechanisms inside us are generally very reliable. And what these mechanisms do next is determined by their prior state and the state of the environment. This is enough to get a serious version of the free will problem up and running.

Consider an example. There are three bagels on the plate and Ruth and Tam have one each. Then, without asking, Tam takes the third and wolfs it down. Ruth complains loudly. Tam is being unfair. She should have shared the bagel, or at least asked Ruth first. But Tam replies that there's no point getting cross because, after all, her impulse was simply the inevitable outcome of the environmental stimulus and the mechanistic processes inside her head. She cannot control these processes, they control her. She has no free will. And, since she does not, there is no point holding her accountable for her actions. There was nothing she could have done about the bagel snatch. And it would be wrong to hold her responsible or to blame her for it.

This sort of story captures a number of elements of the problem of free will. Ordinarily we hold one another accountable for our actions. If I snatch a bagel then, if pressed, I ought to be able to answer for my action. I may try to justify my action, that is, to argue that it was a reasonable thing for me to do. 'You had two bagels last time, it's only fair that I have two this time.' Or I may accept that it was unreasonable, but offer some sort of excuse. 'Look, I know it was wrong, but I was just so hungry.' Or I might admit I have no excuse at all. 'Yes, you're right, it was unfair,' perhaps adding an apology, 'I'm sorry,' or defiance, 'Who ever said life was fair?' In making any of these replies I make it clear that I do consider myself accountable for my action. On a different tack, I might deny that what I did was really an action at all. I might say, 'I know it looks bad, but the fact is a wicked hypnotist programmed me to make the bagel snatch. I had no control over it. It was simply something that happened to me.' In this last case I am not so much accounting for my action, not so much explaining why I did something, as offering an explanation of why something happened to me. If something happens to me, as opposed to my doing something, then, ordinarily, we do not require the person to be accountable. I do not have to account for the things that happen to me, only the things I purposefully do.

In the bagel story, Tam assumes that human beings are complex mechanisms, mechanisms bound by causal laws. This being so, she thinks that it follows there can be no free will. That is, everything that looks as if it is an action is, in fact, merely something that happens to the agent. She might put the point this way: we are simply robots shoved around by the world and our internal states. We might go through the motions of offering justifications or making excuses, but it is all completely idle. For the practice of offering justifications and excuses is premised on the idea that we are accountable for the event in question. And, on Tam's view, we are not accountable for any of these events.

Tam's remarks to Ruth are pretty feeble. In ordinary life, at least, nobody would take this kind of protestation seriously. But when we step back from ordinary life and consider how we can mount a rational response to Tam, the situation is not so straightforward. The sort of scepticism she exhibits can be very compelling. How can we respond?

The first response might be to join Tam in her scepticism. Ruth might say, yes, I suppose you are right. And she might further comment that her agreeing with Tam is itself just one more result of the mechanistic processes in a brain responding to environmental pressures. This is a radical response, and it is important not to underestimate its implications. It entails that one has to give up on the idea of action altogether, to eliminate that category as one with any special explanatory force. It makes Tam's tripping over a stone the same kind of event as Tam's snatching the bagel. As such, the response effectively eliminates the very concept of action. And with this elimination goes the concept of accountability – for if you do not act, what is there to account for – and, hence, the concepts of responsibility, of praise and blame, of morality in general. Indeed, this move even threatens the idea of meaning. If there is no difference between actions and things that happen to Tam and Ruth, how is their apparent exchange of meaningful sentences, sentences which take the form of an argument, importantly different from the bouncing back and forth of noises?

Consider a second response. Here we begin with the idea that the sceptic's conclusions cannot possibly be right. It is, we press, simply self-evident that we are accountable for at least some of our doings. But if it is accepted that the sceptic's reasoning is valid, it must be one of her premises that is at fault. Perhaps, then, Tam is just wrong in saying that people are made up only of mechanistic parts, parts whose operation is bound by strict causal laws. The argument goes like this: because it is clear that people do have free will and because it is also clear that merely complex mechanisms cannot, people must be more than merely complex mechanisms. There must be some 'extra element'. And the extra element must be something beyond mechanism, such as an immaterial soul.

The third kind of response tries to steer a course between the first two. Compatibilists aim to show that the conditions that appear to threaten free will – most generally determinism, in our case mechanism – in fact leave a viable notion of free will intact. While some notion of free will, they argue, is excluded by the problematic conditions, a wholly viable notion of free will is not. Compatibilists, then, aim to show that there is something more subtle wrong with the kind of argument put forward by Tam. Dennett is a confirmed compatibilist, and as such he joins a distinguished line of com-patibilists, including such notables as David Hume (1711–1776) and A. J. Ayer (1910–1989). Although Dennett's compatibilism works out a number of familiar themes, it is a distinctive contribution to the extensive literature on free will. This is partly because of its sophistication and its emphasis on mechanisms that have been designed by Darwinian processes. But, perhaps most important, it is distinctive because of the way Dennett relates the issue of free will to the issue of personal identity and the ways in which we act to shape our own characters.

Before setting out the particulars of Dennett's account, it is worth making a general point that applies to any compatibilist approach. The first is that compatibilists have no truck with the idea that inde-terminism has anything to offer that can soothe the sceptic's worry. Suppose determinism is false. Thus there are different ways the uni-verse can unfold given its initial state and the laws of physics. In effect, it means that the laws of physics do not strictly determine every outcome. There is a bit of slack. This means that in principle it is possible that Tam, instead of snatching the third bagel, left well alone. In fact, for Dennett, as already noted, this is unlikely, since even if determinism is false Dennett expects the mechanisms inside Tam's head to be designed to filter out any indeterminacy that might occur at the level of physics. But, for the sake of argument, let us grant that whether or not Tam snatched the bagel is not determined by her prior state and the environmental stimuli to which she is exposed.

How, the compatibilist asks, is this supposed to support the claim that Tam acted as a result of free will? One thought might be that this bit of indeterminism provides some scope for Tam's immaterial soul to steer events one way or another. But, the compatibilist can reply, are we to suppose that Tam's immaterial soul is moved by no principles at all? If it is not, then Tam hardly seems free, but rather subject to whims of chance. If it is moved by principles, then no progress seems to have been made. For these principles, given the prior state of Tam's immaterial soul and given what is presented to it, will dictate the decision that she makes. And if this is the case, it is unclear that shifting from the material to the immaterial realm has brought any advantages.

I shall not assess the success of this reasoning here. For now, it is enough to note that this kind of reasoning is hotly disputed by those who disagree with compatibilism. But what the reasoning illustrates is the compatibilist conviction that whatever it is that makes the difference between acts of will that are free and acts of will that are not, the answer has little or nothing to do with determinism. We have, then, another instance of Dennett's de-differencing strategy. For Dennett, and compatibilists generally, what matters is not that the act of will is determined, but rather the way in which it is determined. Or, switching away from determinism to the issue Dennett is primarily concerned with, what matters is not that an act of will is the result of the operation of a mechanism, but rather the design and operation of the mechanism that results in the act of will.

8.2   The elements of Dennett's assault

There are a number of interdependent concepts linked to the issue of free will. In *Elbow Room* Dennett works on giving a revised account of some of these concepts with the aim of showing how, once revised, we can see that we both have free will and that we are also made out of no more than cunningly arranged mechanisms. In this section I want to review the concepts that Dennett tackles and comment on his suggested revisions. For each concept there is a claim that Dennett characterizes as a myth and that he wants to dispute. The concepts and the disputed claims are as follows:

- Rationality: mechanisms are and only can be sensitive to causes and not reasons. But to be a *genuine* rational agent is to be sensitive to reasons.
- 'Could have done otherwise' (excluding random factors): mechanisms are such that if, given certain conditions, they operate in one way, then, in these conditions they could not have done otherwise. But for a decision to be *genuinely* free it must be the case that, although you chose to act in one way, you could have done otherwise. If your choices are the result of the operation of mechanisms inside you, then (excluding random factors) it is never the case that you could have done otherwise.
- Control: mechanisms are controlled by their internal states and environmental stimuli. But to be *genuinely* in control of yourself, you must be able to resist the push of your own internal states and environmental stimuli.
- Self-making: the current state of a mechanism is simply a causal product of its prior states and its environmental encounters. But to be *genuinely* responsible for your own character requires that you have made free choices during its formation.
- Responsibility: mechanisms just do what they do; it makes no sense to hold them responsible for their operations. But *genuine* agents make free choices and for this reason, and only this reason, it is coherent to hold them responsible, and hence, coherent to praise or blame them for the choices they make.

Rationality and 'could have done otherwise'

We have already looked extensively at rationality in chapters 2, 3, and 4. Dennett can agree that mechanisms are sensitive only to causes and not to reasons. But on his view agents are not simply identical with mechanisms. Rather, an agent is present when a real pattern of rational activity exerts itself with a certain degree of vigour in the world. And Dennett has shown how such a real pattern of rational activity can be underpinned by the right kind of mechanism.

For Dennett, then, the rationality worry is a red herring. There is no incompatibility between being built from mechanistic parts and being supremely, if not perfectly, sensitive to the power of reason. If to have free will were simply a matter of being able to make rational choices, then Dennett's argument, if successful, would be enough to establish that persons have free will. But this is unlikely to satisfy any but the softest sceptic. For she might concede that we do, more often than not, respond in a rational way to the situations which we face, and still deny that we can make free choices by appealing to one of the other elements just listed.

What about the idea that to be free it must be the case that for any given action an agent could have done otherwise? If determinism is true, then one reading of the proposition 'she could have done otherwise' turns out to be false. Were we to roll back time and play it again, the very same thing would happen. However, for Dennett, as for other compatibilists, the sense which is shown to be false by determinism, is not the sense that is relevant for having free will. Surprisingly, Dennett expresses some sympathy with the project of finding a reading of 'could have done otherwise' such that it is compatible with determinism (*ER*, 131). And he undertakes a detailed analysis of the term 'can' (*ER*, 144–52).

This is quite out of character for Dennett. Throughout his work he tends to avoid such detailed analyses, and indeed explicitly expresses some impatience with them (*ER*, 3–4). Of course, it matters greatly how we understand the term 'can'. When Luther takes his stand against the Catholic Church, he declares, 'Here I stand, I can do no other' (*ER*, 133). There is clearly a sense of 'can' in which he is wrong. He could have gone swimming instead. And as we have just seen there is a sense of 'can' that, given determinism, would make his claim trivial. He could not have done anything else, because he did just what the laws of physics determined he would do. For Dennett, of course, neither of these senses of 'can' are the relevant sense.

However, I do not want to explore Dennett's investigation of 'can' or examine different readings of the 'could have done otherwise' principle. For I do not think that the success of Dennett's project depends on the nuances of such investigations. His position turns on something rather cruder, namely doing away with certain deeply entrenched intuitions adopted by the sceptic about free will. The real work for Dennett to do, and the interesting work that he does, is in offering a modest deflation of free will, and not jumping through complex hoops to show that there is no real need for deflation.

Control and self-control

In the bagel story, Tam claimed she was controlled by her inner mechanism and her environment. The idea that Tam is not really in control can be cashed out in two distinct ways. In one way, Tam could think she is not in control because, quite literally, her mechanism and environment control her. The other way is that Tam could think she is not in control because, despite her best efforts, she is buffeted around by external and internal forces, forces that she is powerless to overcome. In examining the notion of control, Dennett shows that neither of these worries can be sustained.

I begin by looking at the claim that Tam's inner mechanism and environment control her. The first move here is to distinguish between two different senses of the term 'control' (*ER*, 57–61). If we mean by control that 'A controls B if and only if changes in A are reliably reflected or registered in changes in B' (*ER*, 59), then Tam is controlled by her inner mechanism and environment. But in this sense of 'control' it is clearly a good thing that Tam is so controlled. For such control makes it possible that she is sensitive to what is going on in her environment. And it also explains how she can learn: her inner processes are affected by her past encounters and enable her to cope better with future contingencies. Being controlled in this sense is not, according to Dennett, anything that can detract from Tam's freedom.

A second and more relevant sense of control, according to Dennett, is the sense in which 'A controls B if and only if the relation between A and B is such that A can *drive* B into whichever of B's normal range of states A *wants* B to be in' (*ER*, 52). If Tam is being *driven* into states as a result of the *wants* of some other agent, then it is clearly true that she is not free to choose her own paths. But this is not the relationship between Tam's inner mechanism, coupled with the environment, and Tam.

First, the environment is not an agent (*ER*, 61) and so is not even a candidate controller. The environment does not want Tam to do this or that, it has no desires or purposes of its own. It cannot control anything in the second sense of 'control'. It can buffet Tam and upset her plans, but it cannot get her to do what it wants, because it does not want her to do anything. Similarly, the environment can make Tam walk to the left rather than to the right, because one path is blocked by a large rock. But this is not a case of the environment manipulating or controlling Tam, it is simply a matter of Tam noticing what is going on in her environment and responding in the way that is most likely to promote the pursuit of her goals.

Second, Tam's inner mechanism is not an agent either. Tam is the agent, not the collection of her parts. Her inner mechanism does not have its own set of desires. Indeed, Tam's inner mechanism is not somehow independent of, something apart from, Tam.

Consider now a different sort of worry. Tam may be worried that she has insufficient or ineffective control. She may be worried that she is so buffeted about by her environment, and perhaps by certain psychological impediments, that she has very little control. The issue here is not strictly the issue of free will, but rather free action. Perhaps Tam freely wills that she does this or that, but it turns out that her will is ineffective. Her lack of control means she ends up failing to achieve what she wants. Is it at all plausible that Tam has insufficient control in ordinary circumstances, so much so that she might say that she is not accountable for the bagel snatch?

Let's look first at external impediments. Most of the time it is simply implausible to suggest that Tam is so buffeted by her environment that her control is compromised. Humans are very effective self-controllers, that is, they are effective at steering themselves in such a way as to achieve their goals. In part this is because if one method will not work, they are willing and able to try another. If I want to get from Edinburgh to Cambridge to visit my mum, I can achieve this goal even if there is a railstrike. I'll take the bus or plane instead or, at a pinch, hire a car. With a demanding goal such as this, I might be defeated by severe obstacles, e.g. massive flooding and a general strike. But much of the time, as with the bagel snatch, we are more than a match for overcoming environmental buffeting. Even if there is a pretty stiff breeze blowing, Tam is more than capable of flexing her arm muscles to keep her hand on target.

What about internal impediments? To be a self-controller, as all persons are, is not the same as exhibiting self-control. The idea of self-control is quite distinct. A person who has self-control is, to a first approximation, a person who acts upon the desires and motives that she values most highly. A lack of self-control is often illustrated by examples of impetuous action. If I value being polite and I set myself to keep a cool head, I demonstrate my lack of self-control when I throw a tantrum because my name has been spelled incorrectly. 'Get a grip,' my friend tells me. And, in doing so, she is urging me towards greater self-control. The issue of self-control involves very many subtle nuances. For it involves identifying what someone genuinely values – such as politeness – in the face of behaviour that suggests she does not value this at all. These nuances need not concern us here. What does matter for us, is that being made out of mechanistic bits and pieces is not a threat to our achieving self-control.

The kleptomaniac is someone who just cannot stop herself stealing. She lacks self-control. And she does to such an extent that we do not hold her fully responsible for her actions. To say someone is a kleptomaniac, as opposed to a committed thief, is to say that all reasonable steps that she may have taken to curb her stealing have not worked. She may have moralized to herself, she may have rehearsed carefully the negative consequences of her action, she may have tried avoiding opportunities where she could steal, but, nonetheless, she continues to steal. But ordinary weakness is not like this. If we suspect our self-control is threatened by a craving for sweets, we can 'adopt the higher-order strategy of not having sweets around the house, where the temptation would be too great' (*ER*, 63). Dennett describes such a craving as an example of the 'obstacles we carry with us' (*ER*, 63). But like obstacles we encounter in the outside world, there are plenty of methods we can use to steer around them. To lack self-control is for these internal obstacles to be insurmountable or for our methods of avoiding them to be inadequate. Sometimes this is the case, and sometimes it is not. But whether it is the case or not has nothing to do with the fact that we are built out of mechanistic parts. Just as a self-controller built from mechanistic parts can be more or less effective at achieving its ends in the face of external obstacles, so can it be more or less effective at achieving its ends in the face of the obstacles it carries with it.

People, then, are not controlled by the environment or by their insides. And people are sufficiently effective at exerting their will, that it is very rarely the case that they are simply buffeted about by circumstances beyond their control. And whether or not people have self-control is not settled by the fact that their insides are made out of mechanisms, but by the way they behave. Mechanisms can underpin agents who lack self-control just as readily as they can underpin agents who are possessed with a great deal of self-control. But does all this help us with the problem of free will?

8.3 Self-making and responsibility

Even if she is persuaded by what Dennett has argued for so far, the sceptic need not think that the problem of free will has been squarely met. For something could surely be a rational responder, an effective self-controller, and even have some analogue of self-control, and yet lack free will. Consider Dennett's example of the

Mars Explorer. Because of the time it takes to send and receive radio signals to and from Mars, the robot explorers are fitted: 'with (rudimentary) desires – or something like desires – and enough "knowledge" about their circumstances so that they could reliably do the work the controllers would have done, had they been near enough to intervene' (ER, 55).

We do not think, do we, that the Mars Explorer has free will? What does it lack? One key factor is this: when it comes to its successes and failures, the robot is not the agent we hold to account or consider responsible. The buck does not stop with the robot, but with its makers. But for an agent to have free will it must surely be the case that we can say 'the buck stops here' (ER, 76), that we cannot pass the buck on, on to the environment, to the structure of our internal mechanism, to our histories, and so forth. Dennett acknowledges the appeal of this intuition, but does not think it can be sustained. Roderick Chisholm is bold enough to defend the intuition in a pure form, a form that makes it easy to see how and why Dennett wants to reject it. Chisholm writes:

> If we are responsible ... then we have a prerogative which some would attribute only to God; each of us, when we act, is a prime mover unmoved. In doing what we do, we cause certain events to happen, and nothing – or no one – causes us to cause those events to happen. (Chisholm, 1964, 32)

But if we are made from mechanistic parts, we cannot be unmoved movers. So if we sign up to Chisholm's doctrine, we are faced with a dilemma: either embrace eliminativism and accept that people lack responsibility or grant people responsibility at the cost of abandoning naturalism. But, for Dennett, Chisholm's doctrine is a classic example of an appeal to an over-inflated concept. We need to deflate the notion of responsibility, and the closely linked concepts of free will and accountability, and also to talk up the power of mechanisms.

Let us look more closely at what Chisholm thinks is lacking. Dennett has given us an account of how people made from mechanisms can be moved by rational considerations, how they can be effective controllers and be possessed of self-control. But this is not enough for the sceptic. Consider two kinds of worry.

First, while I may be glad that the actions I take are reasonable, what I consider reasonable is relative to my values and preferences. But these values and preferences, the sceptic will press, have simply been imposed upon me. Just as the Mars Explorer has made no choices about what to value in Mars exploration, or indeed whether to value exploration at all, so people are saddled with values and preferences that are not of their own making. If people are made out of mechanisms, devices that operate according to causal laws, how could it be any other way? Being made from a mechanism, not being an unmoved mover, means that I am not free to choose what it is I want, what it is I think most precious. These critical features about my character are given to me, whether I want them or not.

Second, and closely related, while Dennett may have shown self-control to be achievable by agents made from mechanisms, whether we are strong- or weak-willed is not something that we are responsible for. We are all familiar with the way in which we sometimes battle unsuccessfully to carry out the plans and intentions we espouse. These failings may be modest, such as staying in bed for an extra five minutes despite the stern talking to ourselves issued the night before. They may be serious, such as breaking a solemn promise to a friend. On the serious issues at least, we admire the strong-willed, characters who are not victims of everyday human weakness in trying situations. On the trivial ends of things, we often warm to weakness, as manifested in spontaneity, human frailty, and naughtiness. But, in any case, the sceptic's concern is that we cannot help whether or not we are strong-willed or weak-willed, whether we find a balance of integrity and playfulness easy to achieve or a real struggle. If we are built from mechanisms, we cannot choose what kind of character we want to have, we are stuck with what we get.

Making a responsible self

Dennett wants to argue that this style of reasoning sets the standard of what can count as a freely willed choice too high. The sceptic argues that although our actions may be an authentic manifestation of our characters or, as Dennett puts it, our selves, our characters or selves are not something for which we are responsible.

> Unless we can find a way of making a responsible self out of initially non-responsible choices, so that there is a gradual acquisition of responsibility by the individual, we will be stuck. . . . We will either have to deny that anyone ever is the sort of responsible self we all want to be, or we will have to . . . espouse a frankly mysterious doctrine of [an unmoved mover]. (*ER*, 84)

While it may look as though adult decisions are responsible, since they are the product of a character whose ultimate formation is wholly accounted for by non-responsible choices, choices made in the light of non-chosen preferences and values, they cannot be genuinely responsible. If sound, this argument is so powerful that it rules out not only natural agents but seems to rule out supernatural ones too (see p. 256). So how can we give an account of the making of a responsible agent, or, as Dennett often puts it, a responsible self?

Dennett begins by attacking the argument just outlined (*ER*, 84–5). He notes first that the argument appears to have the same form as the argument that there can be no mammals, since, although offspring may and do differ from their parents in various ways, no mammal can be born of non-mammalian parents. But, of course, there are mammals, and, of course, they did not spring fully formed, but gradually evolved from non-mammalian ancestors. Or, again, Dennett asks us to consider the argument that you cannot make a man bald by removing a single hair from his head. If we keep removing one hair after another, at some stage, and exactly when may not be altogether clear, the man will become bald. The mammal argument and the baldness argument appear to be patently invalid. And so if Dennett is right about the parallel, it would seem that the sceptic's argument must be invalid too. It is worth noting that exactly what is wrong with this form of argument – known in the trade as *sorites* or a slippery slope – is controversial. Given this, citing the parallel is not by itself enough to establish that the sceptic's argument is invalid.

Dennett's naturalism urges that it must be the case that the transition from non-responsible agents, such as we are as infants, to responsible agents, such as we are as adults, takes place gradually and by small steps, no one of which could on its own account for the transition, but which collectively can. Here Dennett is accepting one of the points that is important to the sceptic, namely that there is a categorical difference between responsible and non-responsible agents. What he is denying is that the repeated action of non-responsible decisions or choices is incapable of bringing a responsible agent into being.

This move is an instance of one of Dennett's central argumentative strategies. The idea is that something can be levered from one category into another by small steps where the character of each individual step is, of itself, unable to account for the overall change (see *CE*, 421–2 and my discussion of agency in chapter 2). The case of the responsible self exactly parallels the case of the intentional system.

What it is to be an agent is something that we cannot grasp from the design or physical stance (chapter 2). Yet, before we bring the intentional stance to bear, we only have the design or physical stance. If we describe each small step using the design or physical stance, we will never ever describe a transition from a non-agent to an agent. This is why the coming into being of agents can seem quite mysterious. No matter how many mechanisms you add you cannot, it seems, create an agent. All you can create is a fancier mechanism. In one sense this is so. But of course, some fancy mechanisms are open to interpretation from the intentional stance. And some sustain real patterns that are only discernible from that stance. When a mechanism does sustain such an interpretation, then we can say that an agent has arrived on the scene. That is, we can start to predict successfully what it will do by appeal to what it is rational for it to do. And, moreover, we can say that it is falling down, failing to meet normative standards, when it does not do what is rational.

But the vanilla intentional stance, as we have seen in chapters 4, 5, and 6, is blind to the difference between persons and non-persons, to the difference between those that can and those that cannot play the 'question-and-answer game of giving reasons for [their] actions' (CP, 283). Persons arrive when we can start to predict successfully by appeal to the personal stance.

Suppose we begin with a mere intentional system, an agent that is not even in the game of giving reasons for action or accepting praise or blame. We can add, step by step, behavioural capacities that make this agent more sophisticated. But how could any such step or series of steps lever our non-responsible agent into the realm of responsibility? To be responsible is not merely to be able to come up with fancy noises when asked to explain yourself. It is for your behaviour to be interpretable in accord with and answerable to a certain normative standard, namely, that you are the sort of agent that is supposed to be able to give an intelligible account of your action and, in some suitable sense, take ownership of it. It is to be open to criticism when you fail to meet these normative standards.

As in the case of agents, what Dennett has to offer us is not so much an argument as a strategy for achieving reconciliation, a strategy for coming to see that responsibility can be real and yet can be underpinned by processes in which responsibility does not feature. The arguments that he can offer, then, are mainly negative. They are arguments to show what is wrong with the sceptic's starting point, or to show what might be wrong with reductions of the responsible to the non-responsible. In fact, Dennett takes it for granted here that a reduction is hopeless. His case against the sceptic is that, from the sceptic's starting point, the only result will be eliminativism. If Dennett can show that, he can at least show that the fact that we are built out of mechanisms is not the problem. Thus he sees off supernaturalism. Then he need only convince us that eliminativism is not the right option here.

It is important to recognize that so long as the sceptic is allowed to frame the problem it may well be impossible to provide a satisfactory argument against her position. After all, part of what Dennett is trying to do is to deflate our conception of responsibility, not so much that we no longer recognize it, but enough so that it can be accommodated into his naturalistic framework. He suggests: 'If we are to be found responsible at all, it will have to be a modest, naturalised, slightly diminished responsibility, for we are no angels' (*ER*, 158).

Dennett needs to make room for the idea that in human development we go from a stage where it would be wholly inappropriate to hold us responsible for our actions to a stage where it is wholly appropriate via a host of intermediate steps. We have no language to describe these intermediate stages where a person is neither responsible nor wholly non-responsible. We have no words to characterize happenings that are neither wholly on the non-responsible side of the divide nor wholly on the responsible side.

The same point holds true of agents (chapters 2 and 3) and of narrative selves (chapter 6). We have no words to describe the almost-interests of a system that is on the cusp of being an agent. We can either see it as a very poor agent or as not an agent at all. Similarly, we have no words to describe the almost-narrative unity of an emerging self. We can either see it as a very ineffective self, a self that has highly marginal narrative unity, or not see it as a self at all.

In fact, Dennett's comment that we are no angels is itself too concessive. Angels might be perfectly rational. Angels, not being made from mechanisms, might be able to consider all possibilities and consider them in any amount of detail. But, for all that, an angel can no more be a wholly self-made self than a person. For as the sceptic insists, and Dennett concedes, 'a completely self-made self, one hundred per cent responsible for its own character, [is] an impossibility' (*ER*, 156). The idea that we might be 'one hundred per cent responsible' for our own characters is just too demanding. It is not merely inflated in that only supernatural creatures could meet this standard. It is so inflated that not even the supernatural could meet it. The standards required for creating a responsible self must be lowered. But we will also need a positive reason to think that the lowered standard, one which can be met by both angels and persons made from mechanistic parts, is sufficiently high to capture what we care about in our notion of responsibility.

Self-making and the sporting analogy

Dennett tries to offer a positive reason for thinking we are genuinely responsible by way of an analogy with sporting skills (*ER*, 94–9). His idea here seems to be that the acquisition of skill renders certain kinds of explanation of failure unavailable. While a skill is being acquired a person can always insist that she has not quite 'got it' yet or that she is 'only learning'. But once a certain level of skill has been acquired, these kinds of explanations are no longer available. Once she has learned the rules of the game and played a few times, a person cannot plausibly make any special pleas. If she loses it is because she has been outplayed or perhaps because she has been unlucky. But it is not because she does not know how to play. She cannot put that forward as an explanation and expect to be taken seriously.

Dennett wants to argue that something analogous goes on in the case of learning to be an agent. At the early stages we excuse fledgling agents in ways we would not excuse adults. After all, they are simply learning the game of being effective reasoners, of weighing the consequences of their actions, of working out when to make a quick decision and when to spend more time, or when to take a risk and when not. But a point comes, Dennett suggests, when young adults reach a certain level of competency. And once they do, these sorts of excuses or allowances are no longer appropriate.

> [Moral] development . . . is a process that apparently brings people to a plateau of development – not unlike the process of learning your native language. . . . Some people reach the plateau swiftly or easily, while others need compensatory effort to overcome initial disadvantages in one way or another. But everyone comes out more or less in the same league. (*ER*, 96)

Dennett speaks of 'the process of moral development or acquisition of agenthood' as if these two are interchangeable (*ER*, 96). What does he mean by a 'morally developed person' or by someone who has fully acquired 'agenthood'? He seems to mean an agent who is skilled at making effective choices.

But if so there is a serious gap in Dennett's story here. What he seems to give us is a story about how we reach a plateau of competence in prudential reasoning and not in moral reasoning. But it is the latter that is required. In effect, Dennett is offering a story about how we become accountable agents, but not responsible agents. Let me spell out this distinction between accountability and responsibility.

An agent is accountable just so long as she is able, in principle, to defend her action as rational, just so long as she is, quite literally, able to give an account of it. That is, she is not psychologically alienated from her action. She understands and accepts it as something she has done. Being accountable contrasts with being responsible. An agent is responsible for her action when the morally rich acts of praising, blaming, excusing, punishing, and so forth are applicable.

This distinction between responsibility and accountability is reflected in our ordinary judgements. We recognize two quite distinct ways of counting someone's actions as exempt from judgements of praise and blame. The most extreme form of exemption occurs when we judge that a person's values and preferences are so distorted, or her capacity to reason is so impaired, that she is not accountable for her actions. That is to say, we simply do not expect her to answer for what she has done. We do not think that she can participate in the 'question-and-answer game of giving reasons for [her] actions' (CP, 283). This is an extreme and unusual response. We only make it when the agent lacks the minimal capacities for carrying on a rational dialogue that are a precondition for our thinking about them as fully-fledged person in the first place. Just as we do not hold children, animals, or plants accountable for what they do, nor do we with those whose rational capacities are severely impaired. When someone is not even accountable for her actions, we regard her as wholly exempt from praise and blame. Such issues do not even arise.

The second way in which someone's actions can be exempt or more typically partially exempt from judgements of praise and blame presupposes that they are accountable. Consider an example. If your circumstances are very grim, you may quite reasonably feel that you have little or nothing to lose by being punished by society.

No punishment, you reason, would put you in a worse position than you are in now. Nor does being ostracized by the wider community or being held in contempt by it worry you. Perhaps you reasonably feel that your community has already rejected you. And now suppose that you act against the law and against the prevailing moral values. If you are caught, you might rail against the law, against your community, against the prevailing moral values, and so forth. You might try to argue that you are not to be blamed, that you are not fully responsible for your actions, and so forth. And your arguments might be successful. But what you cannot do is argue that you are not accountable for your action. That would make no sense. You can say that you did it, and then add 'and I think I was right', or 'and I am sorry now', or 'I was desperate', or whatever. Whatever we may think of these qualifications, we can make good sense of them. But, unless you have some sort of mental disorder, the reasons we have for exempting you from responsibility are not reasons for exempting you from accountability.

Although Dennett writes about responsibility, for the most part he seems to be talking about accountability. But there is a clear gap between the two notions. Dennett's idea of learning to become an effective reasoner only seems to introduce accountable agents and not responsible ones. Such a reasoner cannot say, when an action has bad consequences, that it was not her action. She cannot disown her action on the ground that she lacks free will and hence is not accountable. She cannot say, she did not perform the action, it just happened to her. Given that she has a certain level of competence in decision-making, consequence-weighing, and so forth, along with the capacity to engage in the question-and-answer game of giving reasons, she just is accountable. What she does, she can answer for.

By contrast consider a case where you have broken a rule in the full knowledge that if detected certain unpleasant consequences will follow. You took an extra bagel, but were found out, and now there will be no more bagels until the end of the month. Given Dennett's account so far, the best we can say is this: 'you took a risk, and this is what has happened'. But what we cannot say is, 'you have done something morally bad'. Of course, taking bagels is rarely so bad that we would want to get too worked up about it. But the point here is that, so far, there are no resources in Dennett's account for us to ground claims about moral good or moral bad and hence to ground claims of moral praise or moral blame. At best we have the resources to say of the agent that she was 'smart' or that she was 'stupid', that she has made better or worse calculations with respect to acting in line with her values.

At least, this is what we will think if we think that we cannot reduce moral notions of 'good' and 'bad' to the non-moral notions of 'achieving my ends' and 'failing to achieve my ends'. If we think such a reduction is possible, then Dennett's story will give us an account of responsibility as much as it gives us an account of accountability. In what follows, however, I shall assume that moral reasoning is not a species of prudential reasoning and hence that there is more work for Dennett's account to do. On this assumption, he has sketched out a story about accountability, but has yet to say anything about responsibility.

8.4　The origins of morality

The final push of Dennett's account, as it appears in *Elbow Room*, takes a very curious form. Dennett begins (155) by saying that he thinks that: 'there is an entirely presentable defence of our desire to preserve . . . [the] distinction between responsible moral agents and beings with diminished or no responsibility' (*ER*, 155). Even if difficult to apply in some cases he presses that the distinction is 'coherent, real, and important'. This is curious because the sceptic could agree with it all and yet not feel her position was genuinely challenged. It is certainly possible to draw a distinction between two categories, categories that we might label 'responsible agent' and 'non-responsible agent'. Or perhaps, if the considerations of the previous section are correct, it is possible to draw a distinction between the 'accountable' and 'non-accountable' agent. While there may be puzzles about whether some agents fall into one category or the other, most cases can be decided easily and without controversy. But this is beside the point. The issue of substance here is what significance such a distinction is supposed to have. The sceptic can agree to a descriptive sorting of agents into the 'responsible' and the 'non-responsible', but she does not think that those in the former category have, as it were, special ownership over their actions that the latter lack, and, further, she does not think that moral praise or blame can intelligibly accrue to any of the actions of those in the former category. And, of course, there is no reason for her to be impressed by a presentable defence of our *desire* to preserve this way of talking. We might want to preserve it for all manner of reasons. But the only reason that will defeat the sceptic is that this way of talking says true things. But, unfortunately, Dennett's defence of our desire to preserve the praise-and-blame way of talking seems to be based on the utility of the practice of holding oneself and others responsible. He puts forward a strong case for its utility. But the sceptic need not attack the utility of the practice. What she attacks is the truth of the claims the practice makes.

However, before turning to see what Dennett can say to *defend the truth* embodied in the practice of holding agents accountable for their actions, it will be useful to see what he says in *defence of our desire* to do so.

The origins of the practice

In effect Dennett offers two arguments for why we desire to hold other agents and ourselves accountable. The first argument is Darwinian. It claims that taking responsibility is a good adaptive strategy for sophisticated planners. To take responsibility here is for an agent to locate the source of a positive or a negative outcome within herself, rather than elsewhere. By taking responsibility for her actions, an agent has the best chance of improving on, as it were, her design. That is, she has the best chance of improving her decision-making procedures in the future. As a strategy, refusing to take responsibility, and blaming the environment or her genes, is terrible. It does not lead the agent to do better in the future, to try to increase her margin for error, or to develop strategies whereby she can achieve her goals even when obstacles or unlucky breaks threaten to thwart her. Taking responsibility, on the other hand, encourages the agent to develop larger margins of error, to be able to get what she wants more of the time. There is a cost, of course. On occasion she may have to accept the costs of being responsible for an action – perhaps being ostracized by others in her community or suffering a punishment – even though that action was the product of a well-designed decision procedure, a procedure which, despite yielding a poor result on this occasion, could not be further improved. But, the thought goes, in the long run it is worth paying such costs. The benefit, namely being an effective (and improving) decision-maker and controller, one that can achieve her ends even when the luck runs against her, is well worthwhile.

As with other Darwinian arguments, this argument does not involve any reasoning on the part of the creature herself. All that matters is that it is the case that one strategy is better than the other, and that variation will generate the better strategy and allow it to compete with other strategies. That is, we suppose that there is a mixture of agents who do and do not take responsibility. Those who do are, by and large, likely to do better for themselves. And note this would be true whether the agent was a conformer or a maverick as far as the moral-cum-legal mores of a community are concerned. Consider the maverick free-rider who takes responsibility for her actions and who looks to find fault with herself when her stratagems go wrong. When things go wrong for her, because she holds herself responsible, she can reflect and adjust her decision-making procedure, improving her margin for error. Were she to blame the environment and leave herself with no failure to account for, she loses an opportunity to improve her decision-making procedure. If the tendency to take or fail to take responsibility is a heritable trait (or if the trait is culturally transmissible), then, according to this argument, we might well expect the tendency to take responsibility to come to dominate the population.

The second argument involves agents reflecting on what would be rational for them to do. Were people to sit down and figure out whether they would be better off holding themselves and one another responsible or not, they would conclude that they would be better rather than worse off. This is based on the premise that people value their self-interest. This argument is a close cousin of the Darwinian argument. The rationale is the same: in one case it is imposed through natural selection, in the other it is recognized through reason and self-consciously adopted. Dennett does not offer the second argument as a serious causal hypothesis. Rather, he suggests that it is a 'rational reconstruction' (*ER*, 158), one that can be used to help to justify our practice of holding ourselves and others responsible. In offering such a reconstruction Dennett is following in the footsteps of Thomas Hobbes (1588–1678) and John Rawls (1971). Both these philosophers offer rational reconstructions of the origins of morality, constructions in which self-interest is taken to be the primary value, and then use the results to justify a richer moral scheme, one that includes values other than self-interest.

The Darwinian argument and Dennett's 'rational reconstruction' argument both defend taking responsibility on the grounds of utility. That is, the arguments explain the origin and persistence of holding ourselves and others responsible, regardless of whether it is literally true that people are responsible, and are in such a way that it could form a legitimate ground for praise and blame. They do so because they can see that it will yield dividends for the individual both directly and also indirectly as a result of the way in which the community impacts upon that individual. Under Darwinian selection, traits that optimize self-interest tend to prosper. And, often enough, when people self-consciously adopt policies, self-interest plays a major role.

The nature of the practice

So far all Dennett has given us is a story about the origins of the practice of holding ourselves and others responsible for our actions, a practice of praising and blaming ourselves and one another. I have done no more than sketch the basic shape of his story here. Dennett provides a wealth of detail in *Elbow Room* and in *Darwin's Dangerous Idea* and, in doing so, does a lot to make his story plausible. That is, he makes the existence of the practice of taking responsibility not only a possible outcome of the Darwinian design process, but a likely one, a 'Good Trick' or 'forced move' (see chapter 7) in the process of refining the design of human beings.

But what we need here is not an account of the origins of the practice, but something that could serve as a reason to believe the claims that the practice makes. Why should we believe that an agent really ought to take responsibility for her actions, when all we have been shown is that it is useful for her to do so? At first blush, it is an open question as to whether our action ought morally to be guided by utility. This does not mean a reduction of one to the other is necessarily ruled out. But it does mean that any such reduction must be argued for. Dennett is aware that if we are ever to enter the moral realm, we need some moral premise. '[My] argument will assume that *something matters* – that some things are for better and some are for worse' (*ER*, 155). But he is simply not clear what the moral premise might be. As already noted, he flirts with the idea that 'what matters' is the Darwinian value of self-interest. But he also claims that other values can be created and have a force independent of Darwinian self-interest. Once we acquire culture, and in particular language, we come to be creatures that by their very nature value 'ought and good and truth and beauty' (*DDI*, 366; and *CE*, 208), as opposed to mere pursuers of biological imperatives. But Dennett, while allowing that such values could come into being, and be distinct from Darwinian self-interest, does not elaborate much further.

It is worth pausing briefly to ask what is at stake here. Darwinism takes it as read that what matters for an organism is its survival and its contribution to reproduction. But without further argument, this notion of self-interest has no moral dimension. It is good for an organism to pursue its self-interest, but it appears to be morally neutral. There is a worry, then, that if we attempt to reduce morality to Darwinian self-interest, that notions such as praise and blame become no more than tools for manipulating oneself and others, tools that either directly or indirectly promote the individual's self-interest. The answer to the question 'Why should I hold myself and others responsible?' becomes 'Because it is useful, it is in your self-interest'. This is different from the expected answer, 'Because, morally, you ought. Because you and others are responsible.'

Although some do try to defend such reduction, any such attempt has to work very hard to deal with what seem like obvious and striking counterexamples. For example, it is not clear that such a view can make blameworthy an undetected action that, were it detected, would be subject to blame. If you can commit your crime unbeknownst to anyone else, and because you are a particularly clear thinker this does not fill you with such bravado that you would take unnecessary risks in the future, then, on such a theory, it is hard to make out how you can be subject to blame. Despite much squirming on the part of its defenders, a reduction of morality to self-interest seems unable to accommodate such examples.

One squirm that could be employed is this. Even though it may yield the wrong result in some cases, it is in an agent's Darwinian self-interest always to stick to the rule 'hold yourself and others responsible'. Perhaps it is 'cheaper' and 'more economic' to be designed to always apply the rule rather than to be designed to look at individual cases. This may be true, but it does not provide the justification we are after. It does not get us the required ought, for it still leaves it open for an agent with extra time on her hands to decide to reject the practice on occasion because it is not useful to her.

If Dennett is to resist the reduction of morality to self-interest, is there any kind of story he can tell for how fully-fledged responsibility could arise simply out of self-interest fuelled accountability? Although Dennett offers no case, by reflecting on his general method, we can see how he might set about constructing one. Just as accountable agents can arise from non-accountable (but rational) agents, so too might responsible agents arise from non-responsible ones. What it is to be an accountable agent is to be prepared to engage in the question-and-answer game of giving reasons for action. To the extent that there is no real pattern that conforms to the rules of this game, there is no accountable agent. But where there is such a real pattern, so there really is an accountable agent. Perhaps a further move could be made, this time organized around the rules or norms of the praise-and-blame game. Very roughly, the argument would go like this. To the extent that there is no real pattern that conforms to the rules of the praise-and-blame game, so there are no responsible agents. But where there is such a real pattern, so there really are moral agents.[1] What is going to generate the selection pressures (both across evolutionary time and across an individual's lifetime) that would shape a person's behaviour towards the norms of fully-fledged responsibility as opposed to mere self-interested accountability? This question takes us into very deep water indeed.

Dennett offers us little in the way of help other than, perhaps, some remarks about the way in which language dominates the environment of persons (*CE*, 417). Could it be through language, the constant trading of ideas, that we come to be creatures that see the commitment to the existence of genuine responsibility, of genuine praise and blame, genuine right and wrong, as a necessary condition of being what we are, as a condition without which we would not be fully human?

8.5 Where things stand

What picture of free will does Dennett offer us? As with his discussions of intentionality and consciousness he builds up a picture from the third-person perspective, and then seeks to get us to identify ourselves with what is revealed from that perspective. What is the picture of you from the third-person perspective? Consider the Cogit-8 robot first introduced in chapter 1. The robot is rational. It cannot help but be moved by relevant reasons, whether they are presented to it by a person or by features of its environment. It is an effective self-controller. The world can throw a whole range of novel and bizarre events its way and, by and large, it will be able to pursue its goals regardless. Moreover, though Cogit-8 has a strong desire to crush drinks cans whenever it sees them, it almost always has enough self-control to resist this desire when other agents are in the room. And although Cogit-8 does not make its own character from nothing – for nothing could – no one else makes its character either. Its character is a highly complex result of its innate endowment, its myriad of cognitive and social interactions. But its character is all its own. It was not imposed on it so much as it developed. Moreover, as it developed, it began to be able to make informed choices about which opportunities it wanted to explore and which it wanted to ignore. These, in turn, contributed to its character development.

Cogit-8 is the kind of creature that, following its extensive enculturation, can weigh reasons and assess the consequences of its actions. It took a time for Cogit-8 to become really skilled at decision-making, and, until it got good, its designers cut it a certain amount of slack. At one stage in its development, but before it was judged to have reach the plateau (*ER*, 96, quoted above), it went through a phase of saying 'Don't blame me, I'm only a robot' when it got into trouble. But its designers used to reply, 'You knew what you were doing, so you must accept the consequences,' or 'You don't say that when we praise you for doing well, do you now,' or sometimes simply, 'You're old enough to know better than that.' This seemed to help. Now, when it does try to wheedle out of responsibility, Cogit-8 tries much more sophisticated strategies. More often than not, when it messes up, it just takes it on the chin.

Finally, Cogit-8 just does find certain kinds of reasoning and certain kinds of conduct morally compelling. It sometimes wonders why it should. And its designers have not been able to give it an argument to say that it should. Nor did it find much help when it read Dennett's *Elbow Room*. But, because it cannot help it, it acts as if the practice of holding itself and others responsible, and of engaging in moral praise and blame, makes sense. It acts as if it has free will. And, though it has its doubts from time to time, Cogit-8 thinks it probably does have free will. It certainly thinks that most of the arguments to the effect that it could not are based on a massively over-inflated conception of what free will could be.

Now try shifting to the first-person perspective. Can you identify with Cogit-8? If you are just like Cogit-8 do you think that both you and it lack something, something that, if only it were added, would give you free will? Or do you think that no extra capacity would help either of you – both of you are doomed to be without free will, for there is no such thing? Or do you think as Cogit-8 thinks, that you probably do have free will, and for similar reasons?

Dennett tries to show that any difference you might cite as making the difference between you and Cogit-8 cannot do the job. Either the difference would need to be supernatural – and even then, as we have seen, it is not clear it can do the job – or it would not be relevant difference. However, there is a striking difference between this and all the other cases where Dennett has applied his de-differencing strategy. Nobody would be persuaded that because there was no relevant difference between herself and Cogit-8 that, therefore, neither of them were conscious or neither of them were genuine agents. But anyone can have the concern that if there is no relevant difference between herself and Cogit-8 then neither of them possess free will. As ever with this topic, it can be hard to resist the thought that if we are not relevantly different from Cogit-8 then somehow all our struggles are pointless.

Imagine looking in on a city of agents just like Cogit-8, designed in the laboratory and unleashed to form their own community. In such a scenario we would certainly talk about honourable robots, weak robots. We would talk about robots with integrity and robots who were dishonest, selfish, and cruel. We would talk about robots who were fairly brought to book, and of those suffering miscarriages of justice. But we might also add the caveat that all this talk was mere metaphor. For the robots, made from mechanisms as they are, must lack real freedom. They cannot be good or bad, they are just doing what they must do, given the mechanisms they have inside them.

Dennett will urge us to say that the moral talk about the robot city is not a metaphor. There really are good and bad robots, feckless wasters and admirable achievers. Moral talk is quite appropriate for them, and it is quite appropriate for us. For from the Dennettian perspective, there is no relevant difference between our cities and my imagined robot city. Dennett's hope is that by switching back and forth between stances: between the personal stance and one or other of the non-rationalizing stances, we will come to see that nothing has been left out, we will come to see that we and the robots have a variety of free will. It is less than we might first have hoped for. But the really big prize has been shown to be a mere illusion. A certain kind of radical freedom is not only not worth having, it is not something anything could have. But the variety we have, urges Dennett, is worth having. It makes good sense of our practices of praise and blame, and it allows us to reconcile two realms that could not seem further apart: the moral and the mechanistic.

For my own part, I find Dennett's defence of a deflated version of free will, one that is compatible with our being made from mechanisms, much less satisfying than his deflated versions of agency, the self, and consciousness. In the case of free will there is much more room to insist that Dennett's attempt at reconciliation fails and thus, in the absence of some better reconciliation, leaves us stuck with either eliminativism or supernaturalism. No doubt a more sophisticated scheme of reconciliation could be generated, but I suspect that the topic of free will is one that will continue to generate a serious tension. The revisions that naturalism require us to make of our concepts just are very demanding. We cannot accept those revisions lightly, nor readily find comfort in them. So if an approach such as Dennett's is ever going to work, it is bound to make us uncomfortable at first, and maybe for quite a long while. Dennett's line, of course, will be that such discomfort that there may be is worth bearing, because supernatural views, if they can be made to work at all, do not keep us honest and eliminativist views collapse into a worthless nihilism. If we reject both supernaturalism and eliminativism, our best bet seems to be to embrace Dennett's 'modest, naturalised, slightly diminished' conceptions of agency, the self, consciousness, and free will.

Further reading

There is a large literature on free will. Gary Watson's collection *Free Will* provides a useful entry point and includes a helpful introduction. Some book-length treatments include Kane (1996), van Inwagen (1983), and G. Strawson (1986), who all oppose compatibilism, and Frankfurt (1988) and Wolf (1990), who promote it. 'Freedom and Resentment' (Strawson, 1962) is an important paper which foreshadows certain aspects of Dennett's view, in particular the fact that our psychology conditions us to treat ourselves and others as free.

I have kept my remarks about the 'could have done otherwise' principle to a minimum. Dennett has plenty more to say about it and about different senses of 'can' in chapter 6 of *Elbow Room*. The classic attack on this principle comes from Frankfurt (1969). Dennett attributes the expression 'the buck stops here' to Harry Truman (*ER*, 76). The idea of an unmoved mover originates with Aristotle and is developed by Aquinas in arguments for the existence of God. An introductory discussion of the *sorites* or slippery-slope argument plus pointers to literature can be found in Michael Tye's article on 'Vagueness' in *The Routledge Encyclopaedia of Philosophy* (Craig, 1998). Hobbes's rational reconstruction – the famous 'social contract' – can be found in his *Leviathan*; Rawls's – the 'original position' that is constructed behind a 'veil of ignorance' – is laid out in his *A Theory of Justice* (1971). Hobbes and Rawls aside, there are many attempts to reduce morality to self-interest or something like it. A particularly good example, one that takes its opposition seriously, is Peter Railton's (1984) 'Alienation, Consequentialism and the Demands of Morality'. Dennett discusses nihilism in *Elbow Room* (153–6). For a discussion of what I call the 'peculiar or unnatural' status of norms, see Mackie (1977), who calls such norms 'queer'. Smith (2000) discusses both nihilism and reviews the issue of whether naturalism can accommodate moral norms. For more on the ideas briefly touched on at the end of 8.4, concerning the suggestion that being responsible is a condition of being a person, see Taylor's *Sources of the Self* (1989), chapter 2, and MacIntyre's *After Virtue* (2nd ed, 1985), chapter 15.

Notes

Chapter 1   Dennett and the Philosophy of Mind

1   Here I draw on a discussion by Richard Rorty (1979, 204–5) about the sense in which science does and does not give a complete description of the world. I return to the issue of the different sense of completeness on a number of occasions throughout the book, and on each occasion owe a debt to Rorty's discussion.

2   For those familiar with the terminology, in this section I am talking exclusively about the type-type identity theory.

3   Amongst other variations, functionalists differ in the way in which functional roles are specified, and in whether a mental state is held to be identical with the state that realizes the role or with the role itself. See Block (1980a) for a useful overview. The version I present here is based on David Lewis's formulation (1972; 1980), and is often known as Australian functionalism.

4   See Putnam (1965) and Lewis (1980). Those familiar with the literature may care to note that it is clear how this can be so if mental states are identical to the types of physical states that typically play the functional role in question (Lewis's view). But it is not clear how this can be so if mental states are identical with functional roles themselves (Putnam's view). However, in developing his style of functionalism, Putnam insists on just this feature and, indeed, pillories behaviourism for lacking it. This, I suspect, is a serious tension for his formulation.

5   Common-sense analysis is commonly called 'conceptual analysis', but not by me here. After all, every approach described in this section offers analyses of concepts. Common-sense analysis is conservative, but leaves room for innovation and extensive clarification. Contrast this with Wittgenstein's approach which is radically conservative. This can

make his view more akin to, and an inspiration for, consensual analysis, which I discuss on page 26.

Chapter 2 Adopting a Stance

1 Of course this conception of agency is contestable, though I do not think it should be especially controversial.
2 In the paper from which I quote here Dennett talks about 'believers' and 'true believers', rather than agents and genuine agents. His terminology varies from paper to paper. I stick to agent/genuine agent throughout my text.
3 Searle's emphasis on consciousness is an illustration of the idea of transparency. In the wake of Putnam's (1975a) work very many philosophers have embraced the doctrine of semantic externalism, which claims that the meaning of one's thoughts is partly determined by the environment. This, of course, cuts against transparency. Dennett welcomes the abandonment of transparency – he, like Ryle, is rather sceptical about the extent to which we know our own minds – but abhors the insistence that, whether we have access to it or not, there is, nonetheless, some precise fact about what our thoughts mean. See *IS*, chapter 8, for Dennett's discussion of these issues.
4 The details of Dennett's discussion in *Content and Consciousness* are quite technical, and, unlike the spirit of the discussion, at odds with his mature view. I make no attempt to examine the details here.
5 There are other options. See Elton (1998).
6 In making this point I am assuming the plausibility of a certain metaphysical view concerning identity and constitution, for example, as defended by Wiggins (1980). I think Dennett's position relies on such a metaphysics, and to the extent that the critic is sceptical of this metaphysics she may also be sceptical of Dennett's overall position.

Chapter 3 Real Patterns

1 The distinction between what is directly observable and what is not is notoriously problematic (Bird, 1998, 131–5), but nothing turns on this for the present discussion.
2 See Adrian Cussins (1993) for an excellent discussion of the idea that I am describing as flipping between stances.
3 Philosophers of language may note that this example hints at a way in which Dennett's view can naturally accommodate Putnam's (1975a) idea of the division of linguistic labour.

Chapter 4 Different Kinds of Psychology

1 We might say that no contribution is made to the agent's biographical narrative. See chapter 6 for an explanation of the role biographical narrative plays in Dennett's account of the self.

2 In particular the argument of *Consciousness Explained*, while not making this interpretation of sub-personal meanings explicit, relies on this interpretation. See chapter 6.

3 In fact, if we think, as Dennett does not (MSO 98), that we can find a good theoretical basis for rationality, then there is no reason why our favoured theory of rationality cannot just be plugged into Dennett's account. The only constraint is that it must allow that agents can be rational on occasion, but also that they can fail to be so.

Chapter 5   Explaining Consciousness: The Basic Account

1 The two alternatives here parallel the Orwellian strategy (experiences are quickly forgotten; memories can later be altered) and Stalinesque strategy (unconscious experience can guide behaviour; experiences can be 'faked' later) that feature heavily in Dennett's post-1991 writing. These strategies, which are concerned with fixing the facts about consciousness during short time periods, are described in chapter 6.

Chapter 6   Explaining Consciousness: Developments, Doubts, and the Self

1 I write 'around about time *t*' because of the way the agent level account is elaborated in *Consciousness Explained* (and TO). I write 'her current (or, with caveats, future) reports' because not all later reports of experience should be taken at face value. Indeed, a later report is neither entailed by experience nor entails experience took place. That she had experience *e* might appear to offer a good explanation of the subject's later report, but we may have good reason to say that the subject did not experience *e*. So a later report is not sufficient. For example, if she reported a contradictory experience at or near the time *e* that was supposed to have occurred, the reporting of which she later forgot, we would have grounds to say the first report was veridical and the second not. For an example, see *BS*, 145–6.

2 Specialists may ask whether verificationism is being invoked here. It is not. But when we have a situation in which we can generate no evidence for or against a given fact, we need to inquire into the metaphysical basis of the fact. The point here is that nothing can be found to underpin the facts Chase and Sanborn think pertain. Unless we countenance the introduction of raw phenomenal facts, facts that are wholly independent of sub-personal arrangements – and that is an option – then Chase and Sanborn really do seem to be engaged in an idle dispute.

3 Compare this claim to Wittgenstein's discussion of language acquisition at the opening of *Philosophical Investigations*. According to Wittgenstein, Augustine portrays his infant self as mentally sophisticated but

lacking in vocabulary. By contrast, both Dennett and Wittgenstein think that such a portrayal begs the question of how we come to acquire mental sophistication.

Chapter 7   Dennett's Darwin

1 I shall not comment further on this issue here, other than to say that to the extent that Dennett makes a case for adaptationism (7.2), he challenges Fodor and Chomsky's view.
2 Cf. the discussion in chapter 4 (p. 125) of rationality and counting instances of conformity and deviation from the rational.
3 In an excellent paper, Peter Godfrey-Smith (2000) has independently developed a similar though distinct 3-fold account.

Chapter 8   A Variety of Free Will Worth Wanting

1 A subtle version of this kind of argument, and one that could be congenial to Dennett, is developed by Taylor (1989, Part I). Taylor is somewhat sceptical of naturalism, but that is mostly because he associates it with reductionism. Dennett is an anti-reductive naturalist. His view has scope for moral norms to be free-standing. After all, for Dennett rational norms are free-standing. And Dennett does not think this makes such norms peculiar or unnatural. So he could, consistent with his general approach, say the same of moral norms.

Glossary

abstracta   An abstractum is something that is referred to in a theory that has no concrete characteristics, e.g. a centre of gravity. Abstracta contrast with *illata*. Dennett argues that intentional states are abstracta but should not, for that reason, be regarded as somehow less than real. See chapter 3 and TK.

atomism   The idea that what a mental state is about (its content) is not dependent on the content of other mental states that the agent has. At its most extreme, atomism would allow for an agent with only one belief or for an agent whose set of beliefs were mostly contradictory. Atomism, however, comes in much milder versions. Dennett is fiercely opposed to atomism, and fiercely committed to *holism*. See Fodor and Lepore (1992, Introduction) for a defence of atomism.

awareness₁   Dennett's term in *Content and Consciousness* for awareness that entails the capacity to provide a verbal report. See *narrative awareness* and *CC*, chapter 6.

awareness₂   Dennett's term in *Content and Consciousness* for awareness that entails the capacity to drive non-verbal behaviour. See *behavioural awareness* and *CC*, chapter 6.

behavioural awareness   Awareness that entails the capacity to drive non-verbal behaviour. Contrasts with *narrative awareness*. See also *awareness₂.*

behaviourism   Most broadly the view that the best account of the mind and of intentional states is one which analyses or explicates them in terms of dispositions to behave. Dennett's account of the mind is a sophisticated version of Rylean Behaviourism. This version of the view is concerned to show how we can grasp the mind and its states without appeal to inner criteria. But, unlike some versions of behaviourism, it does not aim to reduce the intentional to the non-intentional. Nor does it attempt to treat intentional states one by one: it is a holistic rather than an atomistic theory. See chapter 1.

Block, Ned Ned Block is a contemporary of Dennett's who has made important contributions to the topics of functionalism and consciousness. In particular, Block (1995) argues that Dennett ignores rather than explains the most difficult aspect of consciousness, namely phenomenal consciousness. He also argues (Block 1981), that all versions of behaviourism are vulnerable to the 'giant look-up table' objection. See chapter 6.

Cartesian Theory A term I use to refer to theories that fix membership of a kind by virtue of inner features. For example, the theory that what makes a tiger a genuine tiger are facts about its insides is a Cartesian Theory. The term contrasts with *Rylean Theory*. Dennett argues Cartesian Theories of the mind are mistaken. See chapter 1.

causal blueprint I use this term to refer to a specification of a system expressed in terms of the causal powers of the various parts and the causal relations between the parts. A causal blueprint of a system, such as a chess machine, requires no grasp of what the system is for. Causal blueprints are abstract. That is to say they do not need to specify what material a system is made out of. Any material will do, so long as the parts, powers, and relations specified by the causal blueprint are present. Hence the very same causal blueprint may be multiply realized. See *design stance*.

Churchland, Paul Paul Churchland is a contemporary of Dennett's who argues that the philosophy of mind should pay serious attention to the results of neuroscience. He is best known for arguing in favour of *eliminativism*, namely, the claim that our ordinary self-conception is badly misplaced and should, for scientific purposes, be discarded and replaced with a theory based on how mechanisms function in the brain (Churchland 1981). See chapters 1–4.

Darwinian stance The term I use for the application of a *rationalizing stance* to the unfolding of a lineage or species over time. In applying the Darwinian stance to a lineage or species we assume that it has persistence and prosperity as its overarching aim and that it is rational. The rationality of the Darwinian stance is very limited. A lineage or species cannot look ahead. See chapter 7.

Davidson, Donald Donald Davidson is a contemporary of Dennett's. He has developed a view in the philosophy of mind that has many parallels with Dennett's own. Like Dennett, Davidson is committed to the idea that mental states are features of an interpretation of an agent, an interpretation that involves an assumption of rationality. But, unlike Dennett, he insists that mental events – Davidson develops his view in terms of events rather than states – are identical with physical events. I have not attempted to examine the subtleties of Davidson's view and its relationship with Dennett's. See Davidson (1980) and, for an accessible introduction, Evnine (1991). Child (1994) provides an extended discussion of the similarities and differences between Dennett and Davidson. Burwood et al. (1999, chapter 5) provide a briefer account.

de-differencing This is the name I give to one of Dennett's most common argumentative strategies. A de-differencing argument picks out a factor that is supposed to make the difference between an entity falling under one kind rather than another. The relevance, coherence, or the nature of that factor is then attacked. Relevance: it is argued that the factor could not do the job, for example, it could not matter, so far as being included or excluded from the kind 'agent', whether something is made from carbon-based chemistry or silicon-based chemistry (chapter 2). Coherence: it is argued that not even angels could be wholly 'self-made selves', and hence the idea that there is a coherent difference between agents that possess this property and those that do not is undermined (chapter 8). Nature: for example, a supposed difference in experience that cannot be discerned by heterophenomenology stands in need of some kind of underpinning. But the only natural candidate, a sub-personal condition, is simply unable to provide a basis for the experiential difference. Hence the idea of a genuine experiential difference in such cases must be dropped, unless, that is, we are permitted to appeal to supernature (chapter 7).

design stance A stance where we predict what a system will do by appeal to assumptions about its design. Dennett uses the term in two distinct ways, depending on how the design of a system is specified. The design can be specified by reference to a *causal blueprint*. In such cases, the predictor (the person adopting the stance) can successfully predict even if she is wholly ignorant of the job that the system is supposed to do. Alternatively, the design can be specified by reference to the job the system is supposed to do, such as play chess or be a word processor. In such cases, the predictor (the person adopting the stance) must know what job the system is supposed to do, though she may be ignorant of the system's causal blueprint. See chapter 2.

eliminativism The response to the tension between science and our self-conception that recommends a radical, indeed brutal, overhaul of the latter to bring it in line with the former. Eliminativism claims that, quite literally, there are no such things as intentional states, persons, selves, and so forth. *Paul Churchland* and *Stephen Stich* both endorse versions of eliminativism. See chapters 1–4.

flipping strategy The strategy Dennett uses to make intelligible the relationship between an agent as viewed from a rationalizing stance (the intentional or the personal stance) and an agent viewed from the design or physical stance. By flipping between the two perspectives, Dennett presses that we come to see how it is intelligible that agents are made out of, though not identical to, design or physical stance systems. See chapters 3 and 4.

Fodor, Jerry Jerry Fodor is one of Dennett's most important contemporaries. Dennett and Fodor seem to disagree about most issues in the philosophy of mind, although they do agree that *folk psychology* is basically correct. Fodor is the most important philosophical sponsor of the representational theory of mind.

folk psychology   The set of predictive and explanatory principles that we use to predict and explain one another's behaviour. Some theorists, such as Fodor, Stich, and Churchland, argue that folk psychology has the status of a primitive scientific theory of human behaviour. Dennett sees folk psychology as a mixed bag, containing some primitive scientific principles but also containing some conceptual truths. See chapter 4.

functionalism   Most broadly the view that the best account of mind and of intentional states is one that analyses or explicates them in terms of their functional role. Here I restrict my use of the term to theories that fix functional role in terms of causal relations. Where this is the case, functionalism is a reductionist theory, for it seeks to reduce the intentional to something non-intentional, namely causal roles. In the wider literature the term 'functionalism' is used in a bewildering number of ways. As I use the term here, Dennett rejects functionalism. But Dennett's own view has been described, both by Dennett and by others, as functionalist. So, a term to be approached with great care.

greedy reductionism   This is a term Dennett introduces in *Darwin's Dangerous Idea*. In that text he contrasts good reductionism with greedy reductionism. Greedy reductionism, he tells us, fails to respect the significance of distinct levels of explanation, thus inviting such absurdities as the attempt to explain human behaviour in terms of neural processes or Darwinian evolution in terms of biochemistry. Good reductionism rejects supernature, but permits distinct levels. In *DDI* Dennett describes himself as being in favour of good reductionism, but against greedy reductionism. Given the way I use the term 'reductionism' in the text (and the way Dennett more often uses it, e.g. in *IS*), Dennett is opposed to reductionism. In my usage, a commitment to 'good reductionism' is no more than a commitment to *naturalism*. See chapter 7.

heterophenomenology   The method of constructing a description of an agent's inner experience (her phenomenology) from the outside. The heterophenomenologist infers from what an agent reports about her inner experience, along with what she does not say and what, in other ways, she is able to indicate, to construct a story about the contents of her consciousness. The story is neutral as to the ontological status of the item mentioned in it. See chapters 5 and 6.

heuristic overlay   A way of labelling (see *intentionalistic labels*) a causal blueprint or a sub-personal account in order to highlight the connections between its parts and processes and activities of the agent which it underpins. See chapter 4.

holism   The idea that what a mental state is about (its content) is partly dependent on the content of other mental states that the agent has. At its most extreme, holism would entail that two agents could not share a single belief unless they shared all of their beliefs. Holism, however, comes in much milder versions. Dennett is fiercely committed to holism and fiercely opposed to *atomism*. See Fodor and Lepore (1992, Introduction) for a critique of holism.

homuncular functionalism The idea of explaining how an agent has the capacities she has by constructing a causal blueprint comprising simpler agents, that is, homunculi (literally, little people). So long as the homunculi exhibit less intelligence, understanding, awareness, etc., than the agent of which they are a part, this approach can be explanatory. Each homunculus can, in term, be analysed in the same way. Ultimately all homunculi are 'discharged', that is, replaced by a component that can clearly be implemented by a mechanism. Dennett has, on occasion, endorsed homuncular functionalism. But he is also clear that this way of constructing a causal blueprint is not always, and perhaps never, the most perspicuous. See chapter 2.

illata An illatum is something that is referred to by a theory that has concrete characteristics, e.g., an electron. Illata contrast with *abstracta*. Dennett argues that intentional states are not illata, but should not, for that reason, be regarded as somehow less than real. See chapter 3 and TK.

intentional stance A stance where we predict what a system will do by appeal to the assumption that it is a rational agent with certain overarching goals and certain perceptual and behavioural capacities. Dennett generally makes no distinction between the application of the intentional stance to persons and to agents that are not persons, nor indeed to lineages (see *Darwinian stance*). Where necessary, I mark such distinctions explicitly in my text, thus drawing a difference between the intentional stance (or, as I sometimes say, the 'vanilla intentional stance') and the *personal stance*. The intentional, personal, and Darwinian stances are all examples of what I call *rationalizing stances*. See chapters 2 and 4.

intentional system Any system which can be 'reliably and voluminously' predicted by means of the intentional stance. More restrictively we might think of an intentional system as one which requires the use of the intentional stance in order for it to be discerned against the background activity of other systems. See chapter 2.

intentionalistic labels Labels applied to a causal blueprint or a sub-personal account that draw attention to the role the parts and processes play in the activity of the agent they underpin. For example, we use intentionalistic labels when describing a brain module as a 'flavour analysis unit' or describing a neural signal as indicating 'that there is a cat on the mat'. See chapter 4.

Jackson, Frank Frank Jackson is a contemporary of Dennett's who works on the philosophy of mind and a range of other topics. He is the author of the 'knowledge argument' (Jackson, 1982; 1986), which seeks to show all third-person accounts of consciousness, including Dennett's, leave something out.

narrative awareness   Awareness that entails the capacity to report or reflect. Awareness that can contribute to an ongoing autobiographical narrative. Contrasts with *behavioural awareness*. See also *awareness*₁.

naturalism   I use the term to describe the view that there is never any need to appeal to supernature in accounting for what we find in the world. With Dennett, I also take this to imply the need to reconcile science and our self-conception. Not all theorists who eschew supernature agree with the need for reconciliation. Wittgenstein and Ryle, and the tradition that follows in their wake, seem happy to ignore the issue. As such they, and their tradition, are sometimes described as being opposed to naturalism. However, it may be that what they really oppose is the idea of reconciliation through reductionism. Better no reconciliation than that kind. Dennett defends naturalism, but when addressing the tension between science and our self-conception aims for reconciliation without reduction.

non-rationalizing explanation   An explanation of an agent's behaviour that makes no essential appeal to what the agent ought, rationally, to do. A non-rationalizing explanation may have intentional or non-intentional antecedents and may explain intentional or non-intentional consequences. See chapter 4.

normative   A norm is a standard or ideal. It describes how something is supposed to be or ought to be. On Dennett's view, whether they always live up to the standards of rationality or not, agents are supposed to. Hence agency is a normative phenomenon.

personal   The personal, or the personal level, is concerned with what persons, as opposed to their parts, do. Typically a person does not do anything in order to, say, discover that she is in pain, recognize a face, or arrange words to form a coherent sentence. There may be steps involved in doing these things, but they are not steps taken by the person.

personal stance   A stance where we predict what a system will do by appeal to the assumption that it is a rational agent and one that engages in the 'question-and-answer game of giving reasons for [her] actions' (CP, 283). See chapters 4 and 8, and 6.3. Contrasts with the *intentional stance* as well as with the *design* and *physical stance*.

physical stance   A stance where we predict what a system will do by appeal to facts about its physical construction. Contrasts with the *design stance* and all the *rationalizing stances*.

Quine, W. V. O.   Willard Van Orman Quine (1908–2000) promoted the idea that philosophy is continuous with natural science. He argued that there were no truths of philosophy that were wholly immune to revision in the light of data from empirical inquiry. Quine is an important influence on Dennett. But although Dennett often says he embraces this doctrine, I argue that his argumentation tells a different story. (See Symons, 2001, for a different reading of Dennett.) Quine also pioneered the idea of interpretation that is at the heart of Dennett's intentional stance. See chapter 1.

rational Dennett gives no precise definition but uses 'rational' as a general expression of 'cognitive approval'. In practice, in different contexts different standards of rationality are appropriate. For Dennett, rationality need not involve self-consciousness or appreciation of reasons as reasons. Hence he talks about chess machines being rational. But, at the same time, what is rational for a chess machine may not be rational for a person. See chapter 4.

rationalizing explanation An explanation of an agent's behaviour that makes an essential appeal to what the agent ought, rationally, to do. See chapter 4.

rationalizing stances My cover-all term for the *intentional stance*, the *personal stance*, and the *Darwinian stance*.

real pattern A pattern that can be found in a description of events that can be used for successful prediction. Dennett argues that in addition to real patterns being a result of regular, law-governed causal structures, some are also a result of regular, norm-governed behavioural structures. Such structures come into being when trial-and-error learning (such as natural selection or lifetime learning) shapes and reshapes a mechanism so that its behaviour falls into line with one or other rational norm.

reduction Where we have two theories that initially appear to describe two quite independent phenomena, a reduction is the process of showing that one theory can, in principle, be dispensed with, the work it does being taken up by the other. So, for example, astronomy and physics initially appeared to describe two quite independent phenomena. Astronomy was reduced to physics when it was shown that physics could account for all astronomical phenomena. See chapter 2.

Rorty, Richard Richard Rorty is a contemporary of Dennett's who is well known for his pragmatic approach to truth. Rorty is highly sympathetic to Dennett's philosophy, especially the idea that there are distinct descriptions of the world, revealed by different stances. Dennett, however, rejects pragmatism. He thinks that there is more to various analyses of concepts being correct than that they are widely, or even universally, accepted by members of the conversational community.

Ryle, Gilbert Ryle (1900–1976) wrote the highly influential *Concept of Mind* (Ryle 1949) in which he develops a distinctive version of *behaviourism*. Dennett embraces a version of Rylean Behaviourism. Where Dennett differs from Ryle is in his concern to show how such a theory can be reconciled with our scientific world picture, and his belief that such a reconciliation will lead to a modest deflation of some aspects of our self-conception.

Rylean Theory   A term I use to refer to theories that fix membership of a kind by virtue of outer features. For example, the theory that what makes a clock a genuine clock are only facts about what it can do, namely tell the time reliably, is a Rylean Theory. The term contrasts with *Cartesian Theory*. Dennett argues that the right theory of mind will be a Rylean Theory. See chapter 1.

Searle, John   John Searle is a contemporary of Dennett's who has produced influential work both in the philosophy of language and the philosophy of mind. He is particularly well known for his Chinese Room thought experiment (Searle 1980 and 1992) and for his insistence that no version of functionalism, let alone Dennett's behaviourism, can account for consciousness (Searle, 1992).

sphexishness   Dennett uses this term to describe a tendency to get stuck in a rut. The Sphex wasp finds itself stuck in a repeating pattern of behaviour which, from the outside, we can see is quite irrational. But the Sphex itself cannot find a way out. Dennett suggests that all agents made from mechanistic parts will be prone to some degree of sphexishness. Agents such as human beings are largely immune from sphexishness because they have a whole battery of cognitive strategies which they employ, not least the capacity to monitor the success and failure of particular strategies that they are trying out. See chapters 4 and 8.

stance   See *physical stance, design stance, intentional stance, personal stance, Darwinian stance*.

standard naturalistic picture   A set of assumptions about what should and should not be counted as part of nature. In this picture, to be real is to be part of a regular, law-governed causal structure. Dennett opposes this picture, arguing that there can be *real patterns* that are underpinned in a different way. See chapters 2 and 3.

Stich, Stephen   Stephen Stich is a contemporary of Dennett's who works on the philosophy of mind and the nature of rationality. Like Dennett, Stich rejects a reduction of the intentional to the non-intentional. Unlike Dennett, this leads him to embrace eliminativism. Stich also rejects the idea that there is any one conception of rationality shared by all persons, and hence rejects a major plank of Dennett's system. See chapter 4.

sub-personal   The sub-personal, or the sub-personal level, is concerned with the parts that make up the agent as opposed to the agent itself. The sub-personal focuses on the view of an agent that you get if you adopt the design or physical stance. The terminology can be slightly misleading. In Dennett's work, where the term is taken up elsewhere, and throughout my text, referring to the sub-personal level does not imply that the agent at issue is a person. Though Dennett's later work tends not to use the term 'sub-personal' very often, I argue in the text that personal/sub-personal distinction is alive and well in his argumentation. See chapters 4, 5, and 6. See also *personal, non-rationalizing explanation, homuncular functionalism*.

system   Dennett uses this term to refer to any entity whose activity we are interested in predicting. A person can be thought of as a system as, indeed, can a rock. But most often the term system is used when the entity in question demonstrates some sort of complex behaviour.

Wittgenstein, Ludwig   Wittgenstein (1889–1951) wrote *Tractatus Logico-Philosophicus* (1921) and *Philosophical Investigations* (1953), arguably two of the most important works in twentieth-century philosophy. Dennett is influenced by the later work in which Wittgenstein emphasizes, amongst other issues, the importance in looking at how words operate in their ordinary contexts and the danger of taking them out of those contexts. For Wittgenstein the dangers are, in the main, the generation of spurious philosophical puzzles.

Bibliography

Dennett

Books and Key papers by Dennett (both collected and uncollected) are referenced by letter codes (see Abbreviations). Other papers are referenced by date. Where a paper has been collected I refer always to the collected version.

Other papers cited

Dennett, Daniel C. (1982) 'How to Study Human Consciousness Empirically, or Nothing Comes to Mind'. *Synthese* 59, 159–80.

Dennett, Daniel C. (1993) 'The Message is there is no *Medium*'. *Philosophy and Phenomenological Research* 53, 889–931.

Dennett, Daniel C. (1994) 'Get Real'. *Philosophical Topics* 22 (1&2), 505–68.

Dennett, Daniel C. (1996) 'Cow-sharks, Magnets and Swampman'. *Mind and Language* 11, 76–7.

Dennett, Daniel C. (2000) 'The Case for Rorts', in Robert B. Brandom (ed.), *Rorty and His Critics*. Oxford: Blackwell, 91–101.

Dennett, Daniel C. (2001) 'Are We Explaining Consciousness Yet?' *Cognition* 79, 221–37.

Other Authors

Akins, Kathleen (1996) 'Lost the Plot? Reconstructing Dennett's Multiple Drafts Theory of Consciousness'. *Mind and Language* 11, 1–43.

Anscombe, G. E. M. (1957) *Intention*. Oxford: Blackwell.

Armstrong, David and Malcolm, Norman (1984) *Consciousness and Causality: A Debate on the Nature of Mind*. Oxford: Blackwell.

Ayer, A. J. (1953) 'Freedom and Necessity', in his *Philosophical Essays*. London: Macmillan. Reprinted in Watson (1982), ch. 1.

Bennett, Jonathan (1964) *Rationality*. London: Routledge and Kegan Paul.

Bennett, Jonathan (1976) *Linguistic Behaviour*. Cambridge: Cambridge University Press.

Bermúdez, José Luis (2000) 'Personal and Sub-Personal: A Difference without a Distinction'. *Philosophical Explorations* 3, 63–82.

Bird, Alexander (1998) *Philosophy of Science*. London: UCL Press.

Blackmore, Susan (1999) *The Meme Machine*. Oxford: Oxford University Press.

Block, Ned (1980a) 'What is Functionalism?', in Block (1980b), 171–84.

Block, Ned (ed.) (1980b) *Readings in the Philosophy of Psychology*, vol. 1 London: Methuen.

Block, Ned (1981) 'Psychologism and Behaviorism'. *The Philosophical Review* 90, 5–43.

Block, Ned (1995) 'On a Confusion about a Function of Consciousness'. *Behavioral and Brain Sciences* 18, 227–47. Reprinted in Block et al. (1997) (page references are to this reprint).

Block, Ned, Flanagan, Owen and Güzeldere, Güven (eds) (1997) *The Nature of Consciousness: Philosophical Debates*. Cambridge, Mass.: MIT Press.

Burwood, Stephen, Gilbert, Paul and Lennon, Kathleen (1999) *Philosophy of Mind*. London: UCL Press.

Chalmers, David (1996) *The Conscious Mind*. Oxford: Oxford University Press.

Charles, David and Lennon, Kathleen (eds) (1992) *Reduction, Explanation, and Realism*. Oxford: Clarendon Press.

Child, William (1994) *Causality, Interpretation, and the Mind*. Oxford: Clarendon Press.

Chisholm, Roderick (1964) 'Human Freedom and the Self', in Watson (1982).

Churchland, Paul M. (1981) 'Eliminative Materialism and the Propositional Attitudes'. *Journal of Philosophy* 78, 67–90. Reprinted in Churchland (1989).

Churchland, Paul M. (1988) *Matter and Consciousness: A Contemporary Introduction to the Philosophy of Mind*. Cambridge, Mass.: MIT Press.

Churchland, Paul M. (1989) *A Neurocomputational Perspective*. Cambridge, Mass.: MIT Press.

Churchland, Paul M. (1995) *The Engine of Reason, the Seat of the Soul*. Cambridge, Mass.: MIT Press.

Churchland, P. S. and Ramachandran, V. S. (1993) 'Filling in: Why Dennett is Wrong', in Dahlbom (1993), 28–52.

Clark, Andy (1989) *Microcognition: Philosophy, Cognitive Science, and Parallel Distributed Processing*. Cambridge, Mass.: MIT Press.

Clark, Andy (1993) *Associative Engines: Connectionism, Concepts, and Representational Change*. Cambridge Mass.: MIT Press.

Cohen, J. (1981) 'Can Human Irrationality Be Experimentally Demonstrated?' *Behavioral and Brain Sciences* 4, 317–31.

Cowey, A. and Stoerig, P. (1991) 'Reflections on Blindsight', in A. D. Milner and M. D. Rugg (eds) *The Neuropsychology of Consciousness*. London: Academic Press, 11–37.

Craig, Edward (ed.) (1998) *Routledge Encyclopedia of Philosophy*. London: Routledge.

Crane, Tim (1995) *The Mechanical Mind*. London: Penguin.

Cussins, Adrian (1992) 'The Limitations of Pluralism', in D. Charles and K. Lennon (eds) *Reduction, Explanation, and Realism*. Oxford: Clarendon Press, 179–223.

Dahlbom, Bo (1993) *Dennett and His Critics: Demystifying the Mind*. Oxford: Blackwell.

Davidson, Donald (1973) 'The Material Mind', in P. Suppes et al. (eds), *Logic, Methodology and the Philosophy of Science*, vol. 4 Amsterdam: North Holland Publishing Company. Reprinted in Davidson (1980), 245–59.

Davidson, Donald (1980) *Essays on Actions and Events*. Oxford: Clarendon Press.

Dawkins, Richard (1976) *The Selfish Gene*, 2nd edn, 1989. Oxford: Oxford University Press.

Dawkins, Richard (1982) 'Universal Darwinism', in D. S. Bendall (ed.), *Evolution from Molecules to Men*. Cambridge: Cambridge University Press, 403–25. Reprinted in Hull and Ruse (1998).

Dawkins, Richard (1986) *The Blind Watchmaker*. London: Longman.

Dawkins, Richard (1995) *River Out of Eden: A Darwinian View of Life*. London: Weidenfeld and Nicolson.

Dawkins, Richard (1996) *Climbing Mount Improbable*. London: Viking.

Dretske, Fred (1995) *Naturalising the Mind*. Cambridge, Mass.: MIT Press.

Dunlop, Charles E. M. (ed.) (1977) *Philosophical Essays on Dreaming*. Ithaca, NY: Cornell University Press.

Dupré, John (1993) *The Disorder of Things: The Metaphysical Foundations for the Disunity of Science*. Cambridge, Mass.: Harvard University Press.

Ellis, A. W. and Young, A. J. (1996) *Human Cognitive Neuropsychology: A Textbook with Readings*. Hove: Psychology Press.

Elton, Matthew (1998) 'Dennett Explained? A Critical Study of Dahlbom's *Dennett and His Critics*'. *Minds and Machines* 8, 394–413.

Elton, Matthew (2000) 'Consciousness: Only at the Personal Level'. *Philosophical Explorations* 3, 25–41.

Evnine, Simon (1991) *Davidson*. Cambridge: Polity.

Flanagan, Owen (1992) *Consciousness Reconsidered*. Cambridge, Mass.: MIT Press.

Fodor, Jerry (1974) 'Special Sciences, or: The Disunity of Science as a Working Hypothesis'. *Synthese* 28, 97–115. Reprinted in Fodor (1981) and Block (1980b).

Fodor, Jerry (1975) *The Language of Thought*. Hassocks, Sussex: Harvester Press.

Fodor, Jerry (1981) *Representations: Philosophical Essays on the Foundations of Cognitive Science*. Cambridge, Mass.: MIT Press.

Fodor, Jerry (1987) *Psychosemantics*. Cambridge, Mass.: MIT Press.

Fodor, Jerry (1992) 'The Big Idea: Can there be a Science of Mind?' *Times Literary Supplement*, 3 July 1992.

Fodor, Jerry and Lepore, Ernest (1992) *Holism: A Shopper's Guide*. Oxford: Blackwell.

Fodor, Jerry and Lepore, Ernest (1993) 'Is Intentional Ascription Intrinsically Normative?', in Dahlbom (1993), 70–82.

Frankfurt, Harry (1969) 'Alternative Possibilities and Moral Responsibility'. *Journal of Philosophy* 65, 829–33.

Frankfurt, Harry G. (1988) *The Importance of What We Care About: Philosophical Essays*. Cambridge: Cambridge University Press.

Gardner, Sebastian (2000) 'Psychoanalysis and the Personal/Sub-Personal Distinction'. *Philosophical Explorations* 3, 96–119.

Godfrey-Smith, Peter (2000) 'Three Kinds of Adaptationism', in S. Orzack and E. Sober (eds), *Optimality and Adaptationism*. Cambridge: Cambridge University Press 2000.

Gould, Stephen Jay (1989) *Wonderful Life: The Burgess Shale and the Nature of History*. New York: Norton.

Gould, Stephen Jay (1992) *Life's Grandeur: The Spread of Excellence from Plato to Darwin* (published in the US under the title *Full House*). London: Vintage.

Gould, Stephen Jay (1997) 'Darwinian Fundamentalism' and 'Evolution: The Pleasures of Pluralism'. *New York Review of Books* 12 June and 26 June 1997.

Gould, Stephen Jay and Lewontin, Richard (1978) 'The Spandrels of San Marco and the Panglossian Paradigm: A Critique of the Adaptationist Programme'. *Proceedings of the Royal Society of London* B205, 581–98. Reprinted in Sober (1994) (page references are to this reprint).

Gould, Stephen Jay and Vrba, Elizabeth (1982) 'Exaptation: A Missing Term in the Science of Form'. *Paleobiology* 8, 4–15. Reprinted in Hull and Ruse (1988).

Greenwood, J. (1991) *The Future of Folk Psychology: Intentionality and Cognitive Science*. Cambridge: Cambridge University Press.

Hookway, Christopher (1988) *Quine: Language, Experience and Reality*. Cambridge: Polity.

Hornsby, Jennifer (2000) 'Personal and Sub-Personal: A Defence of Dennett's Early Distinction'. *Philosophical Explorations* 3, 6–24.

Hull, David and Ruse, Michael (eds) (1998) *The Philosophy of Biology*. Oxford: Oxford University Press.

Jackson, Frank (1982) 'Epiphenomenal Qualia'. *Philosophical Quarterly* 32, 127–36.

Jackson, Frank (1986) 'What Mary Didn't Know'. *Journal of Philosophy* 83, 291–5.

Kane, Robert (1996) *The Significance of Free Will*. New York: Oxford University Press.

Kim, Jaegwon (1996) *Philosophy of Mind*. Oxford: Westview Press.

Kirk, Robert (1994) *Raw Feeling: A Philosophical Account of the Essence of Consciousness*. Oxford: Clarendon Press.

La Follette (ed.) (2000) *The Blackwell Guide to Ethical Theory*. Oxford: Blackwell.

Lewis, David (1972) 'Psychophysical and Theoretical Identifications'. *Australasian Journal of Philosophy* 50, 249–58. Reprinted in Block (1980b).

Lewis, David (1980) 'Mad Pain and Martian Pain', in Block (1980b), 216–22.

Lycan, W. G. (1981) 'Form, Function, and Feel'. *Journal of Philosophy* 78, 24–50.

Lycan, W. G. (1990) *Mind and Cognition: A Reader*. Oxford: Blackwell.

McDowell, John (1994a) 'The Contents of Perceptual Experience'. *Philosophical Quarterly* 44, 190–205.

McDowell, John (1994b) *Mind and World*. Cambridge, Mass.: Harvard University Press.

McGinn, Colin (1989) 'Can We Solve the Mind–Body Problem?' *Mind* 98, 349–66.

McGinn, Marie (1997) *Wittgenstein and the Philosophical Investigations*. London: Routledge.

MacIntyre, Alasdair (1985) *After Virtue: A Study in Moral Theory*, 2nd edn. London: Duckworth.

MacIntyre, Alasdair (1999) *Dependent Rational Animals: Why Human Beings Need the Virtues*. London: Duckworth.

Mackie, J. L. (1997) *Ethics: Inventing Right and Wrong*. London: Penguin.

Malcolm, Norman (1956) 'Dreaming and Skepticism'. *Philosophical Review* 65, 14–37.

Malcolm, Norman (1959) *Dreaming*. London: Routledge and Kegan Paul.

Malcolm, Norman (1973) 'Thoughtless Brutes'. *Proceedings and Addresses of the American Philosophical Association* (1972–3). Reprinted in D. M. Rosenthal (1990) *The Nature of Mind*. Oxford: Oxford University Press.

Marcel, A. and Bisiach, E. (1988) *Consciousness and Contemporary Science*. Oxford: Oxford University Press.

Maynard Smith, John and Szathmáry, Eörs (1999) *The Origins of Life: From the Birth of Life to the Origin of Language*. Oxford: Oxford University Press.

Millikan, Ruth Garrett (1984) *Language, Thought, and Other Biological Categories*. Cambridge, Mass.: MIT Press.

Mills, Susan K. and Beatty, John H. (1979) 'The Propensity Interpretation of Fitness'. *Philosophy of Science* 46, 263–86. Reprinted in Sober (1994).

Nagel, Thomas (1974) 'What Is It Like to Be a Bat?' *Philosophical Review* 83, 435–50.

Nagel, Thomas (1979) *Mortal Questions*. Cambridge: Cambridge University Press.

Nisbett, R. and Ross, L. (1980) *Human Inference: Strategies and Shortcomings of Social Judgement*. Englewood Cliffs, NJ: Prentice-Hall.

Papineau, David (1992) 'Teleology and Irreducibility', in David Charles and Kathleen Lennon (eds) *Reduction, Explanation, and Realism*. Oxford: Clarendon Press, 45–68.

Papineau, David (1993) *Philosophical Naturalism*. Oxford: Blackwell.

Parfit, Derek (1984) *Reasons and Persons*. Oxford: Clarendon Press.

Peacocke, Christopher (1983) *Sense and Content: Experience, Thought, and their Relations*. Oxford: Clarendon Press.

Putnam, Hilary (1965) 'Brains and Behaviour', in Putnam (1975b). Reprinted in Block (1980b), 24–36.

Putnam, Hilary (1975a) 'The Meaning of "Meaning"', in K. Gunderson (ed.) *Language, Mind, and Knowledge*. Minneapolis: University of Minnesota Press. Reprinted in Putnam (1975b), 215–71.

Putnam, Hilary (1975b) *Mind, Language, and Reality: Philosophical Papers*, vol. 2. Cambridge: Cambridge University Press.

Quine, W. V. O. (1953) 'Two Dogmas of Empiricism', in his *From a Logical Point of View*. New York: Harper and Row.

Quine, W. V. O. (1960) *Word and Object*. Cambridge, Mass.: MIT Press.

Railton, Peter (1984) 'Alienation, Consequentialism and the Demands of Morality'. *Philosophy and Public Affairs* 13, 134–71. Reprinted in James Rachels (ed.) (1998) *Ethical Theory: Theories About How We Should Live*. Oxford: Oxford University Press.

Rawls, John (1971) *A Theory of Justice*. Cambridge: Mass.: Harvard University Press.

Rorty, Richard (1979) *Philosophy and the Mirror of Nature*. Princeton: Princeton University Press.

Rovane, Carol (1998) *The Bounds of Agency: An Essay in Revisionary Metaphysics*. Princeton: Princeton University Press.

Ryle, Gilbert (1949) *The Concept of Mind*. London: Hutchinson.

Searle, John (1980) 'Minds, Brains, and Programs'. *Behavioral and Brain Sciences* 3, 417–24.

Searle, John (1992) *The Rediscovery of the Mind*. Cambridge, Mass.: MIT Press.

Sellars, Wilfred (1956) *Empiricism and the Philosophy of Mind*. Published as a book in 1997. Cambridge, Mass.: Harvard University Press.

Smith, Michael (2000) 'Moral Realism', in Hugh LaFollette (ed.), *The Blackwell Guide to Ethical Theory*. Oxford: Blackwell, 15–37.

Sober, Elliott (ed.) (1994) *Conceptual Issues in Evolutionary Biology*, 2nd edn. Cambridge, Mass.: MIT Press.

Sterelny, Kim and Griffiths, Paul E. (1999) *Sex and Death: An Introduction to the Philosophy of Biology*. Chicago: University of Chicago Press.

Stich, Stephen (1981) 'Dennett on Intentional Systems'. *Philosophical Topics* 12, 38–62. Reprinted in Lycan (1990) (page references are to this reprint).

Stich, Stephen (1983) *From Folk Psychology to Cognitive Science: The Case against Belief*. Cambridge, Mass.: MIT Press.

Stich, Stephen (1990) *The Fragmentation of Reason: Preface to a Pragmatic Theory of Cognitive Evaluation*. Cambridge, Mass.: MIT Press.

Strawson, Galen (1986) *Freedom and Belief*. Oxford: Clarendon Press.

Strawson, Peter (1962) 'Freedom and Resentment'. *Proceedings of the British Academy*. Reprinted in Watson (1982).

Sturgis, Alexander (2000) *Telling Time*. London: National Gallery Company.

Symons, John (2001) *On Dennett*. Belmont, CA: Wadsworth.

Taylor, Charles (1989) *Sources of the Self: The Making of the Modern Identity*. Cambridge: Cambridge University Press.

Turing, Alan (1950) 'Computing Machinery and Intelligence'. *Mind* 59, 433–60.

van Inwagen, Peter (1983) *An Essay on Free Will*. Oxford: Clarendon Press.

Watson, Gary (ed.) (1982) *Free Will*. Oxford: Oxford University Press.

Wiggins, David (1980) *Sameness and Substance*. Oxford: Blackwell.

Williams, Bernard (1970) 'The Self and the Future'. *Philosophical Review* 79, 161–80. Reprinted in Williams (1973).

Williams, Bernard (1973) *Problems of the Self*. Cambridge: Cambridge University Press.

Williams, George C. (1996) *Plan and Purpose in Nature*. London: Weidenfeld and Nicolson.

Wittgenstein, Ludwig (1953) *Philosophical Investigations*. Oxford: Blackwell.

Wolf, Susan (1990) *Freedom within Reason*. Oxford: Oxford University Press.

Wooldridge, Dean E. (1963) *The Machinery of the Brain*. New York: McGraw-Hill.

Index